Douglas Tate and Dr John Lockley

**This book is for those,
who,
having learned the rudiments of computing,
don't know where to go next.**

Published by Watford Electronics

Published in the United Kingdom by
Watford Electronics
Jessa House,
250 Lower High Street
Watford
WD1 2AN
England

Telephone 0923 37774
Telex 8956095
Fax 01 950 8989

ISBN 0 948663 10 3
Copyright © 1988 Watford Electronics

This book was computer typeset by
Ideal Software Consultants, 11 Hathaway Close, Luton, Bedfordshire.

Acknowledgements

Our thanks to Tim Collins, Dave Fucher and Ian Bishop-Laggett for their help and advice in the preparation of this book.

Douglas Tate is a teacher employed by Bedfordshire County Council.

CONTENTS

GENERAL

1. Introduction   5
2. Uses and abuses of computers   6

HARDWARE

3. Work station design   15
4. DIY alterations   27
5. Hardware additions   33
6. Hardware running BBC Basic   54
7. Networks   60
8. The Archimedes   64
9. Compatibility   76

GETTING ORGANISED

10. Organising your work.   82
11. Keeping control of your software   93
12. Working with discs   100
13. Setting up for a programming session   111

NEAT PROGRAMMING

14. Good style   130
15. Writing structured programs   134
16. Getting the best from BASIC   148
17. Graphics and screen displays   162
18. General tips and hints   174
19. Speeding up programs   197
20. Saving space   201

DEBUGGING

21. Debugging procedures   221
22. Specific Errors   224

USING THE COMPUTER AT HOME AND IN THE OFFICE

23. Standard programs   252
24. Assessing commercial programs   268
25. Making the most of commercial software   274
26. Introducing the computer to the office   279
27. Program protection, data theft and the law   286
28. Selling your own programs   293

1. INTRODUCTION

The potential for the computer is vast, but it is not always obvious how to harness it. You need to be led in the right direction - to see how you can use your computer to advantage: to learn good programming habits, to be shown how to tackle that elusive bug and translate the jargon. You may need help, encouragement and advice - otherwise you'll get lost. Even worse, without assistance you may throw up your hands in horror and commit your computer to its final resting place underneath the stairs.

Your problem is not so much where to go from here, but how. Take heart. Just as a picture on a camera slips into focus with a twist of the lens, so your use of the computer can, with a little guidance, become crisp and sharp. As you understand its potential you can revolutionise your attitude towards it. Your output will become greater in both quantity and quality. In short, your computing will become both useful and relevant.

This book is intended to give you that guidance - to plug the gap between beginner and expert. It is not about a particular computer and although based on the complete range of BBC computers, the language, BBC BASIC, is now run on many other makes.(Nimbus, IBM etc) All these computers have their own User guides, their own quirks and oddities (and advantages). We are not trying to supplant the User guides - in fact, in the course of this book we often refer to them - but instead we want to show a more overall approach. By the time you reach the end you should feel comfortable with your computer and be able to see its possibilities. Our aim is not to teach you by rote how to go about, say, programming, but instead to help you develop an attitude towards computing so that you can think through your problems and work out the solutions that are right for your particular situation.

- o O o -

There are so many potential cross references in a book of this type that it is impracticable to include them all in the text. Those which are substantial are referred to by chapter. In addition there is a comprehensive index.

2. USES AND ABUSES OF COMPUTERS

Let's begin with an overview of some of the things the computer can do - and also some of the things it can't (or, at least, not very well). Many of the subjects mentioned are covered in much greater detail later in the book, but we have dealt with everything in one initial chapter in order to give a broad idea of what the computer could do for you.

WHERE TO USE COMPUTERS

Computers are essentially very fast number-crunchers, and anything that can conveniently be reduced to numbers sits easily on them. (Don't forget that words, music and pictures can be reduced to groups of numbers so this also allows for processing of text, sound and pictures.) Computers also make good filing systems - their facility with numbers allows for fast indexing, and their ability to make comparisons allows for speedy retrieval of appropriate items.

Anything requiring the following computerises well
- a lot of calculations
- sorting
- matching of information
- retrieval of specific information from within a mass of other information
- statistics
- graphic presentation of figures
- storage of large quantities of information for later retrieval
- storage of standardised information that can easily be indexed
- manipulation of information, whether it be text, numbers, diagrams or graphics.

In addition, the computer copes well with large quantities of things, whether it be calculations or data.

WHERE NOT TO USE COMPUTERS

The opposite of these conditions shows when not to use computers.

If you are dealing with small amounts of information, or small quantities of maths, then there is little point in putting it on a computer. A pocket calculator, or a small card-index or notebook may be a more relevant method.

If what you are doing doesn't reduce easily to a numerical form, there is often not much point in using a computer, unless there is something else, such as processing of information,which tips the balance. For example, pictures are not well suited to computer storage - the high definition required consumes vast quantities of memory. However, if you are going to process pictures, that is another matter - having reduced the picture to a set of numbers describing the brightness and colour of each minute square you are now in a position to make changes to the picture by fiddling with the numbers themselves - this is the basis of many video and TV effects.

Again, you would not want to store lots of pictures in computerised form unless your retrieval or manipulation mechanism was more important than the pictures - the Domesday Book on videodisc is a good example of this: the importance of the picture is linked with its ease of retrieval and its relationship with other data.

Try to avoid using computers on information which is not easy to quantify - narrative descriptions, for example.

(Narrative can usefully be computerised if it is allied to an automatic indexing system allowing fast retrieval of appropriate text. This is the basis of much police computer work, where items such as a 'red scarf', or car colour, can be used to trace possible connections from within millions of words of officers' reports.)

Computers are fast, but they are also thick! They can't act on their own initiative, and cannot use any logic other than the logic contained within their operating system and program - hence the apocryphal stories of gas bills for £1,000,069.23! Humans would have spotted that something might just be wrong. So be careful when leaving something important to the judgment of the computer alone - programs have to be very well de-bugged to allow this sort of thing to happen safely. Even NASA, with its vast computer expertise doesn't take risks of this sort. Flight calculations are so complex that they can only be performed by computers - so they have three computers running simultaneously and any difference between the results will be scrutinised most carefully.

Computers are also mechanical. Whilst they are fantastic helpers in graphic design, being accurate, and completely symmetrical when required, they are essentially soul-less creatures and lack any element of humanity or true creativity (as opposed to mere randomness). Think of them as instruments and tools but don't expect them to create true art for you.

Finally, computers make great slaves - and lousy masters. If you can use it as a tool - fine. If you feel you are being used by it then it's bad news. Either re-write your approach to computerisation, rewrite your software, or kick it out and go back to quill pens!

GAMES

You either like computer games, or hate them. There are really only four sorts - the chase 'em and shoot 'em type, the pick-up-the-counters type, the strategy and planning variety, and the solve-the-puzzle type (the so-called 'Adventure Game').

Games do a lot more than you might think. It is said that battles were won on the playing fields of Eton - because future army officers learned teamwork there. So it is with computer games, which can help to develop attention, concentration, co-ordination, strategy, application, the ability to plan ahead, and a very graphic understanding of the relationship between effort, practice and reward.

Some games teach at the same time as being 'just' a game - so the child who plays 'Hangman' or 'Geographical hangman', or 'Simple Simon' with a rhythm or a tune will learn spelling, names of rivers and towns, and musical rhythms almost as a by-product of having fun.

A special mention should be put in here for the disabled, especially the disabled child - there are many teaching games to help such children to develop. The games go down well with the children, and because the computer is infinitely patient and has a one-to-one relationship with the user, the lesson proceeds at just the right pace for each pupil. (See also the section below on the disabled.)

Then there are the true teaching programs - maths, trigonometry, chemistry, typing, gardening. You name it, there's a program to help you with it. The computer is a very patient teacher and doesn't get cross when you make a mistake - but will test you thoroughly at each level before allowing you to go on to the next. This means that you can't skip too far forwards without digesting the early steps properly. This is important because if you try to rush into a subject you will get frustrated and be more likely to give up when later information 'won't fit in'.

However, the computer is not necessarily the answer to every problem, and programs vary in quality. Specialist advice is worth getting - there are teaching resource centres which have information about good quality programs, and your child's school will be able to help.

If you are a teacher you can set up your own teaching programs without necessarily having to learn programming. There are program 'shells' available to allow you to write in your own questions, information and the expected responses. (Microtext is one)

WORD-PROCESSING

Word-processing is just a technical name for typing what you want onto the screen, changing it around at the touch of a key, storing it electronically on tape or disc so that it can be called up at a moment's notice, and eventually printing it out on paper.

The beauty of word-processing is its flexibility. You need to write a magazine article, and you don't want to have to re-type each draft? Simple. Do it on a word-processor, and the only typing between drafts will be the changes themselves. You want to move the third paragraph to the end, and the fifth to where the third originally was? A few key-presses will do it all. If you want, you can check automatically that every word is correctly spelled, using a spell-checking program which you have customised to include all the technical words you personally use. Yours might include "rocker arm", "copper sulphate", "Rachmaninov" or "Zena Skinner".

You want to write a Christmas letter to all your friends with mostly the same information, but a little personal paragraph or two for each recipient? Simplicity itself with even the most basic wordprocessor. Create a basic letter format, and save it. Then call it up, address it to Uncle Fergus, add or delete sections, and print it out. Then call up the basic letter again, and re-personalise it for Cousin Albert.... and so on.

You have a list of customers and their addresses, and you want to send an individually headed letter to each? A mail-merge program will do it automatically. If you have the right sort of database (see below) you could select a special group of customers for your mailshot. (say, all those who had bought left-handed widgets between January and August of last year) (See chapter 23 for further information)

ACCOUNTANCY

You want to keep the books straight in your single-handed business, do wages, VAT and keep track of all those orders? There are many 'INTEGRATED ACCOUNTS' packages which will do the whole job for you - no more headaches with cash-books that don't balance! Or you could purchase individual modules to do just one area of accountancy - such as the cash-book only, or wages etc. If you've ever tried to do wages for a small firm, you will immediately appreciate the saving in time that automated accounts bring. Wages and National Insurance calculations that normally take half a day to do are now complete in (quite literally) two minutes.

You want to find out where all the money is going, and what you could do about it? A SPREADSHEET program helps you to lay out the whole sorry mess and see what would happen if you changed some of your outgoings. Basically, a spreadsheet allows you to ask the question "What if...?" and carries out what may be quite complex calculations to display the results. "What if.... we hire three more staff?: what will happen to our overheads, our production capabilities, our requirements for office space, our cash-flow, our profits, each month for the next ten years?" "What if.... we hire more equipment and sack two secretaries...." "What if.... we get another two salesmen....can we cope with the cash-flow problems: will we be able to cope with the orders....?"

Spreadsheets don't do it on their own! You have to provide the formulae. However, doing the calculations manually is a daunting prospect. The complexity of calculations becomes almost overwhelming when there are a large number of possible variables to be considered, especially where each variable has a knock-on effect on other variables. This is where the computerised spread-sheet really comes into its own.

Spreadsheets are for planning - and not necessarily financial, either. If you can quantify it, it will fit on a spreadsheet. Therefore calculations of loads and stresses on an aircraft wing would fit well on one - if we increased the stiffness of the structure by 5% and we decreased the overall weight of the plane by 4.5% and we increased the length of the wing by 10%, what would happen..... Instead if we increased the stiffness by only 2% but reduced the weigh of the plane still further.......

COMMUNICATIONS

You have a small team of salesmen mobile throughout the country and wish to keep in contact. Use the communicating ability of your computer to leave messages, via the telephone, on an electronic bulletin board. Then you don't have to establish physical contact to transfer the information.

Alternatively, you can do your banking, shop and pay your bills by computer without leaving your home or writing a letter......

ACQUIRING INFORMATION

Using just your computer and the telephone system you can communicate with database computers all round the country (or the world, if necessary). These computers hold vast quantities of information on a wide range of subjects and if you have the authority to do so - which usually means you have to pay a user fee - you may read (and print out) information from these data banks. Thus you can catch up with the news, find out the latest Test score, search for complex scientific information, find out about share movements, check on aircraft and train delays because of the fog, download interesting programs for your micro, see what's on TV (in Iceland!).....

In the United Kingdom the best known databases are Oracle, Ceefax and Prestel: users of Prestel can also get through to other computers in this and other countries, via a facility called Gateway. There are a large number of public, private and commercial databases in the USA and in Europe.

Charges vary. Many databanks, such as Prestel, are accessible on paying a small membership fee, charged on a monthly or yearly basis. More sophisticated databases are usually costly items, charged on a page by page basis. Alternatively, and particularly for search procedures involving professional databases, charges can be levied on the number of 'hits' generated: for example, searching a medical database for all occurrences of 'Freidrich's ataxia' in conjunction with 'liposomal abnormalities'.

In general, the more that the information held on the computer is related to business or the professions, the more expensive it is likely to be.

CONTROLLING EQUIPMENT

You wish to control some electrical operations whose functioning depends on the fluctuation in temperature. Simple, connect a thermometer and the necessary electronics to the computer for tireless control.

The best known control system available at present is the series RED BOXES. The unique thing about the system is that it uses the ring main circuit of your house to send signals from one place to another(like those FM baby alarms!). The system has five boxes: a power switching module, Infra-red detector, Analog - Digital converter, RS232 (for networking etc) and a VERY loud alarm box. The whole thing is 'programmed' by your computer which can then be used for other things. Apparently there is no problem if your neighbour has a similar setup to you, as each set of boxes has a unique code.

DATABASES

You are an avid collector and sorter of details about old cars. Why not keep all that information on a DATABASE. It will all be instantly accessible, you won't mislay information again, and you can instantly sort through your lists for information of a certain type - eg all cars earlier than 1935, with an engine capacity of more than 1.5 litres, made either in Germany or in the United States.

The two key words about databases are 'big' and 'search'. Databases can be huge, but you can extract relevant information from them in a very short time. The bigger the database the more useful is the search facility. The effectiveness of the database is best measured by the quality of its search facility, both in speed and ease of use.

GRAPHICS

As a salesman you might find that a moving graphical presentation on the micro screen helps to get your ideas over quickly and impressively, especially when linked up to displays of financial information, market trends, profit margins etc. Allied to this is the use of the computer for the creation of art-work, either to be printed out or photographed off the screen. Among the advantages of this over the easel are the ability to erase or change incorrect work, to shift work about on screen, to experiment and to be able to use striped or spotted paint!

COMPUTER AIDED DESIGN

A similar idea applies to the creation of technical drawings. The computer can produce 3-D images of your work, rotate it and allow a much more humanistic approach to design than trying to plan everything out on two dimensional pieces of paper.

MUSIC

Music is fast becoming a major area of usage for computers either for the storage of information or in the actual creation of new sounds. This is an area for much fun and experimentation.

There are many very expensive add on gubbins for the computer where in fact the machine usually only acts as storage and sequencer. However there are a number of good programs which make use of the computer's internal chips some even provide hard copy of compositions. Possibly the best device to emerge is the Music 5000 system which adds a true synthesizer to the computer very cheaply and makes it into a real music system. An add on keyboard is available to turn the system into a real time musical instrument. The beauty of the system is that you can get excellent results at a very basic level and yet have a tremendous depth of possibilities.

Having said that some add-ons use the computer 'only' for storage etc, one has to mention MIDI. This is a system which gives a common interface between musical systems, keyboards, sequencers, drum synths etc. There are now one or two systems on the market which use the BBC as a central part of the system. Adverts appear from time to time in the computer press (Micro User seems to have them more frequently than others) but the place to look is in the Synthesizer and electronic music magazines.

The sound system on the Archimedes is very much more comprehensive than on the other machines in the range but is still easy to program. The Welcome disc has a good music editor to start you off. Beware the User Guide: getting music from the Archimedes is not quite the same as with the rest of the range so don't expect it.

DESKTOP PUBLISHING

It is now possible to emulate newspaper layouts with some wordprocessors. Multi-column layouts are quite easy to achieve. However, to incorporate pictures usually means using a special package. There are programs on the market, like Fleet Street Editor and Stop Press which allow you fully to emulate the newspaper style, pictures and all! As they give different facilities it would be wise to have a good demonstration of each before purchase! It is true to say that, at the time of publication, no one firm appears to have produced an easily managable package which gives professional results. It is early days.

WRITING YOUR OWN PROGRAMS

Although at first sight writing your own programs may seem attractive, it may not necessarily be a good idea, particularly for business use. Any program worth doing is likely to be complex, requiring hours of programming, de-bugging and final proving on-site. It is almost certainly more cost-effective to buy a custom-made program and tailor it to your own needs, if one is available. It is certainly less frustrating, especially for the novice programmer! (See chapter 25 on adapting commercial software for your own use.)

On the other hand, you may need a relatively simple business program which is not available off the shelf. In which case, see what you can do! But, be warned, the more complex a program, the longer it takes to prove it works properly - and in business you cannot afford to have inaccurate records or calculations.

Alternatively, you may want to create programs just for the fun of it, or because ultimately you want to sell them. You'll need a lot of patience - good programming is not something you learn overnight. However, it's good fun creating your own software, even if it does take a long time. Seeing your work running correctly for the first time can be a great thrill, akin to the feelings of the climber who's just topped a peak.

THE DISABLED

We have already mentioned learning games for the disabled. In addition to games there are programs and specialised hardware now available catering for all sorts of disabilities both mental and physical. The computer can act as a lifeline for those who find movement (including speech) difficult.

There are word-processors with special keyboards which allow speedy writing by those whose muscle functions are very restricted: this allows greatly increased communication, especially where the quality of speech is poor.

Computers can control electrical items, and a severely disabled person can use the computer to do things that would otherwise be impossible - such as ring a particular telephone number, unlock the front door or turn the heating on and off. All this can be controlled with a simple menu program requiring Yes/No answers, performed through the movement of just one or two muscles on a toggle switch, or by blowing and sucking down a control tube.

If you are disabled, or have a disabled friend or relative, do ask for advice from specialised centres. In the case of children, contact your local Teachers' Centre or get the magazine 'Educational Computing'.

3. WORK STATION DESIGN

HEALTH AND SAFETY

Contrary to popular belief,there are no major health hazards associated with using computers and VDUs. A recent article in the British Medical Journal has analysed all the worries that have been expressed. It concludes:-

> There is no conclusive evidence that the use of VDUs is associated with miscarriages: earlier reports were based on inaccurate statistics.
>
> The radiation (ie X-rays) produced by modern TVs and monitors is negligible (but if you are using a pre-1972 colour television with your micro, this may not be correct, so in this case don't get too near).
>
> VDUs produce extra-low frequency magnetic fields (ELF). There have been some laboratory reports about possible problems with ELF, but the relevance to VDU operators is doubtful, to say the least. In any case, VDUs and television sets produce ELF predominantly to the back and side, and not the front.
>
> The screen produces a high electrostatic field and this may create problems with dry skin and mild eczema, particularly in conditions of low humidity.
>
> By far the greatest problem is operator fatigue caused through a bad working posture and incorrectly adjusted levels of screen brightness.

It appears that working with VDUs doesn't cause eye problems, but may bring them more quickly to the operator's attention.

On the other hand, some people who suffer from migraine may get more attacks whilst working with a VDU. If you have the right type of monitor and it is adjusted correctly (see below) then you will minimise this problem.

Migraine (in some sufferers) is brought on by flashing lights, and the more obvious the flicker, the more it is likely to trigger a migraine. You have therefore to avoid flicker and excessive contrast, especially flicker 'out of the corner of your eye'. If you have problems with migraine, then the following may be of help.

1. Use a VDU with a long-decay phosphor. This gives less
    decay of image intensity between successive frames of the
    TV display, and the result is a flicker-free image. This
    sort of monitor is excellent for database-type work, but
    rotten for fast-moving arcade-like games where the long
    decay rates cause ghosting.

2. It is a help to have a screen with a faster refresh rate,
    but this is a function of the hardware and really only
    applies to business machines.

3. A rock-steady display is essential. It may help to turn
    the interlace off.

4. A slow screen scroll is better than a fast one.

5. Set brightness and contrast to the minimum necessary for
    sensible viewing.

6. Take note of all that we say below about good monitor
    set-up, avoiding reflections on the screen, lighting the
    background etc. It will pay dividends.

Although there are no major health hazards associated with VDU work, there are
nevertheless a number of items that can affect your comfort (and your temper!).
Whether you are a professional or an amateur, your workstation needs to be
designed so that you can work comfortably for long hours.

Whilst they are good in their own field of programming, computer experts can go
completely to pieces when it comes to positioning equipment. The average home
computer workstation seems designed for maximum discomfort and eyestrain, and
the specialist desks sold in the magazines are often a disgrace. Even respected
equipment designers don't help, putting disc drives on top of the computer and the
VDU on top of that, thus bringing the VDU less than two feet from your nose.

Try this experiment. Hold your head erect, and look at the horizon. Now shut your
eyes, count slowly to ten and open them again. You will find that you are looking
downwards about 30 degrees. This is the angle your eyes normally assume at rest.
When you read a book or write a letter you automatically position your head so that
your eyes end up in this position of maximum repose, aiming downwards at about
30 degrees. The distance between head and book is governed by the angle the
eyes need to travel in order to encompass a line of print. In this way the head and
neck are relaxed and you can go on reading for hours.

In contrast, most computer workstations require you to hold your head unnaturally erect with the eyes looking either horizontally or even upwards. The VDU is usually much too close, giving too wide an angle of travel to the eyes, which is uncomfortable.

All this leads to eye strain, neck-ache and a reduced span of concentration.

Holding yourself rigid in one position is not good. There are times when it is better not to have an 'ergonomically designed' workstation if the end result is that you spend hours on end in a fixed position. Sideways movement, especially of the neck and upper body, is the best antidote to a stiff neck and upper back, so make sure there are things you use which are in the wrong place! For example, if you have a book you need to use on your left hand side, store it on the right hand side of your work area, and vice versa. (Back in the days of quill pens this would have meant having the inkwell at the front of the desk, just by your left elbow!)

It is important to have regular rest periods away from the VDU to avoid the all-too-present tendency to seize up solid.

Bashing away at the keyboard for extensive periods can give a painful inflammation of the tendons in the wrist, called teno-synovitis. Prevention is better than cure, and if you find you are starting to ache then STOP - you are overdoing it.

DESIGNING YOUR COMPUTER STATION

1. Find a suitable chair. We are not all the same shape or size,and what suits one person won't always suit another so this will be a very individual choice. The chair should have a back support that puts you in a natural sitting position with your back slightly arched. When you sit down the upper portion of the body should feel that it is standing up!

The height of the chair is an individual choice - we do not all have the same length legs and what fits one person may not fit another. The best chairs will have a height adjustment, and be on castors (but not ones that slide about all over the place - if you have to keep making little movements to keep yourself in the right position your muscles won't relax properly: the same goes for tilting chairs). There should not be too much support near the knees as this is tiring: the thighs should be as near horizontal as possible allowing the lower leg to drop vertically to the floor with the feet firmly placed either on the floor or on a footrest.

Secretary's chairs are pretty good if you can find one to fit you.

2.Now fix the height of the surface on which the keyboard is to stand.

When you type, your forearms should be roughly horizontal, with the elbows vertically below the shoulders. (However, it has recently been demonstrated that a lot of non-typist computer operators prefer to lean back in their chairs, with their arms at a more open angle.) Some people find it easier to have the computer keyboard placed about 4-5 inches from the front edge of the table so that the wrists can rest on the working surface while typing - with the Beeb, this means putting a raised bit in front of the keyboard. This is something to experiment with as some people like a wrist rest and some don't.

There is a separate reason for having the keyboard pushed forward. If you are not a touch typist, and therefore have to look down at the keyboard, then if you have the keyboard jammed into your stomach you will have to bend your neck even more in order to see what you are doing. You are less likely to get neck-strain if you push the keyboard forward, irrespective of whether you also choose to use a wrist-rest.

While on the subject of the height of the work-top, don't forget the width - there needs to be space for papers and books, so that you can copy from them, refer to them, or make notes. You should have shelf space for a few reference manuals, and somewhere handy to keep your discs safely and neatly. You will probably need space for a desk light. In general, work out what space width-wise you think you need - then double or treble it!

3. Now to your VDU. It has already been said that most are too close and too high. We prefer the lower edge of the screen to be level with the top of the computer, or possibly a little lower, and tilted back so that the screen is at right angles to the line from your eyes to the centre of the screen. If you are designing the workstation from scratch it may even be a good idea to make a small well for the monitor to stand in, so that it can tilt backwards at the correct angle and still be at a comfortable height.

Unfortunately some of the later Acorn machines are supplied with such short leads that it is difficult to place them in any other way than with the disc drive behind the keyboard and the monitor piled on top. The Compact and Archimedes are offenders here - the short leads connecting the keyboard to the box containing the disc drives virtually force you to use this configuration. It is possible to get longer leads for the Monitor from places like Watford Electronics, but an easier way is to buy the monitor as a separate item. (Even if it is an Acorn monitor it usually comes with a longer lead than that given with the complete setup ... strange.)

However, the golden rule is to experiment. Just as a chair is an individual choice, so is the final layout of your workstation. You may prefer the monitor higher than the position we have suggested: in that case, fine. But if you find life gets tiring try moving things around a bit: go back to the basic principles we have outlined. Only you can judge.

4. Where to put the paperwork. We said earlier how important it is to position the VDU so that your eyes and neck are at their most restful. Don't forget that you may be looking as much (if not more) at a book of listings, or written material that you are entering prior to word-processing. It is so easy to put the paper to be copied down on the table by the side of the computer - thus ruining the ergonomic work-station that you have so painstakingly created! (your neck will be bent again). In addition, your eyes will have constantly to be re-focussing from the paper to the screen and back again, as these will now be at different distances.

A bookrest placed level with the VDU will solve the problem. A small table-top music stand can be very useful as a book rest.

If your work is mainly copy typing, so that you look mainly at the paper, and less frequently at the screen, it makes sense to have the VDU to one side, and the copy paper in front of you.

CONSTRUCTING A DO-IT-YOURSELF WORKSTATION

Often it is not practical to have the whole of your work surface at the low level needed for the keyboard and monitor, so this portion of your workstation need only be about 22 inches wide. The materials can be quite lightweight, and ordinary Contiboard or Melamine-covered board is suitable. If you want to put it together quickly but still be able to experiment you could use 'corner blocks' (also called knockdown fittings) to hold everything together. For a more stable construction the more permanent screw and dowel method is better.

Rather than digging holes in the work bench, you could have a super-high chair with a foot-rest (unless you suffer from vertigo!) In this case, make certain that the chair is stable and does not have a swivel seat.

(See diagram of Workstation on page 324)

LIGHTING AND PROBLEMS OF CONTRAST

Eye strain is one of the biggest bugbears of computing. There are four distinct causes:-

1. Too much contrast in the field of vision.
2. Too little contrast or too dim a subject, especially when looking at something that is not clearly defined.
3. Poor lighting of paperwork.
4. Unwanted light or reflections on the screen.
5. For those who wear glasses, the distance to the screen is usually too far for reading glasses and too near for the normal long distance ones. If you have an old pair of frames it is practical (and cheap) to get a set of lenses specially made for computing.

Eyes get tired much more quickly if there is too great a contrast in the field of vision.

1. The VDU People get muddled when talking about contrast and brightness. Contrast is the difference in intensity between print and background. Brightness applies to the whole screen.

It is not good to have too contrasty a screen. Unfortunately, a very contrasty picture sharpens up the quality of print and graphics, so it is easy to fall into the trap of using a lot of contrast as at first sight it looks very impressive: however, it makes the screen difficult to work with for anything other than a short period.

It is restful to have the screen looking as much like printed paper as possible - the screen should not appear to be emitting light. If you have too contrasty a screen it appears to radiate light from the print, so turn the contrast down: this usually means you will have to turn the brightness up slightly to get the right effect.

If you have a monochrome monitor, you will find that orange (or green) on grey is much more restful than bright orange (or green) on dense black. With a colour monitor you can experiment with different colours for the background and foreground.

Don't assume that black is the only background colour you can have - it is the colour which creates the greatest contrast, and for word-processing and figure work you don't need a lot of contrast.

On the other hand, detail tends to be lost when the contrast is reduced, so it may be necessary to alter the levels for graphics or games. Don't feel that one setting is right for all occasions.

2. The area behind the VDU, and the room in general. When television first came into our homes it was quickly recognised that a light of some sort was needed in the corner behind it, in order to give the eyes something to focus on besides the screen, and to reduce the contrast between the screen and its surroundings. The same is true of your VDU. It may be necessary to light the wall area to the rear of your workstation, especially if your only other source of light in the room is directed onto your work-top.

Professional computer rooms often use up-lighters to create a gentle, shadowless, all-round light. With uplighters you cannot see the bulb directly, only light reflected off the ceiling, so there are no problems with reflections of the lights themselves off the surface of the screen . If you use uplighters you will probably need additional directed light for your paperwork.

3. Light for your papers and the keyboard creates its own problems. A light that is bright enough for reading paperwork may well be too bright for the VDU and "wash it out", so make sure that you have directed light that does not spill onto the screen. An Anglepoise-type lamp may be the answer.

There should be no spill of light onto the VDU from natural sources either. So don't put the VDU in sunlight.

4. Reflections. Make sure that you minimise reflections of light from the surface of the screen. If they are prominent then you tend to turn up the brightness and contrast to try and hide them. The result is more eyestrain from a screen with too much contrast. Identify the source of the reflected light and deal with it - turn lights off, close curtains etc.

You can buy non-reflective glass screens to place in front of the VDU. There are several different makes available, ranging from about the cost of a good disc program to maybe four times that price. Shop around and see what suits you. Don't bother trying to make your own screen using non-reflective glass of the type used in picture framing. (If you look carefully at your monitor you will see it has a curved screen. Putting a piece of flat non-reflective glass against this screen causes loss of definition, especially at the edges where the screen is further away from the glass.)

Alternatively, and better, buy a monitor which already has a non-reflective screen.

HOUSING THE DISC DRIVE AND PRINTER

Cassette players are usually easy to position. The difficult decisions are:-

Where to put fanfold paper.
where to put the printer.
where to put the disc drive/s.

Many 'professional' units have the disc drive over the computer, and the VDU on top of that. As has been said earlier, this is not a good idea. If you want to save space and have a neat-looking layout, why not build a combined disc housing, printer stand and paper store, to stand on one side of your main set-up?

Unfortunately for our plans, many manufacturers of 40/80 disc drives have decided to place the 40/80 switch at the back! This of course makes any reasonable design out of the question, so we've ignored it and hope that you have a good long arm to reach it or the good sense to buy from those with a decently designed drive. An alternative, if you must have 40/80, is to use the option provided by Watford Electronics with their DFS and switch with software and not mechanically. It's cheaper as well.

Let's assume that you have a printer and double horizontal disc drives.

It is easy to make a support bridge to:-

1.   House the disc drive and provide ample ventilation and access to the rear.
2.   Provide a flat platform for about 2 inches of fanfold paper.
3.   Give support to your printer.

The whole construction will have a footprint (i.e.the size of the area on which it rests) the size of the printer footprint plus about 3 inches behind. The total height would be about 9-10 inches.

The support bridge can be of normal shelf Melamine or Contiboard about 16mm (5/8") thick. You can just hammer nails into it, but screws or corner fittings are more elegant. The tunnel top needs to be a couple of inches narrower than your printer and an inch or so wider than the disc drive which sits inside it. You should find with standard units that there is no conflict of sizes.

At this point you can do one of two things - be masochistic and build a thin shelf inside the tunnel to house the fanfold paper, or take the easy way out and put a cork floor tile on top of the drive for the paper to rest on. The latter has advantages. It provides a non-slip surface for the paper, helps to stop hum from the drive by damping the top cover plate and provides a small overhang at the back to stop the paper flopping onto any heat sinks. It gives the maximum room for paper with minimum height. It is also easy!

This all sounds incredibly simple, and indeed it is, but it works!

STATIC

The problems with static are two-fold. The screen has a considerable static charge created on it in the process of creating the image. This ionises the air in front of the screen and causes particles of dust to be repelled from the screen towards the face of the operator. Both the dust and the ionisation of the surrounding air are thought to affect people with sensitive skins, especially those with eczema. An earthed screen placed in front of the monitor screen will reduce the effects: these are available commercially.

However, recent tests in Sweden showed that most of these screens were ineffective in reducing electrostatic fields, that after six months of use no screen actually worked any longer, and that regular cleaning seemed to accelerate this deterioration of function.

Secondly, it is easy to build up a large static charge just by walking across a nylon carpet in plastic shoes, combing your head, or taking off your sweater. If this static is earthed through your computer it may well corrupt the memory, and many unexplained 'bugs' turn out to be due to this mechanism. If you are running software that has to be accurate (business software for example) then get an earthed antistatic mat for the computer to sit on. If the operator touches the mat before touching keyboard or discs any static will be harmlessly discharged.

One final word about static. You can pay incredible prices for antistatic mats and screen guards. These seem to help your health and the health of your computer but they definitely deplete the wallet. It will have to be up to you. For occasional use of the computer you would be hard pressed to justify £100 for this sort of add-on!

BUYING A MONITOR

Human beings are remarkable creatures, swayed by trivia. Advertising is subtle, although all the subtleties are not well understood, which is why we are not all rich! However, when we choose, for example, a car, we are swayed by the line of the roof, the quality of the advert, the charm of the salesman and tend to forget to ask if it will last to its 500 mile service. Please do not allow trivia to sway you in the choice of a screen at which you are going to look for many fruit(ful/less) hours. It is now possible to buy complete systems, monitor included, usually at a slight price advantage usually. Please beware and still take the advice given below. We have seen some 'system' monitors which were dreadfully set up.

NEVER BUY A SEALED BOX. Always see the set in operation before you buy and make certain that you take away the one you saw!

Allow a few minutes for the set to warm up before giving a judgement.

Ask to see it tied up to your computer, if you can, not a similar one.

If you can do none of these things, at the very least:

Make certain that the monitor is compatible with your computer - there are a number of standards and they are all different!

Look at 80 column print all over the screen. Is it crisp and clear? View the monitor with both interlace on and off. (The interlacer moves the picture up and down slightly to create a more continuous image - but it also makes type wobble slightly. To turn off the interlacing use *TV0,1 followed by a change to any mode other than Mode 7. *TV0,0 turns it back on again at the next Mode change. Mode 7 is always interlaced.) If the picture is not quite in the right vertical position, the *TV command will again help. The first number alters the vertical position one line at a time. *TV1,1 moves the picture UP one line, *TV255,1 moves it DOWN one line. So, *TV254,0 will put the picture two lines down and turn on interlace. Note - it only does this after the next Break or Mode change.

If possible look at a grid on the screen to see if there is distortion in the horizontal or vertical lines. Do the lines crowd together as they come to one side? Is there obnoxious fringing on the lines at any point? You are looking for is perfect linearity and perfect purity of white on all lines all over the screen. You won't find it, but you can come pretty close.

It is worthwhile looking at some of the dual purpose units which are now on the market (TV/Monitor sets): some of these are quite good. (Dare we say it, some are better than so-called monitors.) If possible, do a direct comparison with a 'proper' monitor.

If possible, get a matt, non-reflective screen. If this makes the price too high then get a screen filter.

Finally, if you get the chance, go round a big business computer show and have a look at the professional monochrome monitors. The quality on some of these sets is astounding and will give you a standard by which to judge.

MONITOR SET-UP

Sometimes due to age or mechanical shock a monitor loses its sharp focus. It is possible to set it up again using a grid pattern on the screen, but if you have any doubts about your ability with high voltage electrical apparatus, don't even think about attempting this.

The grid can be made with the following:-

```
  5 REM Grid Generator
 10 MODE 1
 15 GCOL 0,135
 20 FOR X = 0 TO 1236 STEP 128
 30   VDU 24, X; 0; X + 15; 1023; 16
 50 NEXT
 60 VDU 24, 1264; 0; 1279; 1023; 16
 70 FOR Y=0 TO 960 STEP 128
 80   VDU 24, 0; Y; 1279; Y + 8; 16
 90 NEXT
100 VDU 24, 0; 1015; 1279; 1023; 16
110 END
```

Note that the bars are quite thick. If the lines are thinly drawn, it is very easy to mis-interpret the fringes. A very badly adjusted set can show the three colours as separate lines with a gap in between - the width of bar overcomes this.

Yes, the right hand and top boxes are smaller than the rest. This is so that a bar can be on the limits of the screen.

This next program can be used as a Grey scale indicator, or to show the colours next to each other for intensity. Play around with the data to get the colours in the order you want them. The order given here has another function - the colours are in order of intensity as they appear on a monochrome monitor.

```
 5 REM Grey Scale
10 MODE 2
20 FOR X = 0 TO 8
30    READ col
40    GCOL 0,col
50    VDU 24, X * 128; 0; (X+1) * 128; 1023; 16
60 NEXT
70 DATA 135,128,132,129,133,130,134,131,135
80 END
```

Adjust the contrast, brightness and colour until you get a satisfactory balance of contrast, intensity and colour saturation.

No attempt has been made to stipulate the SAFETY PROCEDURES you should observe whilst adjusting a set.

If you don't know them DON'T DO IT.

4. DIY ALTERATIONS

IT'S NOT TOO LATE TO VENTILATE!

Many professional computers have a built-in fan to dissipate the heat (and annoy the operator). None of the Acorn series is provided with a fan as standard. The Compact and Master have a respectable grill to let the heat out in the top, the Archimedes in the side. However, if you expand the Archimedes by adding a Podule you will also need to add a backplate. This has a fan built in as standard.

Do you remember Roy Castle frying an egg on a rock in an American desert during a 'Record Breakers' programme? You might try the same on your Beeb after a short session of frenetic computing!

Perhaps this is a little bit of an exaggeration, but the left hand side of the BBC-B (where the mains transformer is) does get remarkably warm and can cause all sorts of spurious happenings. The situation is worse if add-on boards are present. The higher the use of current, the hotter it gets, and the smaller the reserve of current supply available to compensate for mains variations. As the temperature rises the chips begin to work nearer to their 'limits' and are more likely to generate errors. (Some Add-On Board manufacturers have seen the light and have limited the number of ROMs which may be activated, or even present in the machine, in order to limit the drain on the power supply.)

Eventually total corruption of add-on boards can occur due to overheating as a result of the CPU (central processing unit chip) becoming overloaded. Then the only real cure is to change the chip.

There is an alternative way on the BBC-B to reduce the problem of overheating

BUT A WORD OF WARNING....

do not attempt to do this unless you are competent with tools and do not mind invalidating the guarantee.

The problem is to get rid of the excess heat, and the answer is remarkably simple. There is plenty of room for air to get in and circulate from the bottom - it just needs letting out.

However, there are one or two pitfalls, so be careful.

Having taken the cover off, drill a grillwork of small holes in it above the power supply on the left hand side of the machine cover. Drill from the outside in order to avoid raising burrs on the outside of the case.

How big should the holes be? It would be possible to put some grill cloth behind the holes to catch any falling bits and pieces, but the restriction to the air flow would outweigh any benefit. A compromise is to make the holes small enough and frequent enough to provide a ready airflow and yet stop reasonably sized objects. 4mm diameter holes seem to be about right. A grid of 5 holes across, by 8 from front to back provides quite a nice flow. The size of this matrix is 50mm x 70mm, and is situated with its front edge about 20mm directly behind the rear of the speaker grill.

Now it looks as though termites have been at it! Disguise it by painting a solid black rectangle over the whole area. It now looks like a solid black rectangle with holes in it, but at least it looks designed! Alternatively, do the equivalent of fretwork and drill out your favourite design shape, such as an Owl, or your firm's logo.

The holes which you have drilled will have sharp edges. These can be made smoother by placing a larger drill in the hole and rotating it by hand a couple of times.

A final word of warning - again - make sure you take the lid off the machine before drilling the holes!

HUM & DISC DRIVES

Some people happen to be very sensitive to low frequency sound, hum in particular. It is a fact of life that most electrical gadgets hum: usually it is caused by the transformer. It is difficult and expensive to build a transformer which has no audible hum because the alternating current actually causes the metal core to expand and contract 50 times a second.

The main noise is transmitted through the chassis and feet of the machine, or to the case. In either circumstance it sets the table or cover resonating like a violin, amplifying the noise, and you get carried away screaming after a time. Hum is a health hazard on a long term basis and can cause fatigue for no apparent reason. Get rid of it.

There are a variety of cures.

WARNING - you should not even think about going into a disc drive with a screwdriver to do anything inside.

1. Obtain a Cork tile, as used for floors or walls, or a
    polystyrene tile as used for ceilings, and also some of
    that bubble plastic that is used to wrap delicate
    equipment. (It is also useful for keeping greenhouses
    warm, so you might be able to get a small lump for free at
    your local Garden Centre.) Glue the flat side of the bubble
    stuff to the cork tile. Put this assembly on the table
    bubbles down and stand the disc drive on it. This will
    almost completely remove the hum transmitted through your
    table. Even more effective is to make a sandwich of two
    cork tiles and the bubbles.

2. Quite a lot of hum is radiated by the cover. There are two
    approaches, both of which can be used together. If you loosen
    the cover screws and gently shift and press the cover in
    various ways you will no doubt find a position where there is
    minimum hum. Gradually tighten the screws, listening at the
    same time. This operation is up to your ears! When you have
    a minimum amount of hum, stick another cork tile onto the top
    of the cover with a lot of little blobs of Bluetac - this
    gives a further reduction in transmitted sound. (Bluetac
    rather than Evostick, manufacturers may not take kindly to
    Oriental decoration on a drive returned under guarantee!) Now
    store the printer paper on top of that for even more sound
    absorption. Before you do this, find out if the cover gets
    hot with prolonged use: if it does, you will have to think of
    another ploy.

A word of warning - whatever you do, don't restrict any air flow in any way - it can
prove expensive.

BEND YOUR LEGS

When you first get a ROM out of its packing it will almost certainly not fit in the
socket. This is because the legs are splayed out at an angle. At this stage, if you
are not familiar with chips, panic sets in. The solution is mercifully easy.... Take the
chip and lay it on its side so that all its left (or right) legs are flat on the table. Now
carefully bend the legs a few degrees by manipulating the body of the chip until the
legs are at right angles to the body: then do the other side. If you want to be really
finicky, bend the legs until they match up exactly with the slots - this makes them so
much easier to insert and extract.

This is far more complicated to explain than to do and when you have done it once
you will wonder what all the fuss was about.

REMOVING CHIPS

It is all too easy to damage a chip whilst trying to remove it from its socket. The chip suddenly 'gives', your hand bounces up and then reflexly down, smashing the chip into the board and spreadeagling the legs in interesting asymmetrical patterns.

Extraction tools can be obtained from places like Watford Electronics for about £1.50 and are well worth the expense as chips cost much more than this to replace. An alternative tool may be made out of a small screwdriver bent at about 20 degrees approximately 20mm from the end.

SOUND VOLUME

1.   There are often ways of killing the sound effects in games and word-processing programs through software.

2.   The Master can have its volume reduced to half by altering the set-up configuration. When in this state the first sound of the start noise is switched off.

3.   An alternative is to fit a volume control - then when you next write some music or play that loud space game, your neighbours won't be forced to hear it! It will also turn off that dreadful major 7th you hear when you first switch on. Thankfully the Archimedes has a much more gentle sound reminiscent of an Hotel lobby 'bong'!

For the BBC-B:

There are several sound-control kits on the market which don't involve any soldering and are very neat, but if you scorn the pre-packed approach all you need is a switched jack socket and a 47 OHM Logarithmic Volume control. The wiper is connected to the output, or centre pin of the jack socket. The two outside pins are attached to the loud speaker wires. Make certain that the 0v line from the speaker lead is attached to the earth pin of the jack socket. This will give sound to an external speaker.

If you just want to deal with the internal speaker, you need only extend the two wires which lead to the loudspeaker so that they reach the potentiometer which you can place conveniently in the Econet hole. The two wires from the plug in the board go to the two outer pins. One outer pin and the wiper pin (centre) go to the speaker. There is a little blue (or red or green!) box near the plug which has a screw head in its side. This is the computer's internal volume control which should be turned to maximum when you have fitted your own control. Note that some versions of the Beeb have the volume control the 'wrong' way round, so you will have to experiment to find out which direction increases the volume. Note that this only applies to the BBC-B.

MAKE YOUR SCREWDRIVER WORK FOR YOU

If you are an enthusiast you will have the lid off the thing almost as much as on, mucking about with ROMs. Under these circumstances it may be a good idea to invest in an external ROM box, or a ZIF (zero insertion force) socket, in order to allow you to change ROMs without risking damage either to them or to the insides of the machine.

As with all good ideas there are problems. Some Roms do not work reliably in external ZIF sockets. The carrier board type, such as Spellmaster, Quest Paint and Interword have on-board bank switching and can suffer from timing problems due to the longer cable supplying the socket. We have not personally come across this problem and the system is incredibly useful but we have heard reports of errors.

However, if you insist on fiddling with the innards, do get a screwdriver with a very comfortable grip and the correct size head. There is nothing worse than struggling with an uncomfortable screwdriver that also messes up the screw head. Never buy a cheap screwdriver, they can prove expensive.

Some people leave the lid unscrewed. This is not always a 'good thing', as it is so easy to forget and do damage when lifting the computer. Don't worry about repeated use of the screws - the threads in the plastic really do last.

Whatever you do with the top, do remember that the keyboard must be firmly screwed down. The keyboard circuit board flexes, and this is reduced by a support bar in the machine: many faults are caused by cracked circuit tracks. There is also the problem of the keyboard cable cracking or coming loose. Moral, don't leave it undone.

How do you do the unscrew the thing? (B only) Do you you turn the machine upside down to get at the screws at the front, under the keyboard end? Don't. Instead, pull the machine forwards until it projects over the edge of the worktop. You now have access to the screws from underneath!

SPAGHETTI JUNCTION REVISITED

Do you shudder when you look at the horrid tangle of leads behind your computer set-up? At the last count one of us had 17 leads - flat, round, oval etc. Seven of them are for Mains, and naturally there are seven wall sockets conveniently placed behind the computer.... We jest, of course - it is the usual two-socket position.

When you first start it is quite simple - computer, TV, Cassette recorder: one two-way adapter and one plug by itself. Before you can say 'knife', the adapters sprout adapters and it is getting dangerous. You can get a pair of four-way wander terminals and screw them to the bench - an answer, but a bulky one. On the market now are some miniature mains plug and socket sets for doing just this job. They are not cheap, but they are safe and they are neat.

Cables are another unsightly, irritating, and potentially dangerous problem, especially if they trail across the floor where you can trip over them. The better professional desks have cable guides to keep them under control and out of sight, but you can do a good job without guides by using a little thought and care.

1. Round cables can be bundled together and held in place with wire ties, sticky tape, or a specially designed spiral plastic contraption which looks like a thick cable (wind it round and round your group of cables and they all merge together into one thick cable, which looks very neat). However, it does take a little time to dismantle the cables again, so if you need frequent changes in your hardware set-up, don't use this approach.

2. Don't mix power cables with signal cables unless the latter are well screened. Power cables give off a magnetic field: its effects are greater when power and signal cables run side by side for a distance.

3. Flat cables can be taped to the bench.

4. Try to take cables under the bench, where possible, and attach them to the underside if you can.

5. Use flat commercial cable covers on the floor - you can bury power leads etc inside them, and as they sit much flatter against the floor than do cables, there is less chance of catching a foot in them.

5. HARDWARE ADDITIONS

The minute you buy your computer and get your first micro magazine you will be bombarded with adverts for things that you can add on, to, around or inside the machine. Paddles, ROM's, BASIC editors, discs, separate keyboards, languages, solid state discs, printers, VDU's, shadow RAM, 2nd processors, alternative languages - the list is immense. Some machines have some of these features built in. (You can see which by referring to chapter 6.)

What are they, and which do you need?

1. DISCS

The first and most obvious upgrade from the standard BBC system is a disc drive. The advantages are immense:-

1.   Programs save and load in between one tenth of a second and three seconds, depending upon their length - with a cassette system it can be up to five minutes.

2.   File handling is greatly speeded up, requiring a fraction of the time needed for cassettes.

3.   More importantly, files can be accessed in random fashion - in other words, information from any part of the file can be accessed straight away. For cassettes the only way to access information is sequentially, starting at the beginning and reading right through. This greatly limits the information handling capabilities of the cassette system. It is, for example, virtually impossible to run a business system without a disc drive (or preferably two).

4.   Much more information can be stored on a disc than on a cassette, and in a much less bulky fashion.

The only disadvantage is price: but with the falling costs of hardware the extra cost of a disc system is small.

There are two separate items involved in adding a mechanical disc system:-

1.   The disc drive

2.   The controlling chips (Disc filing system, or DFS) which
     regulate the flow of information to and from the computer

The choice of which DFS and disc system you have will change the way in which
your system works and the speed at which it operates.

1. How many disc drives?

The most basic disc system consists of a single drive, holding 100K of information
on one face of a disc. This sounds a lot of information, but in business, or for
record-keeping of any description, it is really very small. With a single disc drive
copying of discs is a chore - you copy sections of the first disc into the computer,
insert the new disc and copy the computer contents out to it, re-insert the original,
copy it, re-insert the new disc, copy out to it...... twelve times in all for each disc.
It's a fag, it's boring, it encourages you not to take as many backup copies as you
should, and in business is a total liability, because sooner or later you or your
secretary will get interrupted and put the wrong disc in at the wrong time, neatly
corrupting both! (We speak from bitter experience!)

The next type of drive is a double-sided single drive. Here both sides of the disc
are used, doubling the capacity - but copying is still a problem because the old and
new discs have to be swapped again... twenty-four times in all. Oh dear.

Then we come to double drives - either two separate drives connected together, or,
more commonly, two drives built into the same cabinet. In this case, the usual
format is two double sided drives, either stacked one on top of the other, or
mounted side by side. The side-by-side version is preferable. With a pair of drives
stacked on top of one another it is really quite easy to muddle top and bottom
drives, as the openings are only two inches apart: if you do mix them up you can
end up copying the discs backwards, wiping your most recent information. It is
much harder to mix up left and right drive ports as they are so much further apart.

The obvious advantage of two physical drives is in copying - the old disc goes in
one drive, the new in another, issue a command and sit back while the contents of
one disc are copied reliably to the other. And of course, the bigger the system, the
more information it can hold.

2. What sort of drive?

At this point there are a lot of decisions to make, because there are a number of different types of drive available. As well as the single or double-sided drive, there are the number of tracks and the density as well as the disc SIZE to consider.

Number of tracks. Information is laid down on discs in a number of concentric rings, with the same amount of information on each ring. 40-track drives lay down 40 tracks, whereas 80-track drives lay down 80 tracks in the same space - i.e. the track width of a 80-track drive is half that of a 40-track drive. Obviously, an 80-track disc holds exactly twice the amount of information as a 40-track.

Some drives are 40/80 switchable. If you are thinking of buying a switchable drive, it may be worth while making it an 80-track and doing all the switching with software. There are some attractive reasons for doing so apart from the obvious one of cash saving. One of the major irritations with most switchable drives is the fact that the switch is usually at the back. (So much for modern ergonomic design and technology!) However, some manufacturers have seen the light and placed all the switches at the front.

There are utilities which sense whether a disc is recorded 40- or 80-track and act accordingly, so you don't have to do the worrying. (This is likely to save your drive heads hitting the end stops when you forget and try to find track 56 on a forty track disc.) This is not a problem with modern drives, but you should be aware that older drives have this headache (sic!). The models following and including the B+ have a command   * DRIVE num 40
(where num is the drive number) : this sets the machine to 40 track reading and will not allow write access to the disc. Very useful.

In fact there seems no good reason why we need mechanically switched drives.

Be careful when recording data for others to use. The area used for recording is the same for both 40 track drives and 80 track drives, but the recording head of the 80 track is only half the width of a normal 40 track read head. If a disc is recorded on a true 40 track drive and then over-recorded on an 80 track drive, the whole of the old recording is not erased. In effect, you could say that the new recording has a small amount of the 40 recording running down the side of it. This does not matter if the disc is now kept on the 80 machine. However, if it is played on a true 40 drive, the tracks will appear corrupt as the wider head will pick up the new narrow 80 track plus a bit of the old 40 track.

Therefore, if you are going to record on an 80 track drive, only use brand new discs. Even if you reformat you will still get the same problems as before because the formatting is being done with the narrow head. If you reformat on the 40 track drive you will still have problems.

As it is expensive to keep on buying discs, one of the authors has a very large magnet from a motor which is used exclusively for wiping ex-40 track discs very, very clean.

Result - no problems. (This magnet has pole pieces about 4 inches wide and is STRONG. If you decide to do a similar thing, keep it chained in a separate room far away from your other discs!)

Density is slightly more complicated, the more so because the terminology is not exact. On each track of a single density disc there are ten sectors, each with 256 bytes of information. In so-called double density there are usually sixteen sectors, so double density discs store more information per track. (but not twice as much!)

Double density stores more information in a smaller area. Double density systems are faster than the single density systems - they must be. If you have nearly twice as much information recorded on one circuit of the disc, then it stands to reason that you will pick up nearly twice as much information per circuit, ie. faster!

Whether your system supports single or double density is a property of your DFS chip (see below) and not of the disc itself, which can be formatted to any of a number of densities. However, once formatted in a particular density it must be read and written to only by the appropriate DFS. Unless you have two sorts of DFS in your system, or one that is capable of operating in more than one mode you will not be able to read a disc with the 'opposite' density, so make sure when selecting your DFS that you don't become instantly incompatible with your friends' systems, or with commercial software you wish to use.

There is an important practical problem with double density: with greater track number and/or increasing density, more information is being stored in a smaller area. Therefore the quality of the disc needs to be correspondingly higher. Make sure you get the right type for your system.(See below)

The size of your discs is another area for choice. Until recently many professional systems used 8" discs: then came the 5.25" discs which are very common at the moment in all types of system. Recently the 3.5" compact discs, encased in a firm plastic shell, have arrived and will probably become the market standard. Their advantage is a much greater robustness - floppy discs are so easily bent and scratched, and can get dust in them. Compact discs are slightly more expensive, but are more reliable, especially in industrial and dusty environments. (The Archimedes and the Compact use the 3.5" format.)

The controlling chip. This is the other half of the disc system, and a very important part too. It regulates access to the disc, and the efficiency and speed of disc access depends upon how well it works. As we said earlier, the density of the disc is a function of the controlling chip, and not of the disc itself. There are two types of chip: the 8271 which works in single density only, and the 1770 which can work in single or double density. The 1770 can also read 40 track discs in 80 track drives.

> DFS = Disc Filing System
> ADFS = Advanced Disc Filing System
> DDFS = Double Density Filing System

The DFS is fitted to the B, B+ and Master as standard. Problems arise when storing a large number of small files: you can't. There is a limit of 31 files per side set by the catalogue system. This is overcome to some extent by using extra software and a double catalogue, such as the SWAP command on DISC DOCTOR. This can be a bind as it is not standard and has to have extra commands to access the data.

ADFS is fitted to the Archimedes, Master series (including the Compact), and the Electron. It can be fitted directly in the B+ as it has the correct chip but the BBC-B has to have a 1770 chip fitted before it will run ADFS.

1. The system regards both sides of the disc as a single side and allows as many files as you wish. (within the confines of the space!)

2. Each directory can have a name up to 10 characters long, and there can be sub-directories and sub-sub-directories etc, etc (see chapter 12). The directory system can be a little difficult to get to grips with at first but the advantages are immense.

3. You may use meaningful names for your directories as well as for the file name.

4. The ADFS works in Double Density mode which means that there are 16 sectors per track rather than 10 (advertising arithmetic, 2 * 10 = 16 !)

5. The ADFS gives faster access to certain types of file, especially when networking.

6. There is a limit of 45 file names per directory,but no limitation on the number of directories. The ADFS is therefore suitable for organising a hard disc (as is the Amcom DFS which was specifically designed for the job).

7. The ADFS uses the disc space much more intelligently (see below).

The Master has the DFS fitted as well as the ADFS and the Archimedes can work in DFS mode so the problems of compatibility are minimised.

DDFS You pays yer money and takes yer choice and reads yer revues. It is almost impossible to give good advice here. There are so many claims and counter claims. If you really feel that you need this extra type of DFS then do some very careful research and see it in operation before buying. DDFS systems tend to be incompatible with each other, and with everything else. They are fine on their own providing that you do not want to use the discs on another machine not fitted with that DDFS. The ADFS really does a better job of packing data and is a standard system so unless there is a really pressing need, don't use it.

There are alternative DFS systems which are attractive (The Watford DFS is one of the better ones). Again, if you feel that you need the benefits of this system (software switching of 40/80 drives) make certain that you see it in operation. Occasionally a ROM or commercial program will not work with a particular type of DFS fitted, so be aware of the problem and make sure all your intended chips will be compatible.

Solid state discs. These are increasingly available: they store information in electronic form. The computer 'sees' them as a normal physical disc system. The advantage is that they can save and load information much more quickly than a physical disc. In a physical disc the disc has to rotate to where the information resides before it can be picked up - in addition, it may also have to get up to its normal speed of rotation before accessing can commence, and all this takes time. In a solid state disc none of this happens. For someone who has a cassette system this degree of time saving make look miniscule, but the more professional your software becomes, and the more that you depend on indexes and look-up tables for information, the more frequently will you be accessing your discs: if you are looking up indexes, say, twenty times per record then the delay on the disc system is multiplied by a this factor, and this makes for very obvious delays when using mechanical disc systems.

The disadvantage of the solid-state disc is that it cannot be the only disc system, because information is lost once the power is turned off: a back-up disc is essential. Equally, feeding in new programs has to be done from somewhere, so a physical disc must be incorporated into the system at some stage.

It is, however, not a bad idea to have a mixture of physical and solid discs - it is easy to copy across from one type to another, so a useful software ploy would be to begin a program thus:-

1. Insert physical disc containing indexes and copy it across to solid disc.

2. Remove first disc, replace with program disc: load program

3. Remove program disc, replace with disc of customer files.

In this way:-

> the program resides in main memory (where it has to, of course)
> the indexes reside in the solid disc (for fast access)
> the records remain on disc

Access to the records themselves can be that much slower without too much of a problem, and in the event of a power failure the precious customer records stay preserved, whilst the contents of the solid state disc and main memory will be lost.

Solid state discs are now coming on the market in conjunction with a physical disc (Opus): as an external disc system (Morley) - this also has battery back-up so that the disc contents can be preserved when the system is switched off: and as a board that plugs inside the micro - Solidisc (which can also act as a RAM bank and printer buffer). Only the BBC B can have the internal board fitted and this set-up has not always proved trouble free.

In the past Solidisk's sideways RAM boards have not always been reliable, for two reasons. The early versions used edge connectors which have a tendency to slip out of place after a time, particularly with transmitted vibrations from the keyboard. Later versions, particularly the 256 board, use a completely different method of hardware connection, slotting the board into a full socket - which is very much less likely to form a poor connection, or to fall out with vibration, though it is important to make sure that the flying leads are well connected, preferably by soldering rather than just clipping them on.

This does highlight a problem with ALL add-on boards - anything which is merely plugged into a socket can in time slip out or form a bad connection. The problem is greatest where there is a large secondary board attached, and especially where the new board is connected in such a way as to give excessive leverage on the socket. The only real cure for this type of problem is for add-on boards and chips to be soldered in, as often happens with 'business' machines. They are much less likely to form a bad connection when soldered. But DON'T do soldering yourself inside machines or on chips unless you know PRECISELY how to do it! Unfortunately much add-on architecture for the BBC is constructed in such a way that you can't get at it to solder it in place.

Hard discs, otherwise known as Winchesters are the biggest storage source available at the moment that can be both read from and written to. The smallest stores 5 megabytes (i.e. 5 million characters)): professional micro equipment often uses 40 megabytes and upwards. Winchesters are permanent stores of data. They are much faster than discs, firstly because they are always spinning even when not being read so there is no lag time while speed is being brought up, and secondly, as they spin twenty times faster access time is only one twentieth of the time for discs.

The ADFS system is a must for a Winchester in order to allow for enough file-names.

Hard discs too need some sort of back-up. Backup onto floppy discs takes ages - a 5 megabyte Winchester is the equivalent of 25 double sided discs! So Winchesters are more conveniently backed up with a tape streamer, which is a sort of express cassette, but they are expensive and really only for professional systems. Some intelligent hard disc systems remember what changes have been made since the last backup and only backup the changes. This greatly reduces the time for backups. (typically 2 Mbyte/minute) If you are thinking of using a Winchester it might be wise to go to a firm who deals in Networks. They have been using Winchesters for a long time and usually have the expertise to give good advice.

Optical and Laser discs are coming. It will be a little time before they are used as more than a source of data. But.. with the knowledge that they can store the Encylopaedia Brittanica on one surface and hardly notice you will realise that it will be an exciting event when they do arrive. The Domesday Project was one of the first systems generally available. It is now being used in schools (and the Russian Embassy in London!) Soon this technology is likely to make huge picture / text / animated sequence databases of complex and technical information readily available.

3. What quality disc should I buy?

A sad personal story from one of the authors.

It is very easy to be sanctimonious and say, 'only buy the very best and stick to them', but cash seems to limit this idealistic approach and in any case, what is 'the best?. For about 125 discs, and a depleted bank balance, I used single-sided, single density discs from a well advertised firm selling by the 25 and 50. I have a double sided 80 track system. They worked well, both sides, and only one did not format on both sides.

The problem came when one disc failed on the second side with a large amount of data and just before my backup schedule. (doesn't it always!) Sure, it really was the disc. I had been warned by the manufacturers, they said it was suitable for single sided working....it was.

I buy the correct discs for the job now.

Remember, the real cost of a disc is not the disc itself, but the value of the information on it, in terms of time and content.

Talking only of 5 1/4" discs, they come in a variety of 'qualities'. 48 TPI, 96TPI, SS, DS, SD, DD! Sort that lot out. Most reasonable retailers will talk about 40 track and 80 track but here is a list to aid translation.

48 TPI	Suitable for 40 Track
96 TPI	Suitable for 80 Track
SS	Single Sided
DS	Double Sided
SD	Single Density
DD	Double Density

So a 96TPI, SS, DD is suitable for ... 80 track, single sided, double density system.

There is no real advantage in buying a disc which is 'better' qualified for the job than need be. The manufacturers make one quality, the best, and then find out what each diskette is best suited for. One suspects that the vast majority of discs are in fact over qualified but you cannot take the chance.

2.ROM CHIPS

ROM chips are individual programs in chip form. They are used in three ways:

1. Physically resident inside the machine. In the BBC-B this
    can be either in the five ROM sockets on the right hand
    side at the front of the main board or else inserted in a
    second ROM board, which can hold up to the maximum of 16,
    each of 8 or 16K. (Though this maximum is not strictly
    true - there are external boards which can hold many more,
    but only 16 are usable at any one time.)

2. Inserted in a ZIF (zero insertion force) holder and
    plugged into the socket underneath the cut-out oblong on
    the left side of the keyboard on the A, B and B+.

3. Inserted in a CARTRIDGE. Your Roms fit into a plastic box
    with a screwed on lid. This assembly then slots into the
    cartridge socket. The only problem may be with the new
    double height ROMs (Quest Mouse, Spellmaster etc.) which do
    not fit into the standard box. At the time of writing
    there appeared to be no 'fatter' boxes available but they

can be used with the lid off. A point to watch out for is
that Compact cartridges are not compatible, pinwise, with
the Electron or Master 128. So much for standardisation.

4.   Copied onto disc, ROM images can then be copied back into
the machine if you also have a sideways RAM pack (see below).
The copied program is called a 'ROM image'. In this way
you can have a very large number of ROM programs
without overloading the machine's power supply. You must,
however, have the permission of the manufacturer before
copying. Quite a few manufacturers will give permission
and appreciate the courtesy of your call. Some will sell
you a ROM image at a slightly reduced price (because you
are not purchasing the chip itself). This is a healthy
attitude which is too frequently abused by users - yes, we
do mean stealing by piracy.

ROMs contain machine code programs, of the type that you would wish to have
resident inside the machine, ready for use at a second's notice, or even from within
a program of your own. Their subjects include:-

a.   Languages - as well as BASIC (which exists in ROM form
inside your machine) you could have PASCAL, COMAL, LOGO,
FORTH, BCPL, MicroCODIL and at least four versions of C.

b.   BASIC editors which enable you to write programs in BASIC
with much greater ease - rather like having a built-in
word-processor for program editing.

c.   DISC DOCTOR, ENIGMA, ADI and similar - these allow
manipulation of disc information, direct reading of what is
on the disc, formatting of discs, joining of disc files together

d.   Toolkits - for fiddling with BASIC. These are specialised
Editors which work like wordprocessors: see below.

e.   Disassemblers which look at machine code programs and
retranslate them back into readable form.

f.   Graphics - allow complex graphics routines to be performed
with much simpler commands - drawing circles, pie-charts,
bar-charts etc

g.   Spreadsheets   (see Chapter 23)

h. Word-processors (see Chapter 23)

i. Databases   (see chapter 23)

USEFUL UTILITY ROMS

We all have our favourite ROM utilities. The selection below is not definitive but just the ones we find most useful in our line of work.

Toolkit	Beebugsoft
DiscDoctor	Computer Concepts
TED (Teletext Editor)	Watford Electronics
Brom Plus	Clares
Basic Editor	Acornsoft
Caretaker	Computer Concepts
Exmon	Beebugsoft
Enigma	Altra Roms
Disk Investigator	Advanced Computer Products
MegaRom	Chalice
Romit	Beebugsoft
Dump Out 3	Watford Electronics
GXR	Acornsoft

The following 'bits' on each are especially well-used:-

TOOLKIT
(now upgraded usefully to Toolkit-Plus) Old but not aged, this utility is worth its weight in gold for the Util section alone. *FREE gives all the info you need about free bytes, HIMEM, LOMEM etc. *ON error reporting and colour display. *PACK Gets rid of excess spaces and REMs. *RECOVER Bad program reverser. *RENUMBER Good flexible routine. *UTIL excellent search and list for PROCs Variables etc.

DISCDOCTOR
Although a few of its functions have been overtaken by others it still seems the best general purpose ROM - A smooth operator! (It has now gone out of production but is well worth getting if you find it reduced or second hand.) Only works with 8271 chip. (ie. with DFS and not with ADFS) *DZAP look at and edit sectors on a disc *MZAP look at and alter memory. *DSEARCH Look for a string on disc. *EDIT edit the function keys. *FORM a good fast format. *VERIFY a good fast verify. *RECOVER perform surgery on a corrupted disc. *RESTORE works with RECOVER.

TED ((T)eletext (ED)ditor)

This has all the features you could possibly want in a teletext editor including very comprehensive character, line, column and block copying. It has a rather weird layout for the keystrip and the command structure needs a little work before it becomes second nature but it is an essential for anyone seriously devising Mode 7 screens. There are some stunning animated displays on the accompanying demo disk. Apart from all the normal commands: *CONVERT will take a Mode 0,1 or 2 screen and convert it as near as is possible into Mode 7 graphics. *SCROLLBUILD allows the building of 600 line high screens (for scrolling!) The screen will show the ASCII and HEX value at a position and also show the absolute position in screen memory occupied by a character. It is possible to convert the screens constructed for down-loading to Prestel. It is also part of the function to provide your own mini view-data database.

BROM Plus

A close rival to Disc Doctor - many will say better. It has many more commands, and works very well but lacks the one command which would make it indispensable - Disassemble. (Disc Doctor has this.) The FORMAT has the useful ability to do two or four sides at once without issuing further commands.

BASIC EDITOR

We like the Acornsoft BASIC editor immensely as it allows the programmer the similar facilities to those of a word processor. This is the single most useful aid to the Basic programmer we have come across. However, if you are into using Function key colours, it won't do them, and you will have to put them in afterwards. (A very similar program is bundled with the Master series and the Archimedes)

CARETAKER.

*EXPAND - un-compacts multi-line statements for easier reading. *INSERT - puts a program or routine from outside into the middle of a program *KEYLOAD - loads a set of key definitions. *KEYSAVE - saves the above. *PARTSAVE - saves a portion of a program in memory. *SQUASH - gets rid of spaces, REMS and makes multi-line statements.(But you have to be careful, it sometimes compacts lines which it shouldn't). *STATUS - same as *FREE in Toolkit. *RENUMBER - can renumber a piece of code into a different area of the program. Same as renumber and move. Be careful with this ROM - it sometimes interferes with the workspace of other games and ROM's. Its SINGLEKEY function is operative by default and causes some games to 'hang', so it has to be turned off before each game is played.

ENIGMA

Designed to make the most of the single density disc system. It has everything that a good disc debugger ought to have plus one superb command worth the whole price .. REPAIR. This will look at a track and grab back any uncorrupted information. Great - except it only works on the DFS.

ADVANCED DISC INVESTIGATOR
Like Enigma this is a very powerful disc editor, but it works on both the DFS and ADFS.

MEGAROM
If you just had to choose one general purpose rom this one would certainly have to· be very high on the list with over 60 commands! There are some very useful and one or two unusual routines which can do most of the jobs you require. Examples: SNIP gets rid of line numbers from line X to the end of program, KEEP <num> turns off every other ROM but Mega and the numbered one.

EXMON
A good machine code utility - there's not much this one hasn't got! and we like the way it works.

ROMIT
This ROM allows the manipulation of the much under-used RAM filing system allowing you to set up sideways RAM space as a Silicon Disc. There is also the facility to put your favourite programs into ROM image and get them blown into a ROM. This would mean that you could have some of your programs permanently in the machine.

DUMPOUT 3
If you find the need to print screens from the computer then the program you are using usually provides you with a 'DUMP' routine that is appropriate. However, if you are writing your own material then this ROM is essential, especially when it comes to MODE 7 (which is a difficult Mode to dump successfully). Apart from being able to dump in all Modes (including Mode 8!!) it also deals with all the main makes of printer. *GIMAGE prints the screen with size scaling, printer type, tone scale, colour masking, orientation and other parameters. *GWINDOW allows you to specify graphically the area to be printed from the screen for graphics. *TWINDOW does the same thing for text. There is also on-screen help.

GXR
There are two very good graphics ROMs to choose from, the excellent one from Computer Concepts or the GXR (Graphics Extension ROM) from Acornsoft. History has decreed that the GXR is included in the Master series computers as a free ROM and for the sake of programming compatibility this rather rules out the other model. If you buy the GXR, do note that there are separate models for the BBC-B and the BBC B+. The adverts usually make this clear (but not always). The number of commands is too great to mention but the main thing to us is the ease with which circles, ellipses and fills may be specified, to say nothing of the palette alterations.

In chapter 23 we mention the graphics program QUEST. Do note that whereas the QUEST ROM is a PROGRAM chip which allows you to make and manipulate picture material, GXR is a UTILITY chip giving commands for you to use in your programs.

ROM COMPATIBILITY BETWEEN MODELS

This list is not exhaustive and certainly we cannot say that we have personally tested every one.   A large number are known to us, the rest is gleaned from the available literature.

Compatible with B, B+, Master 128 and Master Compact

Mini Office	ROM Manager	Pendown Spellmaster
Starword	Wordwise Plus	Ramrod
Brom+	Icon Master	Advanced disc Toolkit
Advanced Disc Investigator		Viewsheet
Ultracalc	TED	ADE+
Macrom	BCPL	Forth
Comal	Iso-Pascal	Lisp
Logo	Micro-Prolog	Viewstore
System Delta	Starstore	MAX
Dump Master2	Dumpout3	Inter Sheet
Help2	Mega Rom	Inter Word
Basic Editor	AMX roms	Inter Chart
Quest Mouse	Commstar2	Inter Base
Acorn C	Beebug C	TED

Compatible with B only

Exmon2	Beebmon	Graphics Rom
Watford DFS	Watford DDFS	View 2.1
Rom spell	Accelerator	Disc Doctor
Romas	Sleuth	GXR (special)

Compatible with B+ only

View 3	GXR (Graphics Rom, special)

Compatible with B B+

Toolkit Plus	Addrom	Speech
Stargraph	Romit	Replay

Compatible with Master only

Master Replay	Floppywise Master	EXMON (Master)

MODE 7 TELETEXT GRAPHICS

If you are even contemplating making up Mode 7 display screens for your program, do consider purchasing one of the excellent screen editors which are now available. There is something slightly masochistic about writing in yards of code when there are editor programs on tap. They do for for screen design what a good wordprocessor does for creative letter writing: they free you from the drudgery and allow you to be easily creative. (see the section above about particular ROMs)

LANGUAGES

At first it may not seem obvious why other languages are useful, particularly as BASIC can do so much. The real difference between languages lies in the ease which which they manipulate different types of information. Some are good for lists of information - useful in business. Others are particularly good for calculations, or graphics, or design, or....

PASCAL is a completely structured language (see Chapter 15) It is much less 'forgiving' than BASIC, but equally, checks what you are doing much more carefully and allows you to make fewer mistakes. For example, you have to set limits on the values each variable can take - so an out-of range value stops the program (very good if it turns out to be as a result of a 'silly' calculation). It does not support any graphics at all.

COMAL is a sort of super-BASIC. It supports the WHILE function, which makes loops so much easier to construct, and so much less likely to have hidden bugs. It also has many other useful features not least of which is syntax checking on entry!

LOGO This language is best known for its graphics (Turtle) but it is really a very powerful language for list processing and is one of the easiest languages to write simple adventure programs in.

Micro-PROLOG is a fascinating language. Its commands are based on lists and rules, and can explore relationships between items on different lists: this is why it is now being used by programmers interested in artificial intelligence and expert systems. For example, you can search for matching patterns of a family tree by giving data such as 'John Smith and Hilda Brown married and three of their four children were called Esther, Fay and William'. 'Fay's father died of TB'. 'Esther's brother William lived at Eversholt'. 'William died in 1676 one year after his father' - and many, many other snippets of information. From this the computer can compare information on all the lists to derive a family tree, with dates of birth and death, and what each person died of, even though the information is not obviously present - eg in the example given above, it is possible to work out that John Smith died of TB in 1675. This is a simple example, but it could still extract this information even if these entries had been culled from different sources, entered at different times, and mixed in with thousands of other similar jottings. A superb language for establishing patterns and fitting information together: a totally different concept of programming for those whose only experience is with BASIC and similar languages.

C is a relatively new language which was said to be too big to run on the BBC. It isn't! There are at present four different versions. The language is like PASCAL in that it has all the structure that a programmer needs but it is a little more forgiving and easier to use. One small difficulty is the use of different types of brackets which have a vital significance but are difficult to tell apart on the screen. A program is written in a word processor and then compiled to P-code for running. (This is a sort of halfway-to-machine-code code.) C is a portable language, which means that the program written on the word processor may be taken onto, say, an IBM PC, then compiled and run.

3.PRINTERS

When you come to look at printers, the air clears a little and decisions are not so complex. Although there are a lot of different types, they are very distinct and the applications obvious.

Dot Matrix. This type is the most common for use with the home micro and with reason. It is fast, versatile and relatively cheap. The head scans across the page building up each character out of little dots. Speeds of about 80 characters per second can be expected. Don't believe much higher figures,though some can do better than this. You can also print out screen dumps and graphics. NLQ (near letter quality) print is available, built into some printers, or available through a ROM chip with some others, but working in NLQ usually slows the printer down as the head has to make two passes to build up the more complex letter shapes.

Daisy wheel printers work rather like typewriters in that an actual raised character is thrown against the paper. The quality is first-class but the speed is slow, and the noise greater. They cannot print graphics, and have a limited number of type faces on each daisy 'head', though you can stop and change the head. For business both a dot matrix and a daisy wheel may be needed, for their different and complementary characteristics. However, a dot matrix machine with NLQ may be all you need, and it is likely that daisy wheel printers are on the way out.

Colour printers are very expensive and unless you absolutely must have colour in your printing, a waste. (But prices are coming down)

Thermal printers are expensive to run and not really feasible in the home.

Laser printers are exceptionally fast, accurate, versatile and expensive. As with Xerox-type machines the prices are tumbling so fast that it is difficult to tell what will happen in the next few years.

If you need Graphics printing it might be worth while thinking of a flat bed plotter. This works by tracing an actual pen over the paper to produce the image.

One bit of advice. Always see the printer you desire doing the work you want it to do with your computer before buying. If the shop can't show it properly - don't buy.

PARALLEL AND SERIAL PRINTERS

The way in which your computer communicates with the printer is by one of two methods -

Parallel printers accept a complete set of (say) 8 bits which form a piece of information at one go. The processing is done on the printer in parallel the same as in the computer. The advantage of this system is the rapid rate at which the information can be sent. The disadvantages are that at least 10 wires are needed (cost) and the cable needs to be short.

Serial printers need the signals sent one bit at a time. This means that the 8-bit byte has to be split up (extra circuits) and reformed in the printer after transmission which slows things down. The advantages are in the cheaper cabling and the longer distances allowable between printer and computer.

4.SIDEWAYS RAM BOARDS

Sideways RAM boards sit in the same position as a ROM chip, but can also be written to. Sideways RAM is not part of main memory, and doesn't increase the capacity of normal RAM. Nevertheless it is a most useful device, and can function in a number of different ways.

1.   It may be used as a printer buffer.

When the computer is outputting to the printer it will only send information for printing if the printer's own memory has space. The printer's memory is usually small - so the computer has to wait while the printer's memory empties (ie. as text is printed out). Meanwhile the computer is unable to proceed with the program, or transfer to another task. A printer buffer accepts a large chunk of text for printing and feeds it as required to the printer itself. Thus you may get on with another task while the printer is churning away.

Physically, a printer buffer can be within the host computer, within the printer, or as a separate piece of hardware linking the two. Sideways RAM sits within the computer and can be configured as a printer buffer by using appropriate software.

A printer buffer doesn't sound particularly wonderful, but once you have used it you will never want to be without one. They act as a sort of psychic release! Whilst your text is being ground out on the printer you can load, work on and save other programs, send further text to the buffer, and generally use your computer. If you use a printer to any degree this is the single most helpful addition to your hardware.

2. It can store ROM images. A ROM image is the software on the ROM chip, transferred to disc. The image can be copied back off the disc into sideways RAM, where it behaves exactly as though the original ROM chip itself were physically inserted into the machine. There are some differences, however:-

a.   Protection fitted by manufacturers will not allow you to
      run certain chips as a ROM image.

b.   As with ordinary memory, the sideways RAM loses its
      program when the machine is turned off.

c.   A ROM image in sideways RAM can be overwritten with a
      different ROM image without turning off the computer.

This gives tremendous flexibility as you do not need to have all your ROMs physically resident in the machine, with all their consequent problems of extra heat and current drain: it also obviates the need for large ROM boards.

3. With some of the BBC computer range SHADOW RAM may be used to organise the screen image without taking up ordinary RAM, thus allowing the memory available for your programs to remain at about 30K whatever the screen Mode (a very great advantage because the graphics modes gobble up a lot of normal memory for screen work) The Master and the B+ have shadow RAM already fitted as a part of the architecture.

4. Some sideways RAM boards may be configured as solid silicon discs. Beebugsoft has a utility ROM, ROMIT, which will use your RAM for this task. Watford Electronics ROM/RAM board and the Solidisc boards may be configured in this manner.

5. Many sideways RAM boards also incorporate sockets to take extra ROMs. A point to remember here is that it is impossible to increase the number of ROMs plus RAM images beyond 16 at any one time. (HCS have a box which may contain more, but the ROMs are switched in banks of 16)

6. Finally, there are pure ROM boards for adding chips to the original 5 sockets (up to the 16 max). Most of these boards have the facility of adding a single socket of sideways RAM.

We must add to this section a special battery backed RAM board:

PMS GENIE is a small add-on box (internal). It stores information. This sounds very uninteresting until you find that the information is accessible from inside any program you are running by pressing SHIFT/CTRL/G. After using Genie, Escape takes you back to exactly where you were in the original program. We use SPELLMASTER a lot and it is marvellous to be using a word-processor, call Spellmaster to find a word, find you need to do a phone call and so call up GENIE, find the number, add an address to GENIE'S store, press Escape twice and be back in Spellmaster, Escape again and carry on writing! The trick is that GENIE has an internal battery backed memory and 32K of storage space(this may soon be increased to 64k if enough pressure is put on the manufacturers!). Many facilities are provided: telephone and address book, notepad, calendar, calculator (this is great as it uses the computer keys rather than a slow pointer) some look-up tables and a desk diary. Searching, up-dating and print-outs (labels for example) are all available. It is invaluable, although a little expensive by BBC program standards.

5.PADDLES

Paddles are big hand-controllers used almost exclusively in games. You move them around and press buttons on the top in order to operate your game: this gives a much more natural feel of 'steering' your craft/ship/little man around the screen. They are useful too for children and the handicapped, where the fine movements required to operate a keyboard may be missing.

6.THE MOUSE

This is a small box-shaped object with either two or three buttons, attached to the computer by a lead (hence the resemblance to a mouse). You roll it around on the table in front of you and in doing so the cursor moves around the screen. When you have the cursor in exactly the right place, press a switch on the top of the mouse to send a signal to the computer. Its uses include -

-      computer aided design

-      selection of items off menus without needing to learn the QWERTY keyboard

-      selection of type faces or shading in artwork programs (it's rather akin to dipping your pen in a jar of striped

ink, which you then proceed to paint on the screen,
directing your 'paint' with movements of the mouse)

In short, the mouse is useful wherever you have a need for a non-keyboard method
of entry of information, and particularly where there is design involved with placing
of images in positions unrelated to normal line and character positions. Paddle v.
Mouse - It is interesting that these two devices which appear so similar in fact give
two extremely different areas of control. It is almost impossible to play games with
a mouse, whereas a joystick is a joy! The mouse is ideal for graphics and window
applications (ie. picking items of menus, often displayed in the form of little icons),
whereas in this situation the joystick is uncomfortable.

7.SECOND PROCESSORS

These are used to expand the capabilities of your system. For example, the 6502
2nd Processor gives extra memory, greater speed and greater flexibility. The main
bit of the Beeb handles all the keyboard processing and the screen whilst the
second processor carries out all the information processing. There are a variety of
2nd processors each of which has particular areas of strength. In particular the Z80
allows access to programs written in the CP/M operating system - which means a
lot of commercial programs, particularly for business and scientific work. The
second processor has largely been superceded by the Master series which has its
own set of 2nd processor options including the 80186 which runs MS/DOS. This
allows the running of much professional business software.

8.SEPARATE KEYBOARDS

It is possible to get a separate keyboard for the B & B+, so that you can rest it on
your knee at some distance from the guts of the machine. This can be useful if you
like to imagine that you are an executive with an IBM PC, or if for some reason you
cannot find a comfortable position with the Beeb on a desk. Viglen produce a nice
version.

9.LIGHT PENS

Light pens were a bit of a disappointment in the early days due to their lack of
sensitivity and precision. However they are starting to come back again. Basically
the 'Pen' is put on the screen at a point where you want some action to happen. A
button on the pen is pressed and the computer works out the co-ordinates and
takes the appropriate action. Useful as a way of inputting information to the
computer without the need to type - just point on the screen to the answer you want
to give.

A more popular version of this type of device uses a flat plotting board and a mesh of sub-surface wires to sense the pen position. Very sophisticated versions of this are available and used at the highest professional levels particularly for computer-aided design - in this respect it behaves much as does the mouse (see above).

10. ADDING EXTERNAL DEVICES

A large variety of external devices can be fitted, to control or be controlled by, your computer. Some are well documented (printers, disc drives, mouse, joystick etc) and are relatively easy to come to terms with. There are others which demand a circuit knowledge of the way in which they are connected to the outside world. The ways in which such devices may be connected are covered here but details of applications are beyond the scope of this book.

There are three ports that are of use here - the analogue to digital interface (ADI), the user port, and the I MegaHz Bus. The analogue to digital interface changes a continuously varying item (voltage) into a digital form. This enables the output from an electronic device such as a thermometer to be converted into a form the computer can understand and do calculations with. Note that the Compact (and the Archimedes) do not have this port in as standard - the Compact has a cut-down version of it. In both cases extra hardware can be purchased to allow the full ADI to be constructed. The port has four input channels which may be used for four devices (or more if you can arrange external polling of the devices by electrical or mechanical means).

Now that you have a measuring device plugged into the ADI socket the computer can 'sense' some Analogue aspect of the outside world. Next, the computer has to have an output to activate (say) a servo-motor. This is done through the user port or the 1 MegaHz bus. With a suitable program to make decisions about the temperatures that are being sensed you can arrange for appropriate commands to go to a servo motor operating (say) windows or a switch operating a heater. Now you can then control the temperature in your greenhouse!.... or your house central heating... or your lighting system... or a burglar alarm.....

The user port has 8 input/output lines (I/O) plus 2 control lines. Each of these can be programmed to be either In or Out in any combination and this makes it very flexible. Note that the signals here are on/off (Binary) as opposed to continuously variable signals (Analogue). With this port you may, through suitable buffers, control lights, servos etc.

If you wish to have a more comprehensive control of the situation, the more difficult to understand 1Mega Hz port is appropriate. This port gives direct access to the 6502 microprocessor address and data buses, though details of how to do all this are outside the scope of this book.

6. HARDWARE RUNNING ON THE BBC

The original Acorn machine was the Atom which is more or less defunct. It ceased production a long time ago. We understand that the original Atom was designed and constructed on a kitchen table - the results of that experiment have come a long way in the intervening years.

BBC-A

The next one was the BBC-A with 16K of memory. It only had the higher numbered screen modes available. This meant that, due to lack of memory, its use was limited. Upgrade kits were available to convert it to the BBC-B.

No longer in production

BBC-B

Although not their first machine, the BBC-B is really the starting point of the Acorn range. In this book we have taken it as the generic model, noting adaptations and changes from it into other models such as the B+ and the Master.

In its basic form the BBC-B came with 32K of RAM, 8 screen modes, a cassette and ROM filing system as standard. A DFS was not included, but was available. The usual disc controlling chip was the 8271 which allows only single density working. Later conversion kits used the 1770 disc controller chip which is capable of supporting both single and double density. It is therefore quite possible to run the BBC-B with an ADFS system attached. (Please see Chapter 12 for a fuller treatment of the differences between the DFS and ADFS systems).

The BBC-B can have a second processor fitted in an external box - with a Z80 second processor it allows you to run CP/M. The 6502 2nd processor gave more memory and faster running, but other hardware developments meant limited sales and usefulness. The 32016 Co-Processor is an entirely different beast allowing 32-bit working and being supplied with some very good language software, but at nearly £1000 it is hardly a small add-on.

Extra internal boards can be fitted for mounting ROMs and sideways RAM. This additional RAM allows ROM images to be stored on disc, thus reducing the need for physical ROMs in the machine. There is also space for an external ROM cartridge at the left hand end of the keyboard, in what is called, disparagingly, the 'ashtray'.

A tremendous amount of good software has been written for the BBC-B, and particularly a lot of educational software for all ages, as many schools bought BBC-B's for their computer courses. In comparison there is much less business software.

There are many who would say that the BBC-B is too small to use successfully in business: but equally there are many who do use it successfully in just this way. It all depends on what you are trying to do. The 'B' is excellent for standalone tasks such as wordprocessing and elementary spreadsheet work: there is no problem with database work unless a lot of sorting or manipulation of data is required. On the other hand the 32K of RAM is limiting, especially for accountancy work.

No longer in production

ELECTRON

This was rather a blind alley. It has an excellent keyboard and good word processing ability, and is frequently used as a communications terminal. However, it has no facilities for internal ROM insertion and ROMs can only be used by purchasing an expensive add-on unit.

A useful feature on the Electron, not repeated on the other machines, was the single-key entry of BASIC key-words by depressing the CAPS LOCK/FUNC key plus the relevant key. Great for the one fingure typist! This feature is available for the BBC-B in CARETAKER.

*FX 225 disables all user-definable keys. *FX 226 disables FUNC/A to FUNC/P. *FX 227 disables FUNCT Q onwards.

You can reset your machine with *FX226,224 so that you can type in user defined characters direct from the keyboard with FUNCT plus key.

Surprisingly the ADFS was fitted as a standard add-on.

No longer in production

B+

The B+ turned out to be an interim measure between the model B and the Master series. The main feature of the Plus series (64 and 128) was the inclusion of Shadow RAM and later Sideways RAM as standard, so allowing 30K of RAM to be available irrespective of screen mode. The B128 had more memory available - but this was not accessible in quite the same way as with the normal RAM. 8-bit machines can only directly address a total of 64K of memory, and any increase beyond this amount must use software tricks - in the case of the B128 this was achieved by 'paging' memory - which makes memory access slower.

The B+ was a venture which left quite a few people without the software support one has come to expect nowadays. This series was a bit of a backwater.

No longer in production

THE MASTER SERIES

The Master is the logical development of the BBC-B that the B+ was intended to be but didn't become. It is possible with many of the add-on devices which are available to make the BBC-B behave in a manner very close to that of the Master 128. However, there are many very useful features which set the MASTER series apart from the BBC-B.

The Master Series consists of the Master 128, Turbo etc and the Master Compact. Let's take a look at some of the extra features which the Master series has as standard.

The Numeric keypad is a joy to use being much more natural than using the normal number keys for inputting numeric data. In contrast to the IBM PC it does not need to be activated before use.

The Break Key now has a physical lock which prevents it being accidentally depressed. It could have been done in a nicer, less fiddly manner but is a step in the right direction.

The position and North, South, East, West layout of the Cursor keys is an improvement as is the separation of function keys and Break key by a substantial gap. (This has been further enhanced on the Archimedes)

Sideways RAM and Shadow RAM add-on boards are now a thing of the past as they are part of the standard architecture. This gives great flexibility to the machine - no more worries about high resolution screens leading to small program memory. The facility to shift the screen memory into Shadow RAM is optional so that it is still possible to run some programs that resent Shadow. Sideways RAM means that it is possible to load ROM images, store and use fast data, or configure it as a silicon disc etc. Various commands to do with loading and saving images to Sideways RAM are available.

It is nice that the new memory system hardware makes the changing of PAGE a thing of the past. In the BBC-B PAGE was at &E00 for Cassette, &1900 for Disc, &1B00 for Network and &1A00 for the Watford board (sometimes). Now it is always at &E00 unless you want to change it for reasons of your own.

The disc handling is much more versatile. DFS and ADFS systems provide format commands for disc, and display commands for free space. The ADFS is fully explained elsewhere (Chapter 12). The access command in the ADFS is particularly comprehensive. You may set a file to READ only, WRITE only, READ and WRITE, LOCKED or EXECUTE only. The REMOVE command allows you to try to delete a file which may or may not be there without an error message occuring if it isn't. This means that you can now do it from within a program without having to set and reset error trapping routines.

A new feature is the CODE key which allows the codes from 128 upwards to be sent from the keyboard.

Most of the major ROMs work on the Master series. However, there were one or two written specifically for the B+ and some which used the special features of the basic B model. One absence is Disc Doctor, a favourite old workhorse. It is absent because a) it won't work in ADFS and b) the Master memory is allocated in a different way.

Potential add-ons include the 32016 second processor which has a 32 bit/16 bit processor for high level languages and also for speed of number crunching.

The Z80 second processor allows the running of CP/M: bundled with this is BBC BASIC, a Word processor, a database, a spreadsheet, an integrated accounting system, Cis-cobol, and Nucleus, which is a system generator.

The Master 512 has the 80186 second processor which can emulate the IBM PC.

The MASTER 128

There are not so many ROM slots available for internal usage but the cartridge system provides a very flexible alternative. ROMs fit into a plastic box with a screwed on lid, and this assembly then slots into the cartridge socket. The only problem may be with the new double height ROMs, (Quest Mouse, Spellmaster etc.) which do not fit into the standard box. At the time of writing there are no 'fatter' boxes available, but they can be used with the lid off.

ROMs may be turned off and on by software. This has many implications, not least the avoidance of command clashes. This is slightly less flexible than some utility ROMs which allow turn on and off at any time, as turn on in the Master 128 only works at hard Break.

ROMs may be listed to see which are currently active. Function keys may be listed and therefore edited easily.

The wordprocessor View, the spreadsheet Viewsheet and an excellent Basic Editor are included as standard. You either love or hate View, but it's much easier to love a freeby which is so sophisticated! But do read Chapter 23 about other word processors. The BASIC is BASIC IV - a slight upgrade only on Basic II.

The graphics commands which were sadly lacking on the Model B are now implemented. Circles, ellipses, parallelograms, arcs etc are all available now as discrete commands, as are a variety of flood-fill routines for odd shapes. They are all fast.

*CONFIGURE. This allows you to set up various parameters of the machine so that after switching on you don't have to fiddle about every time with tedious changes. Because the Master contains a battery, when power is turned off the machine configuration still remains in a small specialized portion of memory. One very useful Configure parameter is the ability to control the sending of line feeds to a printer. This is dealt with in detail later

*STATUS allows you to see the current setting of the Configuration memory.

Two very useful bits of utility software which come with the Master are BAS128 and Convert. BAS128 allows a full 64k of RAM for programs rather than the 32K which is normally available. Convert tries to adapt programs written for the B into a version compatible for the Master. It works by recognising things like memory shift routines, certain direct memory accesses etc. It is not perfect but pretty good. CHARDES is a program to help you design characters.

THE MASTER COMPACT

The Compact is much the same as the Master except that it has its own inbuilt 3.5" disc drive, but no cassette port, and a less comprehensive Analogue input. It is a slightly cut-down version of the Master - and there is no bundled software. The Basic is BASIC 40. Some corners have been cut but a very creditable machine remains.

The Keyboard is a rubber membrane, rather like that on the Spectrum. At that point the similarity ends. The keys are full travel and the feel of the key motion is quite pleasant, quite good for touch typing as there is a subtle 'grip' to the them.

The PORTS are a little cut down. No true Analogue port but a mouse/joystick port. There is a parallel port but the pins are different to the standard Beeb. The disc drive connector is also different but this does not matter as it connects directly to the main disc drive box which is supplied as standard.

The supplied disc drive (3.5" type) seems to be the way the market is going (and a good thing too!). It seems a little strange that this is different to the Master but of course the Archimedes has gone down the same road so may be it is the Master which is the odd man out.

The bundled software looks a little sparse with View and Viewsheet left out but is still a considerable advance over the original BBC-B Welcome tape! The Graphics Extension ROM software makes it all worth while.

THE ARCHIMEDES

The Archimedes is a completely new concept in computing. Related to the BBC-B in many ways structurally but architecturally very different, this machine bears the same sort of relationship to its predecessor as a Porsche does to a Model T Ford.

Because the Archimedes presents such a leap forward in computing we have devoted a whole section to discussing its structure and use, so please refer to Chapter 8 for the full details.

The rest of this section is intended as an introduction to the Archimedes as a member of the Acorn family, rather than as a detailed breakdown of the workings of the machine itself.

The Archimedes is a 32 bit machine, using RISC technology - which means it is fast - very fast: its BASIC runs faster than assembler on the 'B'! It comes in various formats with one or two 3.5" drives and can also have a hard disc. When the 3.5" drive is used as a 640K disc it is compatible with the Compact but in 800K format it is not compatible.

The standard disc filing system is the ADFS but the DFS is supplied on the Welcome disc as a ROM image. The Archimedes is fastest running its own 32-bit programs, but it can emulate the 6502 second processor, so enabling BBC-B type software to be run. It can also emulate MS-DOS: alternatively there is an IBM podule which is a physical add-on rather like the IBM special graphics cards. All these additions are intended to allow the use of the vast range of commercial IBM compatible software.

If it really will run established business software without snags, then it should become one of the foremost computers of the late eighties and early nineties. Not only will it access the existing pool of commercial software, but it will also run most existing Acorn-orientated software - which means that it will get the best of both worlds, the business market and educational software.

7. NETWORKS

The idea of a network is to provide communication between computers and a common source of stored data. There are a number of ways in which this is done in the big wide world of business but BBC networks have so far been mainly used in education.

In essence, a network allows common access from numerous terminals to a large amount of storage space in one place, usually on a Winchester. This space is used for two main functions, the storage of Library programs and data and the provision of individual secure storage space for users. All computers on the network are joined with a common set of wires along which signals travel. Each computer is identified by an 'electrical' code which diverts programs and data to the correct computer. There is obviously a queueing system but this is usually hidden from the user by the speed of access. (This speed of access is going to become very evident soon as the computers with larger memories demand longer programs. As a program becomes ten times as long, so the access time becomes ten times longer.)

If the Winchester holds libraries of software to be used by all computers on the network, it can only be with the specific agreement of the owner of the software Copyright. Usually special Network version must be bought which carries with it a licence to use in a specified manner. Many commercial houses give a very good discount for Networks. The BBC usually charges only twice as much for its network versions as for single user programs, which is excellent. Many firms have a sliding scale depending upon the number of stations: some give Carte Blanche; some try to charge the full cost of the software for each machine. You MUST find out what the agreement is before purchasing. There are software houses with a healthy attitude where you may discuss an agreement if you have unusual uses or demands - on the other hand some software houses do not seem interested in talking to customers. It is our opinion that software houses should gain from multiple usage, but we feel that those who do have a realistic view of the level of increased charge, particularly in the field of education, will be the ones to survive.

The two main versions of networks for the BBC machines are Enet and Econet. Each of the two systems has one computer which is dedicated as a file server. This computer can be used as a computer, but it is disrupted by any network traffic. The fileserver usually has a printer attached to allow stations to print remotely. The main differences between the two systems to the user are at the detail level and a matter of preference.

Each has a "communication between computers" facility and allows a teacher to 'talk' to a pupil or observe what is going on at a remote station.

There are certain types of shared software which pose problems, notably databases. It is a good idea to make absolutely certain that each program works 100% on your network system before you purchase.

One problem with networks is really the problem of Winchesters. As a Disc gets used, so files are created and destroyed. In the process small gaps build up between files which are too small to store programs. In this way it is possible to get to the situation where 10% of your storage space is unusable. On the ordinary business PC with built in Winchester this problem causes a considerable slowing down of disc accessing time. Due to the nature of the beast, compacting is not an easy task: it can be done but it takes a considerable amount of effort. The best solution is to back up the files every so often, then return them, one by one stacked close together. This sounds messy and is.

For all the furore about networks and networking, they are still in their infancy. There are a multitude of different systems of nets, STAR, RING, SPUR, BALANCED LINE, each with its own merit and usage. Hopefully some semblance of order will emerge!

Networks are of major importance in business, where it makes more sense to have just one central database. This stops unnecessary duplication of information, and prevents the problem of information being correct in one file and incorrect in another, to say nothing of the inconvenience of ensuring that all files are kept up-to-date with the same change of information, (such as an address). Secondly, in business there is frequently far too much information input to the complete system for just one terminal to cope with. Whilst it is possible to have lots of little computers dotted round, all doing their own bit of the work (like word-processing or accounts) this is seldom effective because so much in business is inter-related (customer addresses, mail-shots, invoices, accounts, overdue bills, orders, stock control). Without a central database there is the problem of duplication of information, of individual databases getting out of step with one another, and the most obvious problem that the right hand computer doesn't know what the left hand computer is doing.

The other way to deal with inputting and accessing all this information is to have one central database with lots of points of access. The old concept was a big central processor and database with a lot of dumb terminals accessing it. All the computing power was held centrally and the terminals were nothing more and nothing less than input/output devices. This had two effects. Active terminals have to share the computing power of the main processor so at peak times each terminal might perhaps get only a two hundredth of the time of the central processor: not good for speed of programs! In turn, this also requires the central processor to be very fast indeed to cope with the rush - which means expense. Finally, if the central computer goes down, the whole system collapses - not good for business!

The alternative way is to create a network (otherwise known as distributed computing). Each terminal is a small computer in its own right, accessing data from a central point, perhaps sending printing to a central point also, though this doesn't have to be the case. Because the terminal is a computer in its own right it is not slowed down by the activity of others on the network - the only limiting factor is how much data transfer is required from the file to the terminal. (With a central processor everything had to be transferred - screen displays, computing, input/output - the lot.) Secondly, a smart terminal with a small amount of computing power doesn't cost that much. Thirdly, if one terminal goes wrong it doesn't bring the whole system crashing down. Another can be unplugged, transferred to the problem site, and used to do the first terminal's job. Fourthly, replacement or addition of terminals is easy, and usually cheap. The current trend is to use microcomputers which can be bought off the shelf and plugged directly into the system without extensive changes to hardware or software. Finally, it is often cheaper to have a network than a massive central processor.

There is one major requirement of the software for a network. It is essential that a record cannot be altered by more than one terminal at once, as otherwise mayhem ensues. This principle is called 'file locking'. If it is not carried out and two terminals try to access and alter the same file all sorts of spurious things can happen. (eg PC A is dealing with a customer and inputting to the file details of a new order and an alteration to an outstanding order. After a few seconds PC B wishes to process the outstanding order being accessed by PC A. On a good system PC B would be locked out until PC A had finished and closed the file, means that PC B cannot alter the data which PC A is accessing and possibly give rise to lost or incorrectly updated data)

ECONET

Econet is a network system which has grown up with the BBC. The system stores files in a tree directory system (ADFS) and is similar to the storage structure in business PCs. As a result it can be a little bewildering at first finding routes to a particular branch. However, this soon becomes second nature. There is a great deal of software written with Econet in mind, and it is the most widely used networking system for the BBC computer range. Computers are joined to a single cable which a new computer can plug into. There is a limit of about 250 computers which may be put on this network(!) but even this may be exceeded by splitting into two or more networks and using a special 'bridge between network' system. We think it is safe to say that there will not be too many networks of this size in the present school system.

ENET

This network started out looking in use more or less like an ordinary disc drive to the user. The command and storage structure was the same as that of the DFS. The main problem was that it took an effort to run Econet programs on Enet. This problem has now been solved. We personally prefer this system as security tends to be better for the individual and there are more teacher-orientated commands. The ability to FORCE programs down the network to selected stations and to SHOW (demonstrate) a program on a remote set of screens is very valuable.

8.   ACORN ARCHIMEDES

OVERVIEW

The Archimedes is the latest in the Acorn series of microcomputers, and is by far the most powerful. Whereas all previous Acorn machines were 8-bit, the Archimedes is based on 32-bit technology, which means that it can manipulate information in much bigger chunks - four times larger than on the old Acorn machines. In turn this means that it can process data very much more quickly. A second advantage is that 32-bit machines can address much more memory than 8-bit machines, and so 32-bit machines can have very much bigger memories - the biggest version of the Archimedes so far has 4 Megabytes!

The microprocessor used in the Archimedes is a Reduced Instruction Set Chip (RISC). Because it has far fewer internal instructions to decode than other processors it can find and execute an instruction very quickly. By using this processor in conjuction with custom video and memory controllers, the Archimedes can run interpreted programs such as BASIC very quickly, typically at 20-30 times the speed of the BBC-B. Programs running directly in RISC machine code are executed at about 4 Mips (4 million instructions per second). Other more complex processors in competitors' machines may run at 10 or 18 MHz, but each of their instructions needs several clock cycles to execute - bringing most of the operating speeds down below 4 Mips. (The current RISC chip has been run at up to about 18 Mips but in order to increase the speed of the present machine significantly it is understood that very much more expensive memory chips would be needed. This would place the machine in a totally different market.)

You have to think in a different order of magnitude when using a machine such as the Archimedes. With the A310 version running BASIC, having set aside some memory for high resolution colour screens, sprites and relocatable modules (see later) about 694 KBytes of memory are left for your programs and data! Although it is daunting to think of writing a BASIC program using even a fraction of this space, The main point is that for the first time on a BBC machine it will be possible to set up large arrays and store amounts of data which may then be interrogated at very high speed. This is otherwise currently available only on the larger PCs, which offers interesting commercial possibilities.

The machine has *CONFIGURE options which are really a super-set of those used to set up the Master 128 and are retained in battery-backed CMOS RAM in the same way. In the A310 machine there is enough room to assign plenty of space for relocatable modules and sprites.

The Archimedes comes in the 3-box format of keyboard, monitor and monitor stand, with the monitor stand containing all the major electronics, power supply and 3.5 inch disk drive(s). There is a detachable keyboard on a long lead, typical of the convenient arrangement used on 'business' machines. (Acorn almost achieved this set-up with the Master Compact but unfortunately linked the keyboard to the main box with a mass of short wires.) A mouse is standard with all machines.

The disk unit is inclined slightly backwards in order to make it easier to insert disks. Unfortunately the front of the drive overhangs the keyboard connector, which makes connecting up the keyboard rather fiddly.

Two main families are available - the A300 series, also called the BBC computer, and the A400 series. The main differences between the 300 and the 400 series relate to the maximum amount of RAM and how many add-on 'podules' can be used.

Machines in the A300 series are the A305 (512 Kbytes of RAM), and the A310 (1 Mbyte). The A400 series starts with the 1 Mbyte A410 and goes up to the 4 Mbyte A440, which includes a 20 Mbyte Winchester. If you think that you may require very large amounts of memory and are likely to need a Winchester then the A400 series is likely to be most suitable: otherwise the A310 is likely to offer you enough space and facilities. The A305 is probably not quite big enough to make use of the major facilities that the Archimedes offers - in particular, it is likely to run out of memory quite quickly if it tries to run some of the standard CP/M or MS-DOS based business software packages.

All machines come with 512K of ROM which holds the operating system, ADFS, ANFS (Advanced Network Filing system), BASIC, and other utility modules.

HARDWARE COMPATIBILITY WITH THE 'B' SERIES

The Archimedes has parallel printer- and RS232- ports, so printers used with the 'B' series will also work with the Archimedes. However, both ports use different sockets, so you will need to purchase new leads.

There is monochrome video output to a phono socket, but colour output is to a SCART plug, which means that normal RGB colour monitors can only be used if they have a SCART socket as well. (The monitor supplied by Acorn for the Master Compact does have both these sockets and is quite suitable for use with the Archimedes. The only drawback is an aesthetic one - the yellow colour of the B series does not quite go with the pale cream of the Archimedes!)

Unfortunately there is no socket on the Archimedes to plug in external 5.25 or 3.5 disk drive units, because all models have at least one 3.5" drive built in. It would probably not be too difficult to arrange a piggy-back affair inside the 'box' to bring a lead to the outside world for your disk drive units. There is a podule planned to allow external drives to be fitted.

No user-, analogue- or 1 MHz bus- port exists on the basic machines. However, an internal hardware 'podule' is available which provides them.

Because there is sideways RAM no sockets are available for additional ROMs, unlike the BBC B and Master series machines, though an add-on podule for ROMs is planned - software is already provided to access ROM and RAM on these podules.

An Econet socket is provided on the rear of the Archimedes and the machine accepts the same Econet add-on board used for the Master 128. Econet ANFS is included in the software provided in the 512K ROM. Problems will continue to exist when using non-econet networks until manufacturers have produced code of their own. This will have to be loaded from disc if the additional expense of more add-on boards is to be avoided.

SOFTWARE COMPATIBILITY

The Archimedes is provided with BBC BASIC V. This is a very enhanced version of the previous BBC BASICs and maintains an excellent degree of compatibility. A BASIC program from a BBC-B or Master can be transferred to an Archimedes and all the original tokens and syntax will be recognised. As long as the program does not 'poke' directly to memory - especially the screen memory - the program will run, very quickly.

The memory map of the Archimedes is totally different from that of the BBC-B or Master and so programs are likely to crash if they involve downloading techniques or 'poking' memory which the BBC B set aside for buffers. Most downloading routines can easily be stripped from programs. They are usually there just to overcome the memory limitations of the earlier machines. Using buffers for storage is another memory saving technique frequently used with the earlier (smaller) machines and in the Archimedes can normally be got round by reserving the necessary space with a DIM command.

It also possible to make the Archimedes behave in a very similar way to a BBC-B, Master or Compact by using the 6502 Emulator. This is a software module (see later) which enables the Archimedes to run both 6502 machine code and BASIC programs. It also configures the lower part of the memory map to be very similar to a BBC B. As long as the machine code obeys the same rules as BASIC - no 'poking' to the screen or to pieces of hardware that do not exist (eg user ports etc.) - the emulator will interpret the machine code instructions and the program will run. The speed is only slightly slower than it would be running the program in the original BBC-B. The Emulator even runs software such as VIEW (normally used in sideways ROM on the BBC-B) as long as a disc image of the software is called from within the 6502 emulation. In this environment the Archimedes operates in a similar fashion to a BBC-B with shadow RAM - 30K of space is available in all screen modes, PAGE is set to &800 and HIMEM is at &8000.

Notice that earlier the term 'transferred' was used when describing the use of BBC-B software on the Archimedes. The computer uses a different filing system from the BBC-B and so cannot load programs which are stored under DFS. Instead, the Archimedes supports two versions of ADFS (Advanced Disc Filing System). The first is the same as the one used on the Master 128 and Master Compact and creates 640K of disc space using both sides of a 3.5" disc. Therefore a 3.5" disc from a Compact may be read and written to directly by the Archimedes. The second type of ADFS creates an 800K storage on a 3.5" disc.

Discs may be formatted in either mode. The type of disc formatting is automatically assessed when it is used, the Archimedes adjusting the ADFS accordingly. So direct disc transfer is easy if your existing system uses ADFS and 3.5" drives. If you use any other system for storage then the simplest method for transfer is to connect the RS423 port on the BBC-B to the RS232 port on the Archimedes and run a simple program to copy the files across. Such techniques have been covered in editions of 'Acorn User' magazine.

FILING SYSTEM EXTENSIONS

Filing systems on the Archimedes are given some nice additions which make them friendlier to use by comparison with the Master 128. All files are 'stamped' with the current time and date, accessed from the internal clock. The file type is also recorded. Information on the files in the current directory is accessed with the *INFO command. *LCAT and *LEX give similar information for the currently selected library. Files may be *STAMP (ed) to update their date of saving.

It is not necessary to have BASIC active in order to run programs. Simply typing *<program name> will load in a program and activate BASIC if it is needed for the program. This offers interesting prospects in the light of the availability of other languages. There is nothing to stop a suite of programs containing a mix of machine code, BASIC, Pascal, Fortran and any other language which the system can run. Each program could call another in a different language which would then be activated to RUN. These facilities are offered by the FILESWITCH module in the Archimedes and are not specific to any one filing system.

The ADFS is very similar to that on the Master 128, but includes some simple extra commands to facilitate file closure and EXITing from Winchester systems.

GRAPHICS

If we look at the graphics available on the Archimedes, again we are moving in a different world. Modes 0 to 7 are the same as for the BBC B series machines, but there are an additional 10 modes offering a variety of colours and characters per line.

If you have a medium resolution monitor the Mode with highest resolution is 640 x 256 with up to 256 colours. There are also modes which offer 132 characters per line - useful for spreadsheet work if your eyes are good and the screen is clean! If you have the money to spend on a multisync monitor then there are three more modes available which offer 640 x 512 resolution with up to 16 colours available.

In screen modes offering up to 16 colours, the defaults chosen are as for mode 2 on a BBC-B. They are easily changed, however, and any 16 from 4096 may be used at one time. In 256 colour modes, 64 colours are easily available, with subtle shade changes produced using the BASIC command TINT which gives the 256 colour range.

Handling sprites on microcomputers has always been rather difficult and cumbersome. Sprites are a collection of graphic shapes making up a total graphic which occupies more than one character size or graphics plot. A typical sprite would be a spaceship in an arcade game. The Archimedes includes commands to make the use of sprites extremely simple. They may be created using a sprite generator which is supplied on the Welcome disc. Thereafter they may be loaded, saved, merged with other sprite files, plotted on the screen with one simple plot command and flipped in the X and Y axes. It is also possible to define any area of the screen as a sprite and save it to sprite memory, to be replotted later or used as desired. The amount of memory set aside for sprites within the computer is determined by the command *CONFIG SPRITESIZE < X > where X is the number of 32K banks of memory you wish to be reserved for sprites. Commands for loading and saving whole screens are also provided.

This use of sprites coupled with the high processing speed makes for very smooth and rapid graphic animation. It also allows windows on the screen to be saved and swapped around very simply using BASIC. The Archimedes includes a BASIC Desktop program which is downloaded from ROM at switch-on and then operates a windows environment at high speed. (In a 'windows environment', possible courses of action appear in a box on the screen, which looks rather like a piece of paper - the window is actually at the edge of the 'paper'. Successive commands result in the laying down of further 'Pieces of paper' partially overlaying what is already there. These pieces of paper can be pulled around in any direction, and can be lifted off to reveal the original 'paper' underneath. Thus the screen gives the impression of individual pieces of paper laid on top of one another - which doesn't sound very much! - except that for many people it is much easier to work with a windowing system as it gives the impression of a desk-top (and therefore looks more 'natural') and secondly it is possible to see the previous command menu whilst working on the current one, thus giving a much greater sense of 'knowing where you are' within the system.

The Archimedes' windowing system gives facilities comparable with IBM's etc. but actually runs more quickly and more smoothly!

MICE

The mouse supplied with the Archimedes is identical to that currently sold by AMS for use with their Super-Art packages for the BBC-B. It has three buttons and uses a plastic roller-ball. Much thought has gone into making use of the mouse and linking it to graphics on the screen. BASIC V has MOUSE commands which are extremely simple to use.

eg MOUSE X%, Y%, Z%

will give the X and Y coordinates of the mouse on the screen (in the range 0-1279 for X and 0-1023 for Y). Z% will hold information about which button is being pressed. (Z% is a 3 bit number with 1 bit for each button.) The mouse may be linked to a pointer on the screen, with the firmware (supplied) handling all the complex routines necessary for a pointer to flow over text or graphics on-screen without leaving a mess. Restriction of the area of activity of the mouse on the screen is also very simple. By using the command MOUSE RECTANGLE followed by coordinates, the mouse is confined within the area of screen defined. This is extremely useful when implementing windows on the screen operated by the mouse.

The following program shows a simple demonstration of the use of the mouse. It is a painting program which offers 64 colours and flood-fill. All colour selection is from the mouse. The following new BASIC V commands have been used which simplify the whole program:

RECTANGLE <left X, bottomY, rightX, topY> - draw rectangle on screen. RECTANGLE FILL may also be used to produce a rectangle filled in the current foreground colour.

MOUSE <X%,Y%,Z%> - as described above.

FILL <X%,Y%> - performs a flood-fill in the current foreground colour in all directions from the specified coordinates until a non-background colour is encountered.

OFF Turns the cursor off

```
 10 REM >64ART
 20 ONERROR OSCLI"POINTER 0":COLOUR63:END
 30 MODE15:OFF: REM select 256 colour mode, no cursor
 40 FORcolour%=0TO63:COLOUR128+colour%:REM draw palette on screen
 50 VDU32,8,10,32,11:NEXT
 60 A=255:VDU23,A,A,A,A,A,A,A,A,A: REM redefine CHR$255 to block
 70 COLOUR128:col%=63:OSCLI"POINTER 1": REM turn mouse pointer on
 80 PROCshow:PROCrectangles:REM draw borders + colour
 90 REPEAT:PROCmouse:UNTILFALSE:END
100 DEFPROCshow: REM show present colour selected
110 COLOURcol%:VDU31,70,0,A,A,A,31,70,1,A,A,A:ENDPROC
120 DEFPROCmouse: REM get mouse X,Y and buttons pressed
130 MOUSE X%,Y%,Z%:IF Y% > 960 THEN PROCpalette:ENDPROC
140 IF Z%=0 THEN MOVE X%,Y%:ELSE IFZ%=4 THEN DRAW X%,Y%:ELSE IFZ%=2
        THEN FILL X%,Y%:ELSE IF Z%=1 THEN RUN
150 ENDPROC
160 DEFPROCpalette:REM if pointer is in palette area then select
170 IF X% > 64*16 THEN MOUSE TO 64*16,Y%:REM new colour
180 MOUSE X%,Y%,Z%:IF Y% < 960 THEN ENDPROC
190 IF Z%=4 THEN col%=X%/16:GCOL0,col%:PROCshow:PROCrectangles
200 ENDPROC
210 DEFPROCrectangles: REM draw screen borders
220 GCOL0,63:RECTANGLE0,0,1279,1023:RECTANGLE0,0,1279,960
230 GCOL0,col%:ENDPROC
```

BASIC V also includes the commands CIRCLE and ELLIPSE which offer similar facilities to the RECTANGLE commands for their relative shapes. The command BY is added as an extension to the MOVE, POINT and DRAW commands.

eg MOVE BY 100,200

gives an offset to the current graphics postion. It is equivalent to PLOT 0.

The MODE command may now be used to generate a value.

eg M% = MODE

would give integer variable M% the current value of the screen mode.

LINE is used to draw between two screen locations. It is equivalent to MOVE followed by DRAW.

The command WAIT has been added to enable programs to synchronise animation effects with the scanning of the display screen. This removes 'flicker' problems which otherwise can occur.

COLOUR and GCOL have also been extended to allow for the redefinition of colours and to allow full access to the colours available in 256 colour modes.

eg `COLOUR C%,R%,G%,B%`

C% is the logical number of the colour, and R%,G% and B% are the levels set for the red, green and blue components of that colour. They may hold any value between 0 and 255 and are varied in steps of 16 offering 16 discrete levels for each of the primary colour components. (Values between the '16' steps are rounded down to the next step, equivalent to num DIV 16) Simple mathematics shows that this gives a total choice of 16 x 16 x 16 colours - 4096 in all.

SOUND FACILITIES

The Archimedes includes a sound synthesizer which offers up to eight channels in stereo. The enhanced scope which this gives music enthusiasts is quite stunning.

As with graphics, additional commands are provided from within BASIC V to enable the sounds and rhythm to be controlled simply. They offer scope for program enhancement ranging from a simple alteration to the beep of the BBC to full blown music synthesis. Unfortunately this subject is so big that it is impossible to do it justice within the limitations of this book. The BASIC commands which control Sound are slightly changed and not well documented in the guide.

ADDITIONS TO BASIC OFFERED BY THE ARCHIMEDES

In addition to commands to make use of the enhanced graphics and sound capabilities, BASIC V also offers some improvements to its more mundane commands and structures. The more interesting ones are as follows

APPEND - used to append a file to a BASIC program. Very useful! Avoids all that *SPOOL business.

CASE - Part of the CASE..OF..WHEN..OTHERWISE..ENDCASE construct. Looks impressive but how is it used?! The best way to demonstrate this is with a small, if petty, example:
```
10 INPUT A$
20 CASE A$ OF
30 WHEN "DOG"
40    PROCdog
50 WHEN "CAT"
60    PROCcat
70 OTHERWISE PROCunknown
80 ENDCASE
90 ..........rest of program
```

71

Here a value for A$ will be requested at the keyboard. If it is equal to "DOG" then the procedure 'dog' will be called, then on return from that procedure the program will move to line 90 without examining 50 to 80. Similarly if the value entered is "CAT" then the corresponding cat procedure will be executed. If no matches are found then the commands following OTHERWISE will be executed. ENDCASE terminates the construct. Although here only one line and a procedure is offered for each possible match, any number of statement lines can be used for each WHEN command. This PASCAL-like procedure is very neat in use and can be applied to all variable types. It reduces the need for complex IF statements (and therefore reduces even more the need to use that potentially dangerous key-word GOTO)

EDIT - This command causes the the BASIC screen editor to be entered. This is a machine code program which is supplied as part of the ROM in the Archimedes (and is in fact very similar in use to the Acornsoft BASIC Editor, familiar to many BBC-B users). It offers on-screen editing, upward scrolling, and search and replace facilities so that BASIC programs may be edited in a similar way to text on a word-processor. An earlier version of the program is supplied on the Master 128.

ELSE - Part of the IF..THEN..ELSE construct which has been improved to enable multiple lines of statements to be included, instead of them all having to be included in one program line. ENDIF is used to end the contruct.

*ENUMDIR $ FRED produces an ASCII file of all file names in the $ directory and saves in the file FRED - very useful for menu screens.

LINE INPUT (also INPUT LINE) - Allows commas, leading spaces and trailing spaces to be entered in an INPUT command. INPUT on its own strips leading and trailing spaces and will ignore all input after a comma. If you use INPUT A$, and then give as the answer "12, Acacia Avenue", only "12" will be stored (as a string) in A$. On the other hand INPUT LINE A$ will give you the full reply. INPUT LINE does in fact appear in BASIC II, but is not well documented.

LISTO - Has been improved and now also offers the facility to split multi-statement lines. Ideal for trying to debug those crunched programs - but there's little point in crunching a program on the Archimedes, with all that space available!.

LOCAL ERROR - This is used to modify the error handler temporarily and then uses RESTORE ERROR to reset to the original error handling routine.

QUIT - Statement to leave BASIC and return to the operating system.

SUM - This command is used with arrays either to concatanate the strings in the array or to provide the sum of a numerical array.

SWAP - Provides a very simple way of exchanging current values of either variables or arrays.

eg SWAP A%,B% SWAP A$,B$ SWAP A(),B()

WHILE - Part of WHILE..ENDWHILE loop. (See Chapter 16) The loop is only executed if the statement is true. This is the third of the three main loop stuctures. (FOR - NEXT executes a fixed number of times, REPEAT - UNTIL executes at least once and until the UNTIL condition is met, WHILE - ENDWHILE will skip the structure if the condition is fulfilled before the loop is executed)

Passing information to and from Procedures and Functions has been greatly enhanced in Basic V. In previous versions of BBC-BASIC it was possible to pass variables into a procedure. However, sequences of variables (ie. arrays) could not easily be passed without a lot of jiggery-pokery, and results from procedures had to be passed out in the form of Global variables.

BASIC V allows the passing of arrays although one has to be careful. If your machine is fairly full up and you try to pass a large array, the machine may seize up. The reason is simple: the passed array is created as an entirely new array which has had the contents of the old one passed into it. This has the advantage that alterations may be made to it without affecting the main array but creating space for this new array uses up memory. The other major point is that variable values may be passed out of the procedure as well as into it.

An additional bonus is the limited error checking which is provided on program entry. If you have unmatched brackets or parentheses then you will be informed after the program line has been entered. This is extremely useful where a long series of brackets has been used.

BASIC V also supports the use of PROCEDURE LIBRARIES. These are routines which are not part of a main program but may be accessed as though they were. This facility is very useful where standard routines are used frequently in several programs. Using standard procedures in this way generates consistency in software production and encourages good program structuring. The libraries may be loaded from disc into an area which BASIC will reserve in one of two ways.

1.   LIBRARY <filename> reserves space amongst the current variables, arrays etc and the library is placed here. This library will be destroyed when either NEW or CLEAR is used or a new program is loaded.

2.   INSTALL <filename> reserves space for the library at the top of user memory, with HIMEM being lowered as necessary. This library will then remain intact and may be accessed by

several separate programs, being unaffected by NEW, CLEAR or MODE changes. However a hard break (CTRL/BREAK) will clear it.

Libraries are saved initially as normal programs containing just functions or procedures. They must not contain any references to line numbers such as GOTO, and the line numbers used for the procedures are irrelevant. Any number of libraries may be loaded using LIBRARY or INSTALL, so long as sufficient memory is available.

MODULES

The Archimedes supports the use of relocatable modules. These are machine code routines which may be either chip based or loaded in from disk. They act in a similar way to the sideways ROMs on the BBC-B except that in the Archimedes all the modules may be active at the same time as they occupy individual areas in the computer's memory map.

Modules can act in a variety of ways. Some offer enhancement to the operating system, controlling the mouse, pointers, sound etc. Others offer routines such as the BASIC editor. BASIC itself is a relocatable module, blown into ROM. Not only resident in ROM, it is also supplied in RAM version on the Welcome disc. This may be loaded and run in place of the ROM version and gives even faster performance.

Other modules are provided to give hard copy of the screen on Epson printers and a Debugging module for machine code users. The filing systems for disc (ADFS) and networks (ANFS) are also supplied in ROM form as modules.

Modules also available are the 6502 emulator, mentioned earlier and an IBM emulator which allows the Archimedes to simulate an IBM environment and access MS-DOS disks and programs. Under this Emulator programs such as Lotus 1-2-3, MS-Word, Supercalc 3 and dBase III can be run. Because all instructions have to be interpreted, even with the tremendous speed of the RISC chip some functions will run more slowly than on the original machines. These emulators do offer extra facilities to the Archimedes in terms of software compatibility but we strongly recommend that if you intend to run either a BBC-B or IBM program on the the Archimedes under an emulator, you MUST see it running fully first, with all functions of the program, before committing yourself. Also remember that disc formats differ with different companies. If you buy 'IBM' software to run with the emulator, make certain that the disc format is correct for the Archimedes.

The ability to add relocatable modules gives the Archimedes terrific flexibility. If there is a demand for an extra facility or emulation then no doubt either Acorn, or more probably an enterprising third party, will supply the necessary software in the form of a relocatable module.

* commands to handle modules are provided, eg *RMLOAD, *RMTIDY, *RMCLEAR and *RMREINIT. The last command is used to reinitialise the module after a *RMKILL command has effectively removed the software from the machine. Modules which are ROM based have their status stored in CMOS RAM in the same way as that used for the ROMs on the Master 128.

Finally - for all users of the Archimedes: ensure that your printer has plenty of paper. Press CTRL-B or enter VDU2. Then enter *H. . - including the second full stop.

You will then be presented with about 11 sheets containing a summary of all useful commands for the operating system and modules active in your machine. This summary will prove to be far more useful and easier to follow than most of the User Guide provided with the machine.

9. COMPATIBILITY

The most common question that is asked about a new machine is "Will my existing programs run on it?" The answer is not simple and depends upon a large number of factors. They are:-

1. The language and which version of that language is used.

2. What physical form the program and files are stored in.

3. What software protocols have been used to lay down files.

4. The memory and hardware requirements of the program.

5. Whether the program is written 'legally'

6. Whether incompatibility can be resolved through the use of a second processor.

Programs and files are compatible IF they are written in a version of BASIC which is equal or lower than the one in your machine, IF they are written on a medium which is accessible by the machine i.e. five and a quarter inch disc, three and a half inch disc, or cassette, and IF the style of laying down the information on the disc is the same i.e. single or double density, Acorn, MS-DOS or CP/M format.

Let us look at these in detail.

1. THE LANGUAGE

BASIC (which stands for Beginners All purpose Symbolic Instruction Code) is a language which although possessing a general structure has, like English, a large number of dialects. All the Acorn machines use a dialect called BBC-BASIC but as time has gone on various extra elements have been added. There are now five versions of BBC-BASIC, BASIC I to BASIC V. If your machine is one of the early BBC A or B's then you may have BASIC I. To find out which version you have, press BREAK, then type in REPORT <Return>. If the Copyright message is dated l981 then you have BASIC I - if l982 or later you have BASIC II. Later BBC-B's and the B+ have BASIC II, the Master has BASIC IV and the Master Compact BASIC 40. The Archimedes has BASIC V.

The good thing about BBC BASIC is that a program written for a lower level of BASIC will always run on a machine with a higher number BASIC, as all features of any BASIC are implemented in all upgrades. (In other words it is 'upwardly compatible'.) However, the reverse is not true - there are certain elements of the higher numbered BASICs which do not appear on any of the others. Nevertheless, a program written in one of the later BASICs may well be perfectly capable of running on a machine with a lower BASIC provided that it does not use any of the later features.

This upwards compatibility of BASIC is the reason why many apparently redundant features are included on the later BASICs - commands such as GOSUB which have been almost totally replaced by PROCEDURES and FUNCTIONS. They are only included in the later versions of BASIC so that earlier programs will be sure to run on them.

BASIC comes on a separate chip so that if you want to have a higher version of BASIC in your machine it is possible to purchase one (though at the time of writing BASIC V is only available on the 32 bit Archimedes). If you are running BASIC I then we would strongly advise you to put BASIC II in as there are certain disc and file handling elements on this which are a little better. The differences between BASIC IV, BASIC 40 and BASIC II are not great: but BASIC V, for the Archimedes, contains many extra features.

The compatibility referred to above applies with certainty only to programs that are typed in at the keyboard. It does not necessarily apply to programs that are already on disc or cassette. There are one or two occasions when tokens have been changed so when decoded they represent different keywords (see Chapter 13 for the treatment of tokens). Specifically the token in BASIC I for OPENIN is one of two used in BASIC II for OPENUP.

The new BASIC II token for OPENIN is unreadable by BASIC I. The table below shows things more clearly:-

BASIC I command	read by	BASIC II becomes
OPENIN		OPENUP
OPENOUT		OPENOUT
OPENUP		OPENUP

BASIC II command	read by	BASIC I becomes
OPENIN		Vanishes
OPENOUT		OPENOUT
OPENUP		OPENIN

It is still upwardly compatible, in that OPENUP allows you both to read and write to a disc, whereas OPENIN allows reading from the disc only.

If you try to run a program written under BASIC II on a machine with BASIC I in, or vice versa, you may get some peculiar things happening when you try to access disc files. Suddenly your program which lists in one way is magically transformed by the new machine's BASIC interpreter into a slightly different version on screen - in other words you may write OPENIN on your first machine, save the program, transfer the disc to your second machine, LOAD it in - and find thee command has vanished into thin air. This causes a lot of confusion until you realise what's going on!

Some programs are written in languages other than BASIC and it goes without saying that if you haven't got that language resident in your machine, either as a chip or as a ROM image, then your program will not run.

2. PHYSICAL FORMS OF STORAGE

A further problem is of sheer physical hardware incompatibility. The early BBC machines were fitted with a cassette and a disc interface suitable for 5.25" drives. The Master is fitted with a 5.25" disc interface, but the Compact and the Archimedes have their own internal 3.5" disc drives. It is possible, however, to purchase cables for interfacing between most of the range.

If you wish to transfer programs and files between different machines the first problem is to make sure that the hardware is appropriate. Can you physically plug the appropriate hardware into the new machine? (such as a cassette, a 5.25" disc drive, a 3.5" disc drive or a Winchester). If you can't you may need to use a little subterfuge - perhaps copying from cassette onto 5.25" drive: then 5.25" drive to 3.5" drive - in order to make it physically readable by the new machine. We can't give you a definitive way of doing things because there are so many permutations and combinations of hardware and machines.

If you have found the physical plugs to fit into the physical sockets, do you still have compatibility? Not necessarily. Keeping it in the family, ie. Acorn, you cannot go far wrong, but beware strangers. The case which springs to mind is that of trying to run IBM programs on Archimedes under the IBM emulator. First, does the disc fit the drive? Second, does the track format fit the drive layout? Third, does the information on the disc arrive in the correct order for the emulator and your interface? We will say it again:-

TRY BEFORE BUY.

If you still can't get hardware compatibility you can transfer files between machines using the RS242 serial port: alternatively create your program or file and send it, via a modem, into one of the electronic mail banks such as Telecom Gold. Then access it from the second computer. In this way all hardware incompatibilities are removed - expensively. This works for transference of files between totally different makes where the disc layout and machine architecture is completely different.

If all else fails, you can always re-type in the BASIC listings.

3. ACCESSING STORED INFORMATION

1. The Archimedes is a 32 bit machine - all the other Acorn machines are 8 bit machines. What does this mean? The number of bits in a machine describes the size of the biggest chunk of information that it can handle at one go - the larger the number of bits the bigger the chunks of information that can be processed. It is rather like the difference between simple multiplication and long multiplication. We all know our tables up to l2 x l2. Beyond that we have to multiply by breaking down each number into its component parts and multiplying separately - as we would if we were multiplying l5 x l3. Obviously the more tables that you learned and the higher they go, the less you will need to use long multiplication, and the quicker your calculation will be.

It's the same with the computer. An 8 bit computer can deal with numbers up to 256 at any one time. Beyond this it needs to split numbers into separate parts, just as we split the number l5 into 'l x l0' and '5' when doing long multiplication. The Archimedes, being a 32-bit machine reads in information in bigger pieces and deals with it in bigger chunks, which means that it is much quicker when handling similar sized numbers. However, because everything is written on disc in 32-bit characters a 32-bit machine is therefore not compatible with an 8-bit machine unless extra software or hardware is used to decode 8-bit into 32-bit and vice versa. The Archimedes is fitted with this (a 6502 emulator) and so is able to translate, run and produce 8-bit programs which are compatible with the rest of the Acorn range. It does, however, function significantly more slowly when doing this. A word of warning: while the Archimedes should run any BASIC program written correctly from any of the rest of the range, a program written on the Archimedes will not necessarily run on all of the range unless the use of keywords is kept to the level of BASIC on the second machine. Therefore, don't use CASE or WHILE etc!

2. Storage of programs and files on cassette, disc, or Winchester is done in exactly the same way throughout, that is, in blocks called sectors. But there are other things saved besides just the program - various internal codes are put on the disc along with the file itself in order to show the computer where the file starts and to check that it has been read correctly. These check digits and other information are the same throughout the Acorn range. However, a different style of internal codes is used in disc interface chips from other hardware manufacturers - and this essentially is the difference between a computer which runs in CP/M, MS-DOS and one that runs under the Acorn DFS.

The next problem is that the disc filing system may be fitted to a BBC machine and may lay down its files on disc in single or double density according to the type of chip. A single density DFS cannot read or write to a disc formatted in double density: but the reverse is not necessarily true. (see Chapter 12).

4. THE MEMORY AND HARDWARE REQUIREMENTS OF THE PROGRAM

Some programs are big and require a lot of memory to run them. Other programs are not that big, but require a lot of calculating space. Some require both. The memory requirements of programs are a highly individual thing, and depend very much upon the style of programming as well as the subject. Many standard programs running on business machines require 750K as a minimum! Even the Archimedes in its most basic configuration is too small for some business programs and in fact too small to run some of the demo programs!

If there is insufficient memory for a program it will either fail to load in properly, or crash after a short time - usually just when you thought you'd got away with it! Make sure you know the memory requirements of a program before you buy it, and if in any doubt, try it with real data (not just a demonstration datafile) on your machine.

Hardware requirements are usually very obvious - you may need a printer in place or else the program will hang up. Alternatively you may need a particular ROM chip to be in place (such as DISC DOCTOR if you are using DFS discs with the *SWAP command), a facility for sideways RAM, Shadow memory etc. Make sure you have the necessary bits and pieces as otherwise you'll be disappointed.

There are occasions when even apparent compatibility can go astray, especially if you have any non-standard hardware in place. There can be clashes of workspace between the program and some of your resident ROMs (CARETAKER is a notable culprit here - try *NORMALKEY in order to turn the single-key entry off: otherwise remove the ROM from your machine.) Some programs won't work with certain DFS's - and as some DFSs use more workspace than others you may get unexpected 'No Room' messages.

Finally, there is an odd little bug that has occurred because of a change in the DFS chip supplied as an upgrade to the BBC-B. Most models were fitted with the 8271 DFS controller chip, whereas the B+ has the 1770 (and the B+ also has Shadow memory). There are one or two commercial programs going round that find out if the 1770 is in place, and if it is, issue commands to bring in the Shadow memory.

Unfortunately, if these programs are run on the 'B' which has been fitted with a 1770, then when the (non-existent) Shadow memory is called, the program crashes.

5. LEGALITY OF PROGRAMMING TECHNIQUE.

Although BASIC programs and assembler programs are upwardly compatible throughout the Acorn range, this only applies if they are used 'legally'. It is quite safe to write directly to main memory and screen memory on the 'B' - but it doesn't work if you are using a second processor, nor on the Master series nor the Archimedes. The Master and Archimedes both have a program called 'Convert' which attempts to render 'legal' that which is not - but it can't always achieve this.

6. USE OF A SECOND PROCESSOR

Where you want to use software written under another operating system (MS-DOS, CP/M etc) it is possible to achieve compatibility through the use of a second processor. This fits inside or outside the machine, depending upon which Acorn machine you have, and makes the Acorn machine run as an input/output device which drives the 2nd processor. In effect, the hub of the machine is now the new 2nd processor. There are several different types of second processor available, and if this processor is compatible with the new software you want to run, then you may be successful in achieving this.

-oOo-

But note - there are a lot of IFs. The above can only be a general guide to compatibility or lack of it. There is only one rule - suck it and see!

10. ORGANISING YOUR WORK

BREAK KEY GUARD

The B & B+ suffer from the same malaise: the BREAK key is right next door to Function Key 9. There are some commercial programs which use F9 as one of the main keys, which is a recipe for disaster. Some sense has come to the design of the later models: there is a respectable gap between the BREAK key and other important keys. (Also, the later models have a BREAK lock to prevent accidental use. This can be a mixed blessing.)

If you hit BREAK by mistake, you can often get the program back with OLD <RETURN> and then RUN <RETURN>, but it is better if you can prevent the BREAK key being pressed in the first place because information gets lost to a greater or lesser extent. Unfortunately, with commercial programs it is often impossible to alter the program to get even a limited return to normality.

Here are some ways to reduce the damage:-

1. Avoid using the Function 9 key if possible. A finger slip here can be disastrous.

2. In your own programs it is always possible to program the BREAK key (*KEY 10 OLD M) but this is not always ideal and some information (mainly variable values) gets lost.

3. You can alter the hardware so that BREAK is inactivated, being replaced by a switch at the back of the machine. The Master and Compact have a built-in device to do just this. It is a screw next to the key which needs to be turned with a screwdriver to get Break back again. If you want to leave the Break key locked you can set Configure so that the machine automatically performs SHIFT-BREAK when you switch on.

4. A less dramatic method, but no less effective, is to create a little cardboard well within which the break key sits, protected from accidental knocks but still available for deliberate use.

You need a small piece of thin card: the type used in card indexes is ideal. Cut a rectangle 22mm wide and 90mm long. Starting from one end, score lines vertically down at exactly 20mm intervals. This leaves a piece 10mm long at the end. Cut off the corners of this little bit as it is to be a glue tag.

Bend it at the score lines and glue the tag inside the box tube thus formed. You should find that the resulting structure slips neatly over the BREAK key.

For further information on this subject see the delightful article by Robert Jamieson on CAO in A&B Computing, Vol.1 No.15. Published April '85. (CAO.? - it stands for Computer Assisted Origami!)

OPERATION MANUALS

There are always new and interesting points to be gleaned from manuals, books and journals, even for the most knowledgeable amongst us. To help remember them it is a good idea to have a notebook and a fluorescent marker. A quick slash of the fluorescent pen over an appropriate line, or a jotted note in the book, will quickly draw the item to attention later.

When you start operating a new package always jot down in very abbreviated form the commands and procedures you most frequently use so that you need to consult the manual less often for routine information. If the program uses the function keys a lot, make yourself a function keystrip (see later on in this chapter). It will save a lot of time and energy!

STACKING BOOKS ON SHELVES

The computer age seems to have spawned a generation of spiral wire-backed books. They are a delight to copy from, as they lie flat when open, but they are a pain to get out of a shelf when stacked in a bunch. So - try putting a good old traditionally-bound book in between the spiral bound ones and it becomes easy.

CARE OF DISCS

There are a number of sensible things not to do with discs, all of them very obvious.

1.   If you are going to put your discs into your handbag or
      briefcase, even if they are in a box, do make certain that
      you have cleaned the sand out since last holiday. Bags in
      cars tend to fall over and it is amazing just how little
      muck it takes to get under the cover of every disc.

2. Magnets are fatal to discs. The way that the information
    is laid down includes checks to detect errors in
    transcription. If just one character is illegally altered,
    the check for that sector (of 256 characters) will show an
    error. If the sector is part of a program then the whole
    program will not be loadable. If the sector is part of a
    file, that section will be incapable of being read, and
    probably of being written to. It certainly cannot be
    copied. Either way, if you lose one character, you will
    lose a lot of other information with it, so minor magnetic
    interference can produce effects out of all proportion to
    the physical change it creates.

Unfortunately, you don't need strong magnets to do damage. A friend's children
were playing 'fishpond' with a little magnet on top of a mercifully small pile of discs.
The magnet could just about raise a paperclip with a paper fish attached, so it was
not very strong, yet the top three discs had all developed permanent amnesia and
the bottom one had bald patches.

Magnets are not always obvious. It is good to have a healthy respect for all
electrical equipment (especially if it contains a motor), and electric cables
(especially mains cables).

In general, it is unwise to put discs on top of the printer, disc drive or monitor.
There is rarely a problem with any of these but somewhere, at some time, you are
going to come across a piece of apparatus with less than perfect magnetic
shielding. For example, the speaker at the top left of your keyboard can prove
rapidly fatal.

Tape-recorders, steel rulers and screwdrivers should also be avoided. (have you
noticed how well your screwdriver picks up screws?) Telephones are especially bad
- both the handset and rest contain powerful magnets. And don't use magnetic
paperclip holders, even if you do keep the holder itself well out of the way.
Eventually the paperclips themselves become magnetised. If you use them to hold
listing paper together, then leave a disc on top of the listing.....

3. Discs are very sensitive to dust and smoke. The distance
    between the disc drive reading head and the surface of the
    disc is smaller than the thickness of a human hair, and
    slightly higher than a fingerprint. A smoke particle is
    about the same size, but a grain of dust is huge by
    comparison. Remembering what we said about check digits in
    relation to magnetism, consider the damage that can be done
    if a particle gets between the head and the recording
    surface and prevents the reading or writing of just one character.

In addition, dust between the head and the disc may destroy the head and disc (a head-crash). So - keep dust out of the computer area. If you drop a disc on a dusty floor, throw it away - you may destroy your disc drive in trying the disc to see if it's all right. (There is a hair-raising story of one computer user who dropped a disc in this way, and then proceeded to ruin all 34 of his company's disc drives in 'trying to find a computer that would still run his program'.)

Keep the computer area as dust-free as you can. Don't dry-dust - it only spreads it around: damp dust, but please, not when the machines are switched on! Use covers for the keyboard, disc drive and printer. Don't smoke near the computer - smoke particles are just as damaging as dust. (Never mind the computer, smoking can kill you as well!) Don't touch the surface of the discs - handle them by the cardboard packing only, and at the edges, not over the recording area. Even using a pen to write on discs can damage them irretrievably. See chapter 11 for ways to do this safely.

Finally, try not to use discs as mug mats. They are remarkably resilient, but a little common sense does help. They are not load bearing either!

CLEANING

1.   The monitor screen. Have you looked at your Monitor or
      T.V. screen lately? Can you actually see anything through
      the dirt? Go on, give it, and your eyes, a treat and clean the thing.

Cleaning glass is an arcane art. Just because there are dozens of flashy bottles of window jollop on the shelves of your supermarket doesn't mean that this is the answer. The average window cleaning preparation is like heroin - once you have started using it, you need more. Most of these preparations deposit a thin film of waxy substance on the glass, which positively makes the glass glow, in the right light, at the right angle, but not for long - so you have to clean it again - with more jollop.

Instead of using special cleaners, try ordinary household Ammonia in a dilution of about 0.1 pint to a gallon of water. It cuts through grease and muck and leaves the glass sparkling and clean for a much longer period. (However, do take note of the manufacturers instructions. Phillips specifically warn against using ammonia on their monitors.)

It is often convenient to keep the diluted ammonia in a spray bottle. Switch everything off, cover the keyboard with a cloth, spray the screen and then polish it off with a soft cloth. The only precautions you have to take are the usual ones with liquids and electrical equipment.

2.	The keyboard can become quite dusty if not kept clean.
	This can affect the keys if you are unlucky. The best
	solution is a soft brush and a vacuum cleaner.

3.	The printer. There is not much you can do without
	affecting the warranty. If you are handy with mechanical
	gadgets then the following may prove useful. However, if
	the dog howls every time you try Do-it-yourself, leave alone!

The print head tends to become clogged up after many months of hard labour.
When this happens the descenders on Y and G become faint because they have
become gummed up with dried ink. Undo the print head clip and with a fine camel
hair brush put a little soapy water in the place where the wires come out of the unit
to hit the ribbon. Take out the ribbon and run the printer, using its test program, on
clean paper. When the printing from the soapy water disappears, repeat the
treatment. Do this about 6-8 times. It's cheaper than a new print head.

4.	Disc drives. Don't clean too often. Most head cleaners
	cost about £14 and do more harm than good if used too often.
	About every three months is often enough. (Some people advise
	that you do not clean at all until you start getting errors - not bad advice.)
	Don't go inside the box to do anything - leave well alone even
	if you are a genius with mechanics.

ROM BOX

If you have bought any ROM chips you will also have lots of little bits of black foam
that come with them. In most cases this is conductive foam and can be useful for
storing ROMs once you have transferred them to disc. Put one ROM on each side
of the foam for storage, then place them inside one of those folding plastic double
cassette boxes.

STATIC ELECTRICITY AND ROMS

Some ROMs arrive in a bit of polystyrene tile. Take VERY GREAT care when you
remove it, especially if you are standing on a nylon carpet, it's a dry day and you
have just spent a happy half hour stroking the cat. (Chips are allergic, fatally, to
static electricity) Your best bet is to go through the seemingly pointless exercise of
'discharging' yourself to earth by touching something like the metal case of your
disc drive or the tap shaft on a water radiator.

DISC STORAGE BOXES

If you have any quantity of discs it is a temptation to get a swish box with a little lock and dividers so that no one can get in. Have you ever looked at those locks? The keys are so simple that you only have to sneeze in the vicinity of the lock and it falls open. In any case, a thief will just pick up the box...

Some of these boxes should be avoided. If the lid is removable then it is easy to damage your discs at the back by replacing the lid too far forward, whereupon the lid catches on the back divider causing much innocent amusement for onlookers. Also, the lock at the front can be absolutely lethal as it crashes down on discs at the front that have been left leaning forwards, not back.

The solution - get a box that is hinged at the back. If you want to save money, the next time you buy discs get the ones that come with a hinged box free.

It is worth spending a little time thinking about disc storage. Discs, by and large, look much the same at a distance. They also have a habit of multiplying and trying to find the right disc out of a hundred of the things is not always easy. There are a number of ways of getting around this, the most important is regularly noting down what each contains. However, if you colour-code your discs you are already half way there eg. Blue for Basic programs, White for Wordprocessing, Red for personal finances (how appropriate!) etc. You can get coloured discs from many sources. Usually called Rainbow, they come in Red, Green, Yellow, Blue and White. Some also sell coloured boxes for them but wrapping paper or coloured labels from Smiths are a cheaper answer.

Alternatively, you can use coloured disc labels except that there are never enough of the right type. Another, cheaper and more visible way is to use white write-protect labels. Put one round the END of the disc and colour it appropriately. Buy a set of spirit-based coloured marker pens. The set bought by one of us four years ago is still doing yeoman service (in spite of marauding children).

COMMERCIAL CATALOGUES AND THINGY-BITS'N'BOBS

It is always worth while looking in the professional users catalogues. Two of the better known ones are from MISCO and INMAC. Whilst a lot of the content is not really relevant to the small business or home user you can get a lot of good ideas. There are all sorts of cleaning equipment, dust covers, copy holders, lighting, static preventers, labels, ribbons, things to send your signals down 18 miles of wire without the slightest corruption, and whole ranges of outrageously expensive furniture. You may not want it, need it, understand it, but if just one good idea rubs off it will have been worth it.

RULERS AND MAGNIFYING GLASSES

A ruler is a powerful aid to list copying. It guides the eye, helping to prevent duplication and missed lines.

A magnifying glass on a stand is a definite plus as some of the listings in magazines are very poorly printed. There is a magnifying ruler made of tinted plastic which does its job quite well but is a little expensive. However, it does combine the two functions adequately. The ruler magnifies when in contact with the page and the central yellow strip serves to outline a single magnified line at a time.

If you go to computer exhibitions look out for stands which sell odds and ends of computer bits. They have a delightful oblong magnifying glass on a heavy stand - it also has 'hands' for holding things whilst you solder.

CALCULATORS

Believe it or not, it is a great idea to have a cheap old calculator near the computer. Apart from the fact that it calculates to more decimal places, it is surprising how often a quick calculation can avoid disturbing a running program. Calculators also appear in 'pull down' desk-top programs, but the real McCoy is quicker!

A programmable calculator is also useful if you can put a conversion program into it for HEX and BINARY.

LIBRARIES

It is easy to forget that the local library is cheaper than the bookshop! The library can get virtually any book you request, given time - ideal for deciding if a particular book is worth buying for permanent reference. By the way, we hope that you bought this one.

FANFOLD FEATURED

1.   Fanfold paper makes people lazy. How many people use the
      back of the paper for trial listings etc? The usual form
      is ..Print.. Rip.. Check three lines of program.. Screw
      up.. Throw away. Great for the paper manufacturers,
      rotten for de-forestation and your bank balance. Fanfold
      is easy to insert and feed so why not keep that useless
      used paper for a second go?

2.   Setting the width of the tractors is not always easy. The
     secret is not to do it statically. Get the left hand side
     in the correct place and leave the right hand side
     unlocked. Reel the paper backwards and forwards and the
     right side tractor moves automatically into the correct
     position. While still moving the paper tighten the right
     hand tractor lock.

3.   Tearing paper at its perforation - don't use the paper
     tearer provided, but instead hold the paper vertically with
     the perforation a couple of inches above the tearer. Keep
     the paper taut and flick the perforation at on side of the
     sheet. This starts the tear and the rest is easy.

4.   Bursting the edges of fanfold paper is easier to do if you
     wait until you have a number of sheets. Start the tear as
     though you were tearing a telephone book in two, then place
     the perforated bit along the edge of a table and tear
     outwards along that. The better the paper the better it
     tears, and the smoother the edges.

HANDY REFERENCE TABLES

Some pages of the User Guide are well worth a copying. Mount them on card and
stick them on the wall for reference.

Pages worth doing? How about the following from the BBC-B User Guide

     VDU table (p.378)
     Error Messages(p.482)
     ASCII code (pp.486/7)
     Keyboard Layout (p.497)
     OS Routines (p.452)

Why not make up a short reference book of photostated pages from the various
manuals? (but don't sell it .... Copyright!)

KEY STRIP

If you have a number of programs and ROMs you will also have a considerable
number of Function key strips annotating the use of each key for a particular
program. As the newer programs tend to have two, three and four rows of
definitions for all combinations of SHIFT and CONTROL with each Function key,
the result can be an untidy mess of lots of little strips of paper.

You need a device to hold the keystrips together in a little book, spiral bound along its length. The bottom keystrip fits under the plastic strip above the function keys, and the rest of the 'book' goes over the strip, so it can be opened at any page.

There are a couple of firms producing key strip holders which, whilst being good, are expensive. You can make your own for about 10p.

You need a Stanley knife, a steel rule, thin pen, a steady hand and some thin card. Cut the card into a strip 210mm wide (the width of Keys 0-9 plus about 20mm). Now draw thin lines down the page, starting at the right hand side, approximately every 18mm, until you have 10 columns and a wide band to the left. Next divide the page into horizontal strips about 40mm deep. Each of these is a key strip.

Now find someone who can lay their hands on a plastic ring binder punch, of the type that makes a load of little oblong holes all down the edge of the paper. Good places to try are High Schools and Polytechnics, Libraries, Printers etc. The piece of curly plastic which goes in the holes and makes the thing into a small book costs about 4-8p. Unfortunately, the binding machine costs a lot more.... which is why we suggest you borrow it!

You can write out your own instructions on the key strips, or stick the commercial program key strips onto them. The bottom card slips under the perspex strip on the machine and you can now flip between the strips at will.

When one strip is showing, so is the back of another of the pieces of card. It can be used for several purposes:-

1.   Cryptic comments to remind how to use the program.
2.   Key words to remember.
3.   Your own key definitions to go with the program.

Colour can help a great deal on keystrips - each horizontal row should be a different colour - eg. normal - white, SHIFT - green, CONTROL - blue, SHIFT and CONTROL - red

CLEAN ELECTRICITY

Don't operate your computer in a thunderstorm, ever. Unplug it as well.

1.   Mains surges or magnetic surges from nearby lightning may
      kill it, very permanently. (Chips do not like even small
      shocks, and the magnetic surge from nearby lightning can be
      just as devastating)

2.   Have you noticed the lights dim during a storm sometimes, when an overhead line goes down and the voltage drops? Computers can get very forgetful at times like this. It is possible to lose hours of work.

3.   It is also possible for dips and spikes in mains voltage to put unwanted characters on the discs (which leads to whole sections of discs and programs becoming unreadable).

Have you noticed the flashes of light on the television screen when the fridge comes on? Dips in current come when you switch electrical items on, and there is a corresponding surge back into the mains when you switch them off again. There are special mains filters to get rid of these surges and spikes - use it on the computer, and not on the surge-producing items. Some filters look like an adapter. Plug it into the socket from which you take power for all your computer hardware and it will clean the electricity for computer, disc drive and printer together: as each of these has electronic circuitry, each could be affected by mains surges. Other varieties include the filter built into a four-way strip socket, so the output from all four sockets is automatically clean. The filter will sit there for most of its life doing a magnificent job and you'll think you've wasted your money because nothing happens (that's because it's working!).

Don't tempt fate, though! Filter or no filter, it is not a good idea to put your computer on a spur that also feeds an electric kettle, a soldering iron, a fan, an electric fire or anything with an electric motor in. Lights are usually O.K.

However, most filters are not designed to protect against several million volts. If lightning can travel a few hundred yards through the air, we doubt whether it will stop to have a conversation with your filter, so still switch off and unplug it in a thunderstorm. You have been warned!

CASSETTES

Cassettes are not very practical because they take such a long time to load and save, but there are many who have not yet made the transition to discs. If you have discs, there is no reason why you shouldn't use cassettes as an archive store for precious programs and files, in the same way that one would use a tape-streamer as a back-up for a Winchester hard disc.

(It is perhaps a sign of the times that there is no cassette port on the Compact which, in its parallel role to the Electron, really should have one. The Archimedes does not have one either but that is less surprising.)

One of the saddest sights to be seen is the little lad with a C90 tape jam packed full of programs, trying to find and load a particular one. We do tend to think that it is economical to store everything on one tape. Economical in money, yes. Economical in time, no.

If you must use big tapes then do make certain that you have a recorder with a counter. To prevent programs running into each other, be 'wasteful' and allow 20-30 between programs. Always start on a 10 number - it causes less bother in the long run.

Never start very near the leader tape because some tapes have the first few inches kinked by the central boss of the cassette. It is just not worth inviting this sort of problem so allow about 10 seconds-worth of tape before starting to record.

If you work entirely on cassettes the best way to organise them is to get a couple of dozen 5-minute tapes from your local computer shop and only put one program per side of the tape. Label the edge of the cassette case, either with a number or with the title. (There is nothing more frustrating for your friends than waiting while you interestingly discover what is on your tapes.)

If your computer's tape-recorder is under direct computer control then it is worthwhile having an old spare recorder on which to rewind your tape. This saves your having to unlock the recorder from your computer every time you want to rewind. It also allows you to find a program by using the rev counter at the same time as another program is saving or loading. However, if you are perfect and always think ahead you can get away with the attached cassette by using *MOTOR.

11. KEEPING CONTROL OF YOUR SOFTWARE

DISC HOUSEKEEPING

Software has a habit of multiplying before your very eyes, especially if your are using a disc system where saving a new version of a program can be done so quickly. For example, you may have a sizable program, which is called PROG. Then you make a minor alteration, and save it as NEW, but you don't delete PROG just in case NEW has a mistake on it. Two weeks later you make another change which you save as FINAL, but you forget what the precise difference was between PROG and NEW and so you don't delete either of them. And of course you've got a backup disc with all three programs on. If PROG is, say, 8K long, then in the saving of the final version of one program you have taken up a total of 48K spread across two discs.

Later you come back to make an alteration and can't remember which is the later version - FINAL or NEW. The cure is simple.

1. Save programs regularly, in neat list order (eg prog1, prog2, prog3...) so that the names themselves tell you about the program, and you can tell immediately from the name which version of which program it is.

It is often convenient to use the directories on the disc to help in the grouping of programs. For example:-

A	Assembler listings
B	Basic programs
C	Copy of program on another disc
D	Data files
F	Format files
I	Index files
M	Machine code
N	New version of part of a suite of programs
O	Old version or maybe Object code
P	Proword files
U	Utilities
V	View files
W	Wordwise files ...and so on.

For example, save Wordwise files in the W directory. When you return to the disc after maybe a week or two then it is quite obvious that "W.letter" is likely to be a letter in Wordwise format.

The filing system available with the Master is of even greater help. It is possible to have directories of up to ten characters, and sub-directories, and sub-sub-directories etc. In this way one can set up:-

a directory for Wordwise and call it WW,
a sub-directory for articles called ARTICLES
a sub-sub-directory F for finished articles,
an alternative sub-sub-directory D for articles in the
process of development.

A file might then be called `WW.ARTICLES.F.lawns` the contents of which are pretty self-evident!

Although sequential numbering of programs is a good principle, complications arise with a linked suite of programs (where one program calls another). If you change the name of one program you will also have to alter the program which calls it, so under these circumstances it may be better to leave the names of the programs alone even where they are being altered. Therefore use *RENAME to prefix the original program with an 'O.', thus placing it in the 'O' directory. eg. if the program were called PROG you would enter

```
*RENAME PROG O.PROG
```

Now you know that it's an old program: it won't get called from the original suite because the name has been changed, but you still have the program just in case you don't like the changes and want it back again. Similarly, when working on a new version of part of a suite of programs, store it in the N directory until it is ready for use.

So if you catalogue a disc and find the following, it is pretty easy to work out what program or file is which:-

```
A-PROG            B-PROG

C.adven35         D.address
N.B-PROG          O.B-PROG
W.PROGins
```

There is a linked suite of programs, (A-PROG and B-PROG), a copy of an adventure game - 35th version - which is held on another disc (C.adven35), a data file of addresses (D.address), a new version of B-PROG (N.B-PROG), a previous version of B-PROG (O.B-PROG), and a Wordwise file of instructions for the suite of PROG programs.

2. Keep some form of index on paper, so that you know where a program is likely to be. A spiral bound book (which will lie flat on the desk) or an A4 looseleaf folder are probably the best. Allow a double facing page for each tape or disc surface, and do give a brief description even if only a few key words. It is a known fact that the memory of a once deeply significant title like 'BesFrid' fades from the mind after a week or two.

A great help here is to have an indexer program which reads your disc and automatically prints out a list of the programs and files, with space for you to write down what each does. There is no ideal one on the market but Clare's indexer comes very close and only takes a few seconds for each disc. Note that, because of the different way in which the ADFS stores its catalogue data BBC-B and Master indexers are NOT compatible.

Another nice idea is a program for flicking quickly through the first couple of paragraphs of each text file on disc. There is the option of looking at more if you are not certain which version of a file you have got. (Micro User Oct'85)

3. Discs are cheap. It is much more economic in terms of time to use a separate disc for different types of work - you can find a program much more easily. For example, keep a separate disc for word-processing, another for specific program development, another for database information etc. Also consider the use of coloured discs and disc labels. (See Chapter 10)

BACKUPS

Perhaps you have been working on a program for months, only to find that you've poured coffee on the disc. Although you had several versions of the program on that one disc, none is readable. Just as devastating effects can happen when your computer fails during a *COMPACT operation - this leaves you with a totally jumbled disc from which you may be able to save nothing.

Again, the remedy is simple - always make regular back-up copies onto another disc whether you are writing programs, or creating files of information. It is particularly important to attend to backups if you are in business as the loss of important data may mean the difference between profit and bankruptcy. (Inept computerisation and loss of data is reckoned to bankrupt many companies each year.)

Always save before fiddling with memory directly - if you make a mistake and end up with a 'Bad Program' message you may have to start all over again.

1. With tape. If you are doing a long session, produce an ARCHIVE tape - every so often save the program. DON'T rewind that tape at all. DO call each version saved something different, and in sequence, such as:- PROG1, PROG2.

Set aside a Resident variable such as S% (Save) to remind you of the number of the last version saved. Set S% to 0 at the start of your programming session (or the next number in the series if you have already used it before). Better still is to define a Function Key to save for you and get the key to update the S% at the same time. Something like:-

```
*KEY 0 S% = S% + 1 |M SAVE"prog" + STR$(S%) |M
```

Toolkit from Beebugsoft has a similar routine within it.

Keep a note on paper during the session to note the MAIN differences between versions. You may want to recall an earlier version.

2. On disc the whole thing becomes a lot easier. It is a good idea to take a backup every ten minutes or so. This may seem excessive, but if you make it a habit there can be a considerable saving in frustration. It may be worthwhile keeping the last three versions of a program and deleting all others - so every time you save a new version make a habit of deleting an earlier one.

There are a couple of programs on the market which make this backup job much easier. They are usually called "Library Manager", or something similar. The idea behind them is to allow up to about 100 versions of a smallish program to be stored on one disc.

In most cases Library Managers allow quite a long description of each program to be stored with the title as well. They work by ignoring the conventional DFS catalogue (which only holds 31 titles) and taking a complete sector to store all the information about a program's length, name etc: the subsequent sectors store the program itself. The sector after this stores the next program description, and so on. On small programs this is a little wasteful in space but a marvellous boon in convenience!

At the end of a session an archive disc should be made and kept separately.

If you are regularly using files of information (especially in business), such as addresses, financial information etc, then you should have four data discs in operation. Three are used in rotation to hold up-dated information.

The first day's information goes onto disc 1. At the end of the day, copy disc 1 onto disc 2.

The next day, work with disc 2. At the end of that day's computing, copy disc 2 to disc 3.

The next day, work with disc 3, and then copy to disc 1 ..... and so on.

If today's disc fails, go back to the previous day's disc and you've only lost a maximum of one day's work. This method of working is called "Grandfather, Father, Son" for obvious reasons.

Why have three discs? If a problem develops during copying, you might ruin two discs. You still have the third to fall back on.

And the fourth disc? Use it for weekly back-ups and store it in another building. Then if you have a fire or a theft you won't lose more than a week's data.

Another way of backing up is as follows:-

a. Use disc one as a working disc.
b. Backup disc 2 to 3 (destroying the oldest version)
c. Backup disc 1 to 2 (keeping a record of today's versions)

Although this method uses more transfers, it keeps the same disc for the same job and is therefore easier to keep track of. The disadvantage is that if something goes wrong in copying then you may not find out about it as quickly as with Grandfather, Father, Son. With the GFS method all discs have files which were 'live' at one time, and therefore valid. With the sequential method of copying, if something goes wrong on the transfer from 1 to 2, you may end up copying a duff file from 2 onto 3 and end up with two discs of garbage.

3. Interval between backups

Obviously, you don't have to backup at the intervals stated - instead, work out the need for backups by how much you are doing to your files. If you are changing a lot of file information you'll need to back up more frequently.

If:
    B is the time taken to backup
    V the interval between backups
    F the average interval between disc failures

then if we assume that the time of disc failure is spread out randomly, then the amount of work lost will on average be half the time between backups - i.e.

$$\text{time lost} = V/2$$
$$\text{number of backups between failures} = F/V$$
$$\text{the total time taken for these backups} = FB/V$$

The point beyond which you get no further benefit in backing up is when the total time needed to take the backup copies is equal to the time taken to re-input the lost work.

Therefore:

V/2 = FB/V

which becomes

$V = \sqrt{(2FT)}$

It doesn't matter what units you use, as long as they are the same throughout. Therefore if the time between failures is 50 working hours (=3000 minutes) and the time to back up is 4 minutes then there is no point in backing up more often than

$\sqrt{(2 * 3000 * 4)}$ minutes   = 155 minutes

On the other hand, if backing up only takes 5 seconds (eg. saving a copy of a new program rather than backing up a disc file) then you are well advised to back up every

$\sqrt{(2 * 300 * 0.85)}$ = $\sqrt{(500)}$ = 22 mins

DISC LABELS

Rather than using those rather irritating little sticky labels supplied with discs, try 90*40 mm white sticky labels which come on a roll from Smith's. They stick to most things and have a large expanse of white for marker pens etc. Thus you can write BIG titles: for archive discs it enables you to include more details of the contents.

If your printer supports superscript printing, you can make some stunning personalized labels with a little effort. Your wordprocessor will dictate the way you do this.

If you are working with several different disc formats such as single sided, 40- or 80- track, special formats as used with Solidisc or Disc Doctor etc (to say nothing of CP/M or MS-DOS) then be sure to note the formatting on the disc label. It saves the horrid sound of the drive head banging against the end stop when you get it wrong.... As well as being an unpleasant sound it can do a lot of damage to your drive if you are unlucky. (see below)

40 AND 80 TRACK PROBLEMS

If you do forget how a DFS disc is formatted then use DISC DOCTOR, or any direct disc reader, to look at sector 01 on track 0. If you look at the top right hand side of the display you will see either X1 90 or X3 20. (The X can be any number, don't worry about it!) 190 in Hex equals 400, and 320 in Hex equals 800. This indicates the number of tracks * 10.

Rather odd things can happen if you *BACKUP from a 40 track disc onto an 80-track disc (assuming that the system is correctly set up with one drive set for 40-track working and the second to 80-track). You will find if you *BACKUP that you have lost 100K off the 80 track disc! What happens is that the disc is copied across byte for byte, so the number of tracks available on the first disc (the hex number referred to above) is copied across to the second disc. The second disc is formatted to 80 tracks, but the DFS doesn't know this - because it finds the number 190 transferred from the 40 track disc it thinks that only 40 tracks are being used, and is unaware that the disc has a further 40 tracks which are lying idle. Using your disc editor, change the 190 to 320 and all will be well.

MORAL - use *COPY *.* , this also gets rid of unwanted waste space between files.

WRITING ON DISCS

Once again we come to a DON'T!. Discs are delicate, and you must not press on them with anything that makes even the slightest dent in the disc surface. Unless you are very hamfisted, or impetuous, it is all right to write on a disc label with a felt tip or a marker pen, but a Biro, pencil or fountain pen is asking for trouble. There is a special pen for the less delicate amongst us (actually, a good insurance) called the BEROL Floppy Disc Pen. It really can be worth the pennies - the 'nib' is designed to bend before you can get enough pressure on it to mark the disc surface.

NOTEBOOKS

When you are doing a Magnum Opus in programming, or even an Opus Minimus for that matter, it is very useful to have a spiral bound shorthand book beside you. Use A4 if you have large handwriting.

What's it for? Jotting down all the things you have to do as they occur to you. Then when you have done them you can cross them out. Put the date down, and if you are doing more than one version of the program, put the version number by the suggestion. When your program is completely finished, you should have a book full of crossed out notes with nothing left unattended to. Then you know you've not left anything incomplete!
(For the programmer this is possibly the most useful tip in the whole book!)

12. WORKING WITH DISCS

AUTO-START YOUR DISCS

If you have only just started working with discs you may be tempted to load programs the hard way -

    `*.` <RETURN> (to see what's on the disc)
    `CH."PROG"` <RETURN> (to load and run the program)

This is a bit slow, and for those of you in business, likely to scare your secretary to death as all those funny filenames flash past her gaze. (Was she really supposed to load in your private financial program? She thought she'd try CHAINing in something else, just to see what happened....)

The answer is easy - make it automatic. If the disc is set up correctly, then pressing SHIFT and dabbing BREAK causes the computer to search the disc for a file called !BOOT, load it in, and do what it commands - which usually means CHAINing a specific program.

So how do you set up a !BOOT file? Simple. With a fresh disc in the drive type in

    `*BUILD !BOOT <RETURN>`

and you will get automatic line numbers given to you. When you have entered all appropriate commands press <Escape>. The disc will whirr, and the file is saved (overwriting any existing !BOOT file).

Now you have to let the computer know to search for a !BOOT file, so type in `*OPT4,3` <RETURN> and this tags the disc - you can check this by cataloguing the disc with `*.` <RETURN> and you will see in the top right hand corner "Option 3 (EXEC)".

(The various alternatives provided by the *OPT command are as follows:-

    *OPT4,0 SHIFT/BREAK OFF
    *OPT4,1 SHIFT/BREAK Load !BOOT
    *OPT4,2 SHIFT/BREAK RUN a M/C prog called !BOOT
    *OPT4,3 SHIFT/BREAK EXEC a file called !BOOT   )

If your disc is for word-processing using Wordwise your !BOOT file could be:-

```
001 *W.
```

where 001 is a line number generated by the machine.

On pressing SHIFT/BREAK the !BOOT file with its single command would be loaded, landing you immediately in Wordwise.

That's a bit of an improvement. If you do this to each of your discs, CHAINing the appropriate program then you can issue the same command to start off any disc. This can be very useful in preparing programs for people unfamiliar with the computer - if the instruction to start off is always

"Insert disc: Press SHIFT/BREAK"

then entering a new program or suite of programs is easy.

If you have a Master or a Compact there is one more thing you have to do before the computer automatically searches for a !BOOT file - you have to adjust the configuration of the computer to activate autobooting when SHIFT/BREAK is entered. Please refer to the User Guide for information about this. Once the configuration is set then you don't have to adjust it again. Note that you still have to set your disc with OPT 4,3 (say) in order that the correct action is taken on AUTO BOOTing, as with the DFS.

Elsewhere (Chapter 25) you will find instructions for creating a small program to set the red keys prior to going into Wordwise. You could now improve your !BOOT file in one of two ways:

-    include all the commands in the !BOOT file itself. This is
     a little bit messy if you use *BUILD as it's not quite as
     easy to edit as a normal program)

-    make the !BOOT file CHAIN a second program with the main
     program in it. This is easier to change, but uses up a
     file-name on your disc. In this case the !BOOT file reads

```
001 CHAIN"Keyset"
```

The program "Keyset" would set the red keys: the final instruction is *W., which calls Wordwise.

A neat variant on this theme, useful if you have a number of different programs on the one disc, is to have a standard !BOOT program for each disc, which CHAINs a second program which catalogues the disc, and asks for a single character entry which directs the computer to CHAIN your chosen program.

This listing contains no frills and is only included to show one method. If you read this book carefully you will be able to construct a better (but larger) Menu program.

```
 10 MODE 7
 20 number= !  (where ! is the number of programs on the disc)
 30 FOR loop=1 TO number
 40    READ prog$
 50    PRINT TAB(3) loop;" ";prog$
 60 NEXT
 70 DATA Alien Invader,Database,Fred's Jokes
 80 REPEAT
 90    J=GET-48
100 UNTIL J >= 1 AND J <= number
110 IF J=1 CHAIN "Aliens"
120 IF J=2 CHAIN "DDBase"
    .
    .  .  .  . etc
```

(Alternatively, use DISC DOCTOR from Computer Concepts, where you can use M/BREAK to do the same thing. Note that BASIC programs must be in the '+' directory and machine-code programs in the '-' directory for this to work.)

PROBLEMS WITH !BOOT FILES

Have you ever had a !BOOT file which doesn't seem to do quite what it ought? On some machines spurious effects occur when pressing SHIFT/BREAK. It seems that on pressing SHIFT/BREAK spurious characters go into the keyboard buffer and are read in unintentionally when an input is required in the !BOOT file, or even in the program that is subsequently CHAINed.

Cure... simply put *FX15,0 as the first line of the !BOOT file. This gets rid of everything in all the buffers.

TINKERING WITH !BOOT FILES

A !BOOT file is not like a normal BASIC program. It is not stored in the same way and cannot be LOADed or CHAINed, (but you can *EXEC !BOOT from the keyboard). Nor can you SAVE a program and turn it into a !BOOT file by *RENAME. You cannot use GOTO or IF in a !BOOT file, nor GOSUB,

PROCedures or functions - it takes its instructions in order, from top to bottom, and in no other way. You can't ask questions in a !BOOT file - but you can issue lots of complicated commands.

So what is it? It is really a program which is stored exactly as it is typed in from the keyboard, without the use of tokens (Chapters 13 & 21) - the correct name is a SPOOLed file. When it is read back (EXECuted), the computer behaves as if it has been given a whole set of instructions typed in at the keyboard. This is why you cannot use GOTO or jump around in the program: and why you cannot rename a BASIC program to become a !BOOT file, because the EXEC procedure doesn't decode the tokens.

This sounds silly, doesn't it? But on the computer things are usually done for a reason, and there is a great advantage in EXECing a program: it is not part of main memory, and therefore cannot be wiped or interrupted by inserting a command such as *COPY into it. Therefore you could start off your suite of programs by *COPYing a program from drive 2 to your RAM board, then COPYing a second program from drive 1 to the RAM board, then copying a third program, then setting the red keys....etc etc... then CHAINing the main program. If you tried this in BASIC the remainder of your program would be wiped out during the execution of the first *COPY command.

A !BOOT file is an excellent way of setting up your computer ready for action - keys set, files in all the right places, main program in place and RUNning.

If you want to see the contents of the !BOOT file just type in *TYPE !BOOT <RETURN>. Altering a !BOOT file is fiddly - any mistake means entering the whole thing again. A reliable method is to call up your existing file with *TYPE or *LIST - then if you type in *BUILD !BOOT <RETURN> you can use the copy key to enter as much of the original file as you want.

There is an easier way, using Wordwise, or any wordprocessor that will SPOOL a file. Go into the Wordprocessor, and load !BOOT. You will notice that it does not have line numbers. Make any changes you want, then save the result using the SPOOL option, using the file name !BOOT again.

You can, of course, create a !BOOT file afresh on the wordprocessor. Write it, without line numbers, with a <RETURN> at the end of each command line. Alternatively, if you need the last line to have information in it but no <RETURN>, then simply leave <RETURN> out.

There is another advantage in creating the !BOOT file in this way. *BUILD requires a lot of working space as a fixed length file of several K on the disc. If your disc is nearly full, you will not be able to *BUILD and save the !BOOT file, however short it may seem to you. Using the above method with a word processor it is possible to SAVE even with a nearly full disc.

DIRECTORIES AND LIBRARIES

The directory acts rather like a page number in a book - you can't read from the page until you have opened it up.

With the DFS when you catalogue the disc (with *.<RETURN>), the current directory is shown at the top on the left hand side. Unless you tell it differently, the directory is $, so think of the disc as being permanently opened at a page labelled $, on which you can write or read back your programs. If you want to change directory, type in *DIR N where N is the symbol of the new directory. Then, effectively, the computer closes the first page and opens a new page. Let us assume that you have just typed in

```
*DIR W <RETURN>
```

If you now catalogue the disc you will see that all the programs that were originally up at the top have now been printed at the bottom, each with "$." in front of their name. Any files or programs you have in the W directory will be showing at the top of the list, but without the "W." as the name of the current directory is indicated at the top of the disc catalogue.

You can access files resident in another directory, whilst keeping in the current directory - instead of CHAIN "PROG" you have to give the fuller file specification which includes the directory (if you don't include the directory in a file specification it is assumed to be the current directory). If PROG is in the $.directory and you have now changed to the W directory, to CHAIN PROG you have to write CHAIN "$.PROG"

And if you wanted a program on another disc you would have to give the full file specification - drive number, directory, program name. eg ":0.$.PROG"

Why bother? You can keep control of your software better by storing related programs in one particular directory (for a full treatment of this subject, see Chapter 11). This can be done in simple form on the BBC-B, or in much more detailed and complex form with the Master which allows directories and sub-directories, and acts as a mini-filing system.

If you can stand it, there is a very good tutorial on the ADFS with all the machines which use it. Just in case you do not want to go to the expense of turning on the machine, here is a diagram of the way the ADFS stores its files in a TREE structure.

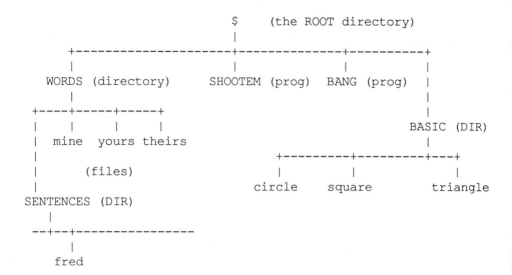

```
                              $      (the ROOT directory)
                              |
      +--------------------+--------------+----------+
      |                    |              |          |
   WORDS  (directory)  SHOOTEM (prog)  BANG (prog)   |
      |                                              |
  +----+-----+-----+                                 |
  |    |     |     |                              BASIC (DIR)
  |  mine  yours theirs                              |
  |                        +---------+---------+---+
  |        (files)         |         |           |
  |                      circle    square     triangle
SENTENCES  (DIR)
     |
  --+--+----------------
     |
   fred
```

The Root directory can have files and programs in it ($.SHOOTEM $.BANG) and it can also have directories which contain files ($.WORDS.mine $.WORDS.yours $.BASIC.circle). Directories can have sub-directories which also have files and sub-sub .... ad nauseam. ($.WORDS.SENTENCES.fred)

Note that the sub-directory system does not work with the cassette filing system.

WORKING WITH THE ADFS

We have already mentioned the advantages of the Directory system (above, and Chapter11). The fact that you can have directories and sub-directories allows for much greater precision in filing. No longer do you have to try to remember what F.FETELET means. If you store it as '$.Wordproc.WW.Fete.Circular' it tells you all you need to know. ("A Word-processed (Wordwise format) circular letter about the Fete").

By selecting your pathway (the way through the directory sequence) carefully, you can place yourself in the right position to see on the catalogue only items that are relevant to your current needs. If you want to look at 'Letters about the coming fete', then first choose the directory path-name *DIR $.Wordproc.WW.Fete after which on cataloguing the disc you will see only the contents of the 'Fete' directory. Alternatively, if you leave yourself in the 'WW' directory, you can see what other categories of letters and articles you have stored.

Moving around the directories is very simple. To go back to the parent directory (i.e. the directory which contains your current directory), simply type in *DIR ^ - e.g. if you are in directory 'FETE', typing in *DIR ^ will take you to directory 'WW'. If you are in directory 'FETE' and want to save an article about computers, then if you save it under the filename "^.Computers" it will be filed in the 'WW' directory, this being the parent directory of 'FETE'.

Another convenient way of moving around the directory system is to use the command *BACK. This takes you to the previously called directory (not necessarily the parent directory). For example, you may have a database of addresses about the Fete, stored under the full file-name of "$.Database.Files.FeteAddres". First access the directory containing this file (*DIR $.Database.Files). Now access the directory which contains the circular letter (*DIR $.Wordproc.WW.Fete). If you now type in *BACK you will immediately be back in the database file directory: type *BACK again and you will return to the directory containing letters about the fete.

This takes a long time to explain but only a few seconds to understand! Essentially *BACK allows you to oscillate with ease between files in widely separated directories - great for database and mail-merge work! *BACK can be used both in command mode and from within programs.

All this assumes that you have been careful to file all your letters in the right place! It's a great temptation just to bung in the nearest available disc and SAVE to that. A little discipline here reaps great rewards later.

Just how you use the directory system is up to you. The example assumes that you are the sort of person who files things by what they are (ie. letters, files, programs) rather than by what they relate to (The Fete, Computer information, address lists). You could just as easily have done it the other way round, and filed everything about the Fete in one directory - but then you wouldn't be able to tell which was a database file and which was a letter... unless you create sub-directories. Then, in the future when you want to combine all your address lists you have to remember that the 'Fete' directory has an address file lurking in it somewhere.....

The way you choose to file things always ends up in compromise, as every librarian knows. To put it another way, if you have a file about 'Motoring', and a separate one about 'Insurance', where do you put information about Motor Insurance? This sort of thing can cause great difficulty in locating information later on. It can be bad enough with just a few files: if you use a hard disc there may be hundreds of directories and sub-directories, and thousands of files. Under these circumstances you need a consistent plan over naming and placing files as otherwise you will lose things - frequently!

Besides the advantages of the directories, the ADFS has a number of extra facilities available.

*CDIR creates an (empty) directory, for filling up later. *CREATE reserves space for a file (so reducing the chances of the 'Compaction required' error where an initially small file outgrows the space available for it). *SPOOLON extends a spooled file, and *APPEND extends a *BUILD file without causing 'Can't extend' problems.

Note however that whereas *TITLE in the DFS titles the disc, *TITLE in the ADFS re-titles (not renames) the current directory. The difference is important. You can have a directory accessed as 'WW' (as above), but you can title it 'Wordwise'. The title is a description, rather like a REM statement and does not form part of the path-name of the file.

*COPY in the DFS copies a file or files from one disc surface to another - in the ADFS this command copies a file from one directory into another.

The ADFS works more intelligently than the DFS in its use of available disc space. The ADFS contains a map of unused disc space and if an existing file becomes too long it finds a bigger space to put it in, automatically transfers it, then continues to extend it. Only when a larger space cannot be found is the message 'COMPACTION REQUIRED' displayed.

As with the DFS compaction routine, the ADFS system pushes files close together, collecting unused space in single (and therefore more useful) big chunks. Unlike the DFS, a compaction routine may need to be repeated several times in order to compact the whole disc, until there are no holes in the map. (*MAP lists the 'holes' available, whilst *FREE shows the total amount of free space remaining.)

THE LIBRARY

Libraries are little-used on the Acorn DFS, mainly because they are not explained in detail. (It is really only of use if you have dual disc drives or a double-sided single disc and use machine code utilities from disc.)

To remind you, if you issue a command prefixed by an asterisk, the computer treats it as an operating system command, and searches through all the on-board ROMs to see if it matches with any of their commands (eg *DRIVE 0 will end up with the DFS). If no match is found it is then offered to the discs to see if a machine code program of that name exists.

Imagine you have a disc full of machine code utilities which you want to call whilst in the course of running a program in drive 0. In this case you would have your disc of utilities in, say, drive 1 under a directory of, say, M. This you choose to use as your library, so the *LIB M command merely tells the computer where to look for this collection of machine code programs.

You can change the library with the command *LIB, either directly from the keyboard, in a program, or in a BOOT file. If you want to set the library to directory M on drive 1, then issue the command

```
*LIB:1.M
```

Now, every time an unrecognised * command is issued, first disc 0 will be searched, and then disc 1. This can save a lot of fiddling with *DRIVE and *DIR eg. *explode instead of *:1.M.explode!

A slightly more flexible method, useful if you have a lot of different utilities, is to set the LIB to $, the default directory on the appropriate drive. ie *LIB :1.$. This will mean that any *<filename> without a directory will be directed to drive 1, $ directory even if the default for normal files is a different directory letter. If a directory letter is given the file will of course be looked for in that directory. This means that you have two default directories, one for machine-code programs and one for all other applications.

On the ADFS the usual ploy is to create a directory in the Root called LIB or LIBRARY or even LIBERTY. The first three letters must be LIB.

DAMAGED DISCS

If you have a damaged disc, then if you are lucky only one particular program or file will be affected, and everything else can be accessed. DO NOT ATTEMPT TO SAVE TO, OR TO *COMPACT A DAMAGED DISC - you may lose everything on it. It may be appropriate to *COPY all unaffected files to an unaffected disc (You cannot *BACKUP a damaged disc as the routine will fail when the damaged portion is reached.)

Now look at the damaged file. You may be able to recoup some of it by looking at the catalogue (sectors 0 & 1) and finding the start sector of that file using Disc Doctor. If you can find it then all you need to do is to go through the file on disc until the sector cannot be read, RECOVER up to there and possibly the bit beyond. You won't get it all, but there is a lot of saved typing time!

However, if you have an error on the first track of a disc you may lose the whole of your catalogue. In this, even if cases the rest of the disc is unaffected you cannot access anything because the computer doesn't know where to look for each program or file. (It uses the catalogue information to find it.)

Instead, if you have an appropriate disc editor then you can recover from this potentially very serious situation using a command such as *RECOVER, which is a command which loads a predetermined number of tracks into memory. (The command which goes with it, *RESTORE, we never use because there is a simpler way of doing things.)

Using ENIGMA is even easier - with this utility if you have a disc with a damaged track then use *VERIFY to find out which track then type in *REPAIR <Drive Number> <Track Number> which loads the sectors on that track into memory. The utility reformats the track and asks you whether you want to save back the data onto that track.

If you recover a program or a file in this manner you don't even have to look at what is on the track itself - BUT if there has been damage to a track there is the possibility that you have the odd error either in the text or in the program - like thisb(!) So you will have to check that your program or data is correct - but at least you've rescued it from oblivion.

1. TEXT FILES

If your disc is full of text files for say, Wordwise, proceed as follows:-

1.   Start at sector 2 (the one after the catalogue) and load a
        wodge of sectors into memory. Something like ...

        *RECOVER 0 2 90 1900 0

Where 90 is the number of sectors being loaded.

2.   Now do a sum... PRINT ~90 * 256   answer = &5A00
3.   Save this lot to a new disc with   *SAVE wodge1 1900 +5A00
4.   Next *WORDWISE and LOAD wodge1

5.   It is now possible to look at this lot and selectively
        save files out of it using markers and option 3. (You will
        have to save to another disc, of course!)

By doing this to the whole bad disc you should be able to save everything, even semi-corrupted files, which you will have to alter later.

2. BASIC PROGRAMS

Not quite the same as above, but similar.

1.   Same as 1 above.

2.   Use *MZAP to look at memory starting at &1900. All
        programs begin at the start of a Sector. All sectors start
        at a number ending in '00' e.g. 1B00, 3400 etc. Look for
        the start of a program at one of these points: it will

begin with... 0D 00 0A if your program started on line 10
(0A is the Hex for 10)

3. Set PAGE = & pagenum where pagenum is the address of the start
    of the program you have just found. Type OLD.

4. Save your program to disc by typing SAVE"filename".

5. Do the same again for the rest of any programs left in memory.

6. Now you can reload, list and examine your saved programs to check you
    have no extra rubbish at the end.

If you haven't been able to *REPAIR the disc then once you have recovered as
much as you can you will need to reformat the disc making certain that you VERIFY
it afterwards. (This will check that there is no permanent damage to the disc.) Don't
forget that formatting a disc wipes it, so make sure that you have copied everything
first.

13. EASIER PROGRAMMING SESSIONS

SETTING UP

When beginning a new program, use the following procedure:-

1. Set the function keys ready for programming - see below.

2. Input utility procedures you may need, copying from the store on your utility disc. You might want to use the procedures for double-size type, verification of entry routines, verified answer routines, centered printing.... If in doubt, import the procedure anyway - you can always delete it later if you don't use it. It is a good idea to have a few skeleton programs of procedures already set up with some of your more common procedures in. You will nearly always want to initialise, centralise print, use an answer vetting routine, so why not combine them all in to one big skeleton program?

3. Start your program with some REMs to identify the program and its function.

4. Then start programming.....

MASTER 128 CONFIGURATION

You can save yourself a great deal of time and effort if your MASTER turns itself on with a standard setup tuned to YOUR requirements. Use *CONFIGURE, but use it with care. There appears to be a lot of confusion with the Configuration setup. The purpose of it is to allow you to set up various parameters of the machine so that after switching on you don't have to fiddle about every time with tedious changes. Because the Master contains a battery, when power is turned off the machine configuration still remains in a small specialized portion of memory.

The standard setup will almost certainly not suit many people and the tendency is to dive in and alter everything. DON'T!! The best way to go about the job is to alter only one thing at a time. There are two methods. Either use the configuration screen given in the set of Welcome programs, or use *CONFIGURE and *STATUS (page 244 in the Welcome manual) This latter method seems the less confusing and there should be less possibility of doing harm. BUT - Don't follow the instructions about setting disc drive speed to 3 - on late Masters (with the 1771 chip) and also with certain disc drives this will not allow the drive to be read. If in any doubt, set it to zero or leave it alone. (After all, if it's read the Welcome disc it's OK even if it is not the optimum setup!)

One very useful Configure parameter is the ability to control the sending of line feeds to a printer. This is a pain to do on the BBC-B because it normally requires *FX6 commands in every !BOOT file.

*CON.CAPS It seems strange that the CAPS lock configure suggests ON. Try it at OFF if you are not certain, especially if you are a typist, wordprocessor operator, programmer, games player, fiddling about, ...

*CON. TV 0,1 gives you a stable screen with NO interlace. Try it with TV 0,0 and then try a MODE other than MODE 7. The difference with the setting at 0 is startling - the screen is STILL!

*CON. SCROLL is perhaps the sensible choice. Read page 25 of the Master Guide. The idea of NO SCROLL is good and useful, but only in rather special circumstances. At these times it can be more useful to do a temporary job with VDU.

*CON. BAUD & DATA Most people will buy a parallel printer with their computer. These commands can be left as they are in this case. However, don't forget that some commercial firms sell off their very good printers when a new WHIZZO comes along. These are usually dirt cheap and SERIAL. If you have one of these you will need to dig into the manuals to find the figures for these commands.

*CON. PRINT A very happy command this. On previous BBC machines it was possible for a program to come to a grinding halt if a printer was not attached. This command allows the program to continue if a PRINT command is issued in these circumstances. It is also up to you to decide whether to have automatic control of printer line feeds at your end or the printers (by setting DIP switches).

*CON LOUD Think very carefully before leaving this irritation at high level, especially if you have a Network! 20 Beeping computers can be a menace - though some commercial programmers have the belief that it is clever to beep every time a letter is entered into a computer, even on a word-processor!

PROGRAM TESTING

Don't wait until the program is finished before you test it - instead, test each section as it is typed in, as then you will have more of an idea as to where the fault might lie.

Testing a program is an art. Don't just test for convenient parameters - make sure that it can deal with anything you can throw at it. Many programs work well until they come to 'edge conditions' - eg a program to insert a name in an alphabetical list may not be able to cope with a name which has to be added right at the beginning.

If you have a program to insert items in alphabetical order into an ordered list you could test it in the following manner, each time checking that the name was inserted in the right place:-

1.   Input an ordinary name, eg Hopkins.

2.   Test the 'edges'. Try Aardvark or ZZarg.

3.   Go beyond the edges. (1mith or {ones) - if you were constructing an index you might need to file "*TV0", for example.

4.   Does it matter if you enter upper or lower case? (or, rather, do you mind what it does with different cases?) What does it do with ffolkes or MacTavish? or if you enter sMITH by mistake?

5.   Can it cope with hyphens? Try Smythe-Robertson.

6.   If you hit a number or another non-alpha-character (not necessarily at the beginning of the word) can it deal with it? (you may need to alter the input routine)

7.   What if you enter blanks?

8.   What if there's a comma in the input (eg. "blankets, scouts, for the use of" (INPUT will only accept information up to the first comma or space. If you want to accept these two characters, either use an input vetting routine, or use INPUT LINE instead of INPUT)

8.   What if you enter RETURN on its own?

9. What about combinations of CTRL and other keys? (bit of a cheat this as you cannot guard against all combinations easily - CTRL/L for example)

In general, test the normal parameters, then the 'edges', then beyond the 'edges', then silly values.

This is the sort of testing you should carry out for each procedure you write. If the procedure doesn't use keyboard input you can easily give it special values to work on. You can alter the resident integers i.e. A%-Z% plus @% at the keyboard and the values will not be wiped out when you run the program. eg, at the keyboard

```
A% = 150
PROCdisplay
```

You can give particular test values in the program itself

```
212 X = 5 Y = 67   (note, not one of the normal line numbers)
220 PROC_shoot(X,Y)
```

In order to dissect out bits of the program for testing you can put END or STOP in the program (STOP is often more useful as it quotes the line number and definitely tells you the program has ceased). In command mode you can GOTO a particular line number to start a section of the program. eg.from the keyboard,

```
GOTO 340 <Return>
```

and in order to test a procedure you can call it directly from the keyboard

```
PROC_display
```

These two methods may not work if elements of an array are to be used.

After a program has been run, or you have Escaped from it, all variable values, including arrays, will be preserved so long as you haven't altered any of the lines of the program, or used BREAK. This means that you can find out what they contain at the point the program stopped with questions in command mode, eg

```
PRINT answer$
```
or
```
PRINT house$(6)
```

You can also alter the values given and re-run the procedure (in command mode) to see what happens eg

```
answer$ = "N"
PROC_decide
house$(6) = "Riverside Villa"
PROC_list
```

Having done specific tests, use the whole program for the purpose for which it was intended and see if it stands up to it. It may run out of memory after the first three entries.. or the first thirteen.. or only if the entries occur in generally ascending order of string length.. or if you have a large number of similar entries - eg in Scotland with all the names beginning with Mac (bad news for anyone who's filing into separate 'buckets' for each letter of the alphabet). Then you find silly (but logical) things happen - such as filing MacDonald, MacGregor and Machinery: or your disc files crash up against each other and give the 'Can't extend' message... (DFS) or "Compaction required" .. (ADFS)

Be warned - however much you test, in a complex program you will almost certainly never be able to test for all the possibilities. This is why good custom-built commercial programs require software servicing. It's rather like the rattle in the car which only occurs when going round a left hand corner at between 45 and 53 mph in third gear and accelerating with the wind behind you - it's rather difficult to predict and test in advance!

Therefore:-

1.   Don't be surprised when a program you thought you'd
      debugged runs into problems.

2.   Do insert proper error trapping, which at least will get
      the user out of a nasty situation as safely as possible
      without losing data. It will also prevent the program
      crashing fully.

For further information about testing and debugging programs, see (Chapter 17)

FUNCTION KEYS

Don't forget that if you are doing a heavy programming session the function keys can be set up to aid you. They can save a great deal of time and energy in typing if you put frequently used words, phrases and commands on them.

We tried to think up a definitive list for use in programming, but the potential range is vast, and depends very much on the sort of computing you do. There was someone who came up with a bright idea for a data-bank of sets of definitions which could be called up at the press of...... yes, you've guessed it, a Function key!

They can store:-

1. Words and sequences that you use a lot in programming
    eg.   PRINTTAB(

2. Long words and sequences that you use in wordprocessing
    eg   "the BBC-B microcomputer"; the sequence of commands used to
    throw the printer into large type; or the commands to
    indent a the first line of a paragraph

3. Frequently used command mode commands
    eg.   RUN |M

4. Extended command mode commands
    eg   MODE 7: VDU14|M LIST130, 270 |M

5. Little programs which are really extended direct mode
    commands
    eg FOR N = 1 TO 14 : P.size%(N) : N.|M
    (to display the contents of the array size%(14))

In general, try to make the computer do the work for you: any sequence of key-
strokes that you use frequently (especially awkward combinations) may usefully be
put onto the red keys.

On the BBC-B there is only one page of memory (256 Bytes) set aside for function
key definitions, so you may have to be economical and accept compromises. A
useful ploy is not to write out keywords in full, but refer to them in their abbreviated
forms - they are stored in this abbreviated form and are only converted to full
keywords (ie tokenised) when they are actually used. This procedure will quite
save a few bytes of memory. The problem does not appear so soon with the
Master series as four times as much space is allocated to the keys.

EDITING IN ALTERNATIVE MODES

Don't think that just because your machine switches on in MODE 7 that you should
necessarily use that mode for programming. The disadvantage of Mode 7 is that it
has its own character set which does not always correspond with the printing on the
keyboard.

Alternative modes can be very useful:-

Mode 6 Unlike Mode 7 all the characters are all as printed on the keyboard - and
the minus sign and underline are clearly different.

Mode 3 is 80-column presentation and so allows very much more program on screen at one time. Again, its character set is as printed on the keyboard: however, the small size of typeface and long line-length can be tiring or even difficult to read, especially if you haven't got a medium- or high-resolution monitor.

Mode 0 is also 80 column and if your program is fairly short (or you have shadow RAM) why not try colour. Try the following sequence.

```
MODE 0
CTRL/S 0 4 0 0 0 and then CTRL/S 1 6 0 0 0
0 4 says take background and make it colour 4
1 6 says take foreground and make it colour 6
```

Notice that you do NOT have to press return at any point (and there aren't spaces between the numbers!)

TYPING IN BASIC LISTINGS

Typing in your programs can be a bind if you use AUTO and make a mistake. If you use a Word-processor to type in your listings, try this.

Clear the screen. Type:-

```
NEW   <R>   (R simply means 'Press Return' don't type it in!)
AUTO  <R>
```

Then type in your program in lines as you would normally, but without putting in line numbers. Use <R> between each line. Now SPOOL the result.

```
*SPOOL filename <R> (or use the word-processor's spool
option.)
```

Go to Basic with

```
*BASIC <R>
*EXEC filename <R>       (forget any error messages which
                         may appear on screen during this
                         process)
LIST
SAVE filename <R>
```
And there is your beautiful program, with line numbers.

(You could have missed out the AUTO and put your own line numbers in the original - which would create fewer problems if you are a GOTO fan. However, if you are, this book is probably not for you!)

The reason this works is as follows:-

If you SAVE a program, all the keywords are converted into tokens, which shortens the program. On the other hand *SPOOLING a program saves it to disc exactly as it appears on the screen.

A SAVEd program must be LOADed or CHAINed - during these procedures the tokens are converted back to their BASIC keyword form. On the other hand if you *EXEC a program, although it is coming off the disc, the computer treats it as though it is typed in very quickly into the keyboard.

You cannot *EXEC a program which has been SAVEd because *EXEC does not translate the tokens.

Therefore:-

A SAVEd program must be LOADed or CHAINed because it is stored in tokenised form.

A *SPOOLed program must be *EXECed because it is stored just as you see it.

So in the advice mentioned above you are creating a SPOOLed file, exactly as on screen. When this is *EXECed the first instruction clears the computer's memory: the second sets the AUTO function and automatically creates line numbers: and the rest feeds in the program as though you were typing it in at express speed whilst using AUTO.

MAGAZINE LISTINGS AND ACCURACY

Don't always believe listings in magazines, especially in the April issues. The first issue of a magazine we now rate highly had over 60 mistakes in a single listing. We wrote to congratulate them on a magnificent puzzle but got no reply.

PLAN THOSE SCREENS

It is possible to plan your screens by sitting at the computer and playing with editors or just doing the numbers game. How much more creative to sketch them accurately on a piece of paper. But it's such a fag working on squared paper or those photostated pages from the back of the guide isn't it?

The answer is - don't do it on squared paper, do it over the top of squared paper.

You need a sheet of 5mm squared paper - fairly bold lines are best. On it mark a rectangle 40 squares long by 32 high. Each square represents 32 screen units which is equivalent to 1 character position in 40 character text mode.

Mark the ends of the squares 0, 32, 64, 96, 128, 160, 192, etc. up to 1280 horizontally, to 1024 vertically. (In fact positions 1280 and 1024 don't exist on the screen. Although there are 1280 points on the screen the first is numbered 0 and therefore the last is 1279 (and 1023). More of this below. **)

Mount this on a piece of substantial card and cover it with transparent film (not essential). All you need now are a couple of paper clips and a supply of tracing or grease-proof paper. Drafting sheet, if you can get hold of it, is even better - delightful stuff to work with.

Now you can draw freehand, away from the 'grid', then place the grid underneath the final drawing, ready to plot it out. You can use the grid to position text or graphics accurately, and symmetrically if necessary. At the end of your designing session you can immediately obtain the correct coordinates for every detail of your artwork. This saves time (lots of it!), gives greater freedom for design and allows more accurate placing of the elements of the display.

** A small problem when drawing the screen is our concept of what we think we are doing and what we want are really doing. Consider this problem. Say you wish to draw a set of vertical lines across the screen with a line every 32 positions. Your last line will be 31 positions from the right hand side of the screen if you use:-

```
FOR X = 0 TO 1279 STEP 32
```

This is because the position for the last line should be 1280 by calculation.(0 + 32 + 32 + 32 etc = 1280, not 1279)

But, FOR X = 0 TO 1280 STEP 32 has the same result because 1280 does not exist. If you want the edge of the screen to have a line on it you will have to make a special provision at position 1279:-

```
FOR X = 0 TO 1279 STEP 32: plot line :NEXT
MOVE 1279, 0: DRAW 1279, 1023
```

The trouble is that we tend to think in terms of bounded areas and what we are really doing is plotting a line and then having a blank space. In effect the plot is (Line + space) which is why there is no line at the right hand side. The right hand side of the space comes up to 1279, so, no line at the right hand edge.

USE OF COLOUR

We tend to think of colour only in terms of finished screens in the final program. Here are a few ideas to open your eyes (literally!)

COLOURED REMS

Sometimes it is useful to be able to scan quickly through a listing on screen to find a particular section. An obvious way is to set up a Function key to take you to an appropriate spot, but this is not the best solution if there are several places to look at.

You may put Coloured REMs into listings (for use in Mode 7), or if you have a Monochrome screen, flashing REMs. Use the normal SHIFT/Function key method to put a colour code into the REM. It must be preceded with speech marks, just as in printing normal text. (The '@' sign represents the colour code.):-

```
10 REM "@This is how to do it.
```

Note that you do not need to bother with a set of speech marks at the end of the REM.

However - colour control codes make some printers do odd things, like deleting previous characters, so this method can backfire with printed listings. Therefore if you work extensively with these, try the following method which works only on printed listings. If instead of the colour code you place a printer control code for double size type just in front of the REM statement then the rest of the REM will be printed out in double size. If you pick a printer code that is automatically terminated by a line feed then you don't even need to remember to cancel the change in print mode at the end of the line!

However, putting the printer code in directly is not quite so easy. You can't use CHR$(n) because you need to enter the ASCII code for n directly. So:-

1. Find the printer code you want. On the Epson, a line of double width type is 142, so we'll use that as an example.

2. Type PRINT "X";CHR$(142). The cursor will move down a line and then two positions to the right, having printed "X" and then the character for CHR$(142).

3. Enter:-   `*KEY 0 REM"`
    and use the copy key to copy the single (invisible) character that you printed to the right of the "X"

4.   Press <Return>

Now you have REM"@ stored in function key 0, (where @ is the printer control code). Every time you want to print a REM line in large type use KEY 0 to begin the line.

COLOURFUL EDITS

Editing in Mode 7 is great, but have you tried other Modes in colour? This is a matter of personal taste. Don't forget that reducing the contrast between printing and background lessens fatigue, provided the characters are still distinct.

Here are one or two combinations which you might try. No order of preference is given!

Blue on Green	White on Blue
Red on Yellow	White on Mauve
Blue on Yellow	Blue on Cyan
Green on Blue	Blue on White
Yellow on Blue	Green on Black
Cyan on Blue	

GREY SCALE AND MONOCHROME MONITORS

If you normally program in colour, it is easy to forget those who prefer to use a Monochrome screen and those who are partly or totally colour-blind (about 10% of the male population).

Some colours and colour combinations actually disappear when viewed in monochrome. Colours viewed on a black and white monitor are varying shades of grey, and in order from darkest to lightest (the 'Grey Scale') are:-
Black, Blue, Red, Magenta, Green, Cyan, Yellow, White.
The closer the colours are in the list, the less the contrast between them when seen on in monochrome, so take care that your selection of colours will be readable whatever the type of monitor that is being used. In particular, blue, red and magenta are not very visible against a black background, so you can't use red on its own for danger - in monochrome it's hardly visible. Red on a white background is much more attention-grabbing, and flashing red on a white background even more so.

While mentioning this, there are some programs on the market that offer you the opportunity to alter the colours of text and background. This facility is very useful and is to be commended. Don't ignore this feature if you have a monochrome set: you may find that you can get a more pleasing display by experimenting with what are effectively degrees of contrast.

GENERAL TIPS

MOVING THE CURSOR

A silly one, not obvious until you do it.

If you are to copy a line from near the top of the screen to near the bottom, move the cursor down the screen until it re-appears at the top. This usually takes less time.

To make the line you wish to copy get to the top of the screen so that this becomes even easier, just press RETURN a few times to make everything go towards the ceiling. This is especially useful if there are several lines to be altered sequentially.

UPSIDE DOWN SHIFT KEY

Lower case variable names are a 'GOOD THING' for readability of programs. (Key words in upper, variables in lower). Did you know that the obvious uses of the Case keys are not the only ones? This one is very useful - it means that you type in UPPER case and get lower case on SHIFT! All you have to do is:-

   Press CAPS LOCK and SHIFT at the same time.

Any subsequent use of the Caps lock or Shift lock keys returns all the case keys to their normal setting.

MERCIFULLY SILENT BEEP

Beep can become a dirty word, so why not turn it off with *FX210,1. If you get withdrawal symptoms you can turn it on again with *FX210,0 . Alternatively, fit a volume control (see Chapter 4)

CONTROL YOURSELF

Everyone seems to know about CTRL/BREAK and what you can do with it, but did you know about these:-

   C/BREAK is the same as *TAPE ie Cassette Break
   D/BREAK is the same as *DISC ie Disc Break
   N/BREAK is the same as *NET

It's quicker if you are doing a lot of it.

PICTURE CONTROL

*TV A,B controls the picture. Values of A change the vertical position of the picture on the screen. Values of B change the interlace. To get a slightly steadier picture in all modes except Mode 7, turn the interlace off with *TV0,1. Then change to your new mode. *TV0,0 (and a Mode change) turns interlace on again.

To move the picture up one line use *TV 1   up two lines with *TV 2

down one line with *TV255   and down two lines with *TV 254

VDU IS GOOD FOR YOU

Don't forget to look at the VDU list in your User Guides. There are lots of goodies which we tend to forget. Most VDU commands can be entered from the keyboard as CTRL/key.

CTRL/L clear text screen.   (clear (L)ists)
CTRL/P clear graphic screen. (clear (P)icture)

VDU22,3 or MODE3 is a pain to type in, but how about CTRL/V 3 ie, press the CTRL key and V at the same time then type in 3. (No carriage return is needed)

However, this doesn't reset HIMEM, so is only safe to use this when going from a mode with high screen RAM requirements to one with smaller screen needs ie. Mode 0 (20K) to Mode 7 (1K) or when using Shadow Ram.

MINIMUM ABBREVIATIONS

It's worth while having a look at the abbreviations for keywords in your User Guides. Some are rather like the S**cl**rs single key entry where you have to press more keys than there are letters in the word, but some give a saving. We don't think this warrants photostating the list, but a pencil list (until you know which of them are most useful for your purposes) is a definite plus. Some favourites are:-

CH.	CHAIN	CHR.**	CHR$	CL.	CLEAR
C.	COLOUR	D.	DATA	DEL.	DELETE
E.	ENDPROC	ENV.	ENVELOPE	H.	HIMEM
I.	INPUT	L.	LIST	MO.	MODE
O.	OLD	PA.	PAGE	P.	PRINT
REN.	RENUMBER	REP.	REPEAT	RES.	RESTORE
SA.	SAVE	SO.	SOUND	S.	STEP
U.	UNTIL	V.	VDU		

** This one saves the use of SHIFT

Most of these depend on whether or not you are a good typist. If you are, you probably won't want to bother! The main point is...Does it save time, thought and effort? If the answer to any one of these is no, then it is not worth using.

Even though you type in abbreviations it does not save memory and when you list or print, the words are printed out in full. This is because keywords are stored as 2-digit tokens. For example, the keyword 'PRINT' is stored in memory as D0, (meaning &D0). It does not matter if you put in P. or PRINT it is still stored as D0. Thus, when the machine comes to translate it back again, it simply puts in the full interpretation.

A TOKEN ORDER

Just a little job which should have been done in the Manual, putting the Keywords and their machine code tokens in order. We often need them in Numeric and not Alphabetic order, so here they are.

Note: Some keyworks have a different Token if on the left or right of an equation. i.e. LOMEM= or =LOMEM. These are labelled LEFT or RIGHT in the list.

ALPHABETICAL ORDER				NUMERICAL ORDER			
ABS	ABS	94		80	AND	A.	
ACS	ACS	95		81	DIV	DIV	
ADVAL	AD.	96		82	EOR	EOR	
AND	A.	80		83	MOD	MOD	
ASC	ASC	97		84	OR	OR	
ASN	ASN	98		85	ERROR	ERR.	
ATN	ATN	99		86	LINE	LIN.	
AUTO	AU.	C6		87	OFF	OFF	
BGET	B.	9A		88	STEP	S.	
BPUT	BP.	D5		89	SPC	SPC	
CALL	CA.	D6		8A	TAB (	TAB (	
CHAIN	CH.	D7		8B	ELSE	EL.	
CHR$	CHR.	BD		8C	THEN	TH.	
CLEAR	CL.	D8		8E	OPENIN	OP.	
CLG	CLG	DA		8F	PTR	PT.	(LEFT)
CLOSE	CLO.	D9		90	PAGE	PA.	(LEFT)
CLS	CLS	DB		91	TIME	TI.	(LEFT)
COLOUR	C.	FB		92	LOMEM	LOM.	(LEFT)
COS	COS	9B		93	HIMEM	H.	(LEFT)
COUNT	COU.	9C		94	ABS	ABS	
DATA	D.	DC		95	ACS	ACS	
DEF	DEF	DD		96	ADVAL	AD.	
DEG	DEG	9D		97	ASC	ASC	

ALPHABETICAL ORDER

DELETE	DEL.	C7
DIM	DIM	DE
DIV	DIV	81
DRAW	DR.	DF
ELSE	EL.	8B
END	END	E0
ENDPROC	E.	E1
ENVELOPE	ENV.	E2
EOF	EOF	C5
EOR	EOR	82
ERL	ERL	9E
ERR	ERR	9F
ERROR	ERR.	85
EVAL	EV.	A0
EXP	EXP	A1
EXT	EXT	A2
FALSE	FA.	A3
FN	FN	A4
FOR	F.	E3
GCOL	GC.	E6
GET	GET	A5
GET$	GE.	BE
GOSUB	GOS.	E4
GOTO	G.	E5
HIMEM	H.	93
HIMEM	H.	D3
IF	IF	E7
INKEY	INKEY	A6
INKEY$	INK.	BF
INPUT	I.	E8
INSTR(	INS.	A7
INT	INT	A8
LEFT$(	LE.	C0
LEN	LEN	A9
LET	LET	E9
LINE	LIN.	86
LIST	L.	C9
LN	LN	AA
LOAD	LO.	C8

NUMERICAL ORDER

98	ASN	ASN
99	ATN	ATN
9A	BGET	B.
9B	COS	COS
9C	COUNT	COU.
9D	DEG	DEG
9E	ERL	ERL
9F	ERR	ERR
A0	EVAL	EV.
A1	EXP	EXP
A2	EXT	EXT
A3	FALSE	FA.
A4	FN	FN
A5	GET	GET
A6	INKEY	INKEY
A7	INSTR(	INS.
A8	INT	INT
A9	LEN	LEN
AA	LN	LN
AB	LOG	LOG
AC	NOT	NOT
AD	OPENUP	OP.
AE	OPENOUT	OPENO.
AF	PI	PI
B0	POINT(	PO.
B1	POS	POS
B2	RAD	RAD
B3	RND	RND
B4	SGN	SGN
B5	SIN	SIN
B6	SQR	SQR
B7	TAN	T.
B8	TO	TO
B9	TRUE	TRUE
BA	USR	USR
BB	VAL	VAL
BC	VPOS	VP.
BD	CHR$	CHR.
BE	GET$	GE.

ALPHABETICAL ORDER

LOCAL	LOC.	EA
LOG	LOG	AB
LOMEM	LOM.	92 (LEFT)
LOMEM	LOM.	D2 (RIGHT)
MID$(	M.	C1
MOD	MOD	83
MODE	MO.	EB
MOVE	MOV.	EC
NEW	NEW	CA
NEXT	N.	ED
NOT	NOT	AC
OFF	OFF	87
OLD	O.	CB
ON	ON	EE
OPENIN	OP.	8E
OPENOUT	OPENO.	AE
OPENUP	OP.	AD
OR	OR	84
PAGE	PA.	D0
PAGE	PA.	90
PI	PI	AF
PLOT	PL.	F0
POINT(	PO.	B0
POS	POS	B1
PRINT	P.	F1
PROC	PRO.	F2
PTR	PT.	8F (LEFT)
PTR	PT.	CF (RIGHT)
RAD	RAD	B2
READ	REA.	F3
REM	REM	F4
RENUMBER	REN.	CC
REPEAT	REP.	F5
REPORT	REPO.	F6
RESTORE	RES.	F7
RETURN	R.	F8
RIGHT$(	RI.	C2
RND	RND	B3
RUN	RUN	F9

NUMERICAL ORDER

BF	INKEY$	INK.	
C0	LEFT$(	LE.	
C1	MID$	M.	
C2	RIGHT$(	RI.	
C3	STR$	STR.	
C4	STRING$(	STRI.	
C5	EOF	EOF	
C6	AUTO	AU.	
C7	DELETE	DEL.	
C8	LOAD	LO.	
C9	LIST	L.	
CA	NEW	NEW	
CB	OLD	O.	
CC	RENUMBER	REN.	
CD	SAVE	SA.	
CF	PTR	PT.	(RIGHT)
D0	PAGE	PA.	(RIGHT)
D1	TIME	TI.	(RIGHT)
D2	LOMEM	LOM.	(RIGHT)
D3	HIMEM	H.	(RIGHT)
D4	SOUND	SO.	
D5	BPUT	BP.	
D6	CALL	CA.	
D7	CHAIN	CH.	
D8	CLEAR	CL.	
D9	CLOSE	CLO.	
DA	CLG	CLG	
DB	CLS	CLS	
DC	DATA	D.	
DD	DEF	DEF	
DE	DIM	DIM	
DF	DRAW	DR.	
E0	END	END	
E1	ENDPROC	E.	
E2	ENVELOPE	ENV.	
E3	FOR	F.	
E4	GOSUB	GOS.	
E5	GOTO	G.	
E6	GCOL	GC.	

ALPHABETICAL ORDER

SAVE	SA.	CD
SGN	SGN	B4
SIN	SIN	B5
SOUND	SO.	D4
SPC	SPC	89
SQR	SQR	B6
STEP	S.	88
STOP	STO.	FA
STR$	STR.	C3
STRING$(	STRI.	C4
TAB(	TAB(	8A
TAN	T.	B7
THEN	TH.	8C
TIME	TI.	91 (LEFT)
TIME	TI.	D1 (RIGHT)
TO	TO	B8
TRACE	TR.	FC
TRUE	TRUE	B9
UNTIL	U.	FD
USR	USR	BA
VAL	VAL	BB
VDU	V.	EF
VPOS	VP.	BC
WIDTH	W.	FE

NUMERICAL ORDER

E7	IF	IF
E8	INPUT	I.
E9	LET	LET
EA	LOCAL	LOC.
EB	MODE	MO.
EC	MOVE	MOV.
ED	NEXT	N.
EE	ON	ON
EF	VDU	V.
F0	PLOT	PL.
F1	PRINT	P.
F2	PROC	PRO.
F3	READ	REA.
F4	REM	REM
F5	REPEAT	REP.
F6	REPORT	REPO.
F7	RESTORE	RES.
F8	RETURN	R.
F9	RUN	RUN
FA	STOP	STO.
FB	COLOUR	C.
FC	TRACE	TR.
FD	UNTIL	U.
FE	WIDTH	W.

CHANGING DISC FILENAMES

It can be very irritating if you have saved a program or file, but entered the file name in Lower case when you intended it to be in Upper, or the other way round. You can't use *RENAME directly, because the DFS sees the upper case and lower case versions of the same name as identical, and gives out the error message 'File exists'.

Therefore to change a file name to the opposite case the normal routine is to rename the file as something else such as "TEMP" and then rename it a second time to what you really want it to be. This is tedious and mistakes can easily be made.

Instead, RENAME the directory first, not the filename. Thus:-

```
*RENAME west3x  A.west3x      *RENAME A.west3x  WEST3X
```

This allows the use of the copy key (which reduces copying errors) and the first stage keeps the original name intact: this keeps the name correct on disc for the second stage in case you are interrupted or the power fails.

BUTTERFINGERS WITH *.

How many hundred times have you typed *> in the vain hope that you were going to get a disc catalogue coming up. ANSWER >>> MANY #*%%$#..done it again!

This little machine code program senses your stupidity, divines what you really wanted, presents you with a catalogue, kindly changes the case back from Shift Lock to Caps Lock, (which it thinks you thought you had set) and goes away.

```
 10 REM Butterfingers catalogue
 20 P%=&C02
 30 [OPT3
 40 PHP:PHA:TXA:PHA:TYA:PHA \ store present register contents
 50 LDA #&2E       \ load  full stop
 60 STA &C00       \ store full stop
 70 LDA #&0D       \ load Return
 80 STA &C01       \ store Return
 90 LDA #&0        \ empty Accumulator
100 LDX #&0        \ set LSB of address
120 LDY #&0        \ set MSB of address
130 JSR &FFF7      \ OSCLI   call full stop
140 LDX #&20       \ load Caps Lock number
150 LDY #&0        \ &10=Shift lock, &30=Lower Case
160 LDA #&CA       \ load appropriate Osbyte number
170 JSR &FFF4      \ OSBYTE  set Caps Lock
180 LDA #&76       \ load appropriate Osbyte number
190 JSR &FFF4      \ OSBYTE  set LEDs
200 PLA:TAY:PLA:TAX:PLA:PLP   \ restore registers contents
210 RTS]
```

Type the program in, minus the REMs if you wish. SAVE a copy somewhere, then RUN it. You should see a normal assembler listing. It you do,
*SAVE > C02 C2F C02 to each of your discs. Now whenever you forget Shift Lock this program is called.

How does it work? If you forget to release Shift lock you input *> to the computer, which the computer first tries to recognise as an operating system command. If the command is not recognised, the computer then searches the disc for any machine code program with that title. The program above is saved with the filename "*>" so on typing *> the program is called!

Note, line 140 decides which Case condition you go to. At the moment &20 decides
CAPS LOCK The options are:-

```
Shift Lock...... &10
Caps  Lock...... &20
Lower Case... .. &30
Reverse Shift... &A0
```

With Reverse Shift, you get Capitals as normal but Lower Case on pressing Shift.
(Great for typing in listings.)

14. GOOD PROGRAMMING STYLE

Good programming is like good driving - it's not whether you get to your destination that counts, but how safely and smoothly you do it, and whether or not you get lost on the way. And like good driving, good programming will usually get you there as quickly as possible, consistent with safety.

A good program:
- looks good on the screen
- uses the minimum of key-strokes from the operator
- is properly de-bugged so that it never 'crashes'
- is speedy in operation

The programming itself is:
- neat and easy to read
- easy to alter
- economical on memory and computing time

Therefore so we have to consider programming from two viewpoints - the design of the on-screen operation, and the design of the program itself. Both are important.

ON-SCREEN OPERATION

1. Start and end well.

There should be a title page with a note about the author and the copyright holder, with perhaps a second and third page of instructions, before going into the program proper. At the end of the program, either the screen should be cleared, or a message left saying 'End of program'.

2. Think carefully about the screen layout

Consider making the screen symmetrical rather than having everything crammed up against the left hand side.

What about a border round the whole screen? - it helps the symmetry, and gives a polished look to the layout, without much extra use of memory.

There are three ways of creating a border:-

a. Write a procedure to do it each time - eg, for MODE 7

```
10000 DEFPROC_border
10010  FOR J = 0 TO 39
10020    FOR K = 0 TO 23 STEP 23
10030      P.TAB(J,K) CHR$255;
10040    NEXT
10050  NEXT
10060:
10070  FOR J = 0 TO 39 STEP 39
10080    FOR K = 0 TO 22
10090      P.TAB(J,K) CHR$255;
10100    NEXT
10110  NEXT
10120 ENDPROC
```

b. Write the same procedure as in (a), but use it just the once, then use VDU28 to create a window just inside the border.

```
10 PROC_border     20 VDU 28,1,22,38,1
```

will create a permanent border around the screen and you will be able to use all the screen within it. CLS will clear only the middle part of the screen, and so the border will not flicker either. Neat!

c. In a mode which will accept graphics, much the same technique can be done with graphics commands. Change the background colour, use CLG to fill the screen with colour, then change the size of the screen (this time with VDU 24, as it's graphics) and clear the inner part with CLG (having first redefined the background colour). VDU 24 limits the graphics area only, so remember also to use VDU 28 to limit the area you can write text on.

3. Make it easy for the operator

a. Don't let the screen get too cluttered, especially when inputting information. It is easier on the eye to clear the screen after each question, or group of related questions. It needs very little extra programming to do this, but it greatly increases the user-friendliness.

b.   Draw attention to the next question to be answered - by
the use of colour or flash; perhaps by highlighting the
question or using double height lettering; or by displaying
'blank' characters (CHR$255 or dashes) at the place where
the entry is to be made, thus showing how many characters
need to be entered.

For example, just printing
Date?

is nothing like as useful as
Date ../../..

or alternatively
Date? (DD/MM/YY)

and
Name?

is less helpful than
Name <.........>

It is even neater to arrange for the cursor to leap across
the slashes as numbers are entered.

c.   Reduce the number of key-strokes needed to enter information.

-    Use GET or GET$ to take the next character from the
keyboard, rather than INPUT which requires a <RETURN>. The
more you can use one-character answers the more you can cut
down on key-strokes. Therefore:-

"Do you want to see this again? (Y/N)"

"Enter transaction:-   (C)ash / Che(Q)ue / (W)ithdrawal"

-    Use menus which give single number or single letter options.

-    Use 'default values' - in other words, display the most
frequently expected answer and only ask for further details
if this is entered as incorrect. eg. if most of your
customers have a Manchester address, but could live in any
part of the country, this next routine will stop you having
to type in 'Manchester' each time:-

```
10 PRINT "CITY - Manchester (Y/N)"
20 J$ = GET$
30 IF J$ = "Y" OR J$ = "y" city$ = "Manchester"
      ELSE CLS: INPUT "What city "; city$
```

Unfortunately with GET and GET$ there is no time for second thoughts if you pressed the wrong key! So you will need a final question where all the given answers are displayed and "All correct? Y/N" is requested.

f.   Have error-checks during input of information. If a
       question requires a numerical answer, the program must
       reject any answer with a non-numerical character in it and
       repeat the question until a valid answer is obtained.
       Every keyboard entry should be checked for correct
       character type, correct length of string and make
       allowances for information entered in upper- or lower-case
       characters.

       It is surprisingly easy to create an all-purpose
       entry-vetting routine, and it is easier to do this with GET
       than with INPUT because each character can be vetted as it
       is entered. (See Chapter 18)

There is a further benefit for the operator in using input validation - as each character is vetted when it is entered it is impossible to require a whole line to be re-typed because of an earlier illegal character. Errors are detected as they are made - so re-typing is limited to immediate re-insertion of the correct character. If an audible warning is sounded it also draws the user's attention to the incorrect entry, and may help him to work out more quickly what he should be doing.

15. WRITING STRUCTURED PROGRAMS

As far as possible, try to write "structured" programs. This is the name given to programs in which the main program works by calling up sub-routines, which work by calling up sub-sub-routines..... etc. For example, a program might read as follows:-

```
10 REM "Star wars"
20 PROC_initialise
30 REPEAT
40   PROC_spaceship: PROC_attack: PROC_bomb: PROC_score
50 UNTIL hit
60 ...
```

Then follows the definition of each procedure, each of which may call many other procedures.

It's rather like building a house - the whole thing can be broken down into smaller and smaller units until the final unit (a single brick) is reached.

Why write programs in this way? Simple.

1. They are easier to create
2. They are easier to read
3. They are easier to alter
4. They are easier to de-bug
5. They are almost certainly shorter
6. They may well be quicker

As a rough rule of thumb, wherever the same routine is being used in two different parts of the program, turn it into a procedure. In other words make the computer do the work for you.

You need to write in double size letters in two different places in the program? Write a Procedure - DEFPROC_doublesize(N$,x,y,c) - to place double sized lettering of the contents of N$ at position x,y in colour c; and then call it from the main program e.g as PROC_doublesize("HEADING",10,2,129) in one part of the program and PROC_doublesize("ANOTHER BIT OF PRINTING",20,2,135) on another occasion.

Even neater - define your colours at the top of the program -

```
 30 red = 1: green = 2
  .
  .
760 PROC_doubleheight("Hi!", 6, 5, green)
```

(For the full Procedure, see chapter 17)

You have now written one routine which you can call up at any time. It can save hours of programming time. Not only is it quicker to write PROC_doublesize.. etc, but once the procedure is de-bugged it is always correct, unlike new entries of program lines.

(See the section below on 'Utilities' for quick ways to store Procedures so that you can add one to a program in an instant.)

WRITING STRUCTURED PROGRAMS AT THE KEYBOARD

Even if you can't keep your hands off the computer when programming you can still write structured programs effectively.

It is not the answer to every problem.... but it does make program writing a pleasure, and because the program always RUNs correctly, right from the start, it has a much neater 'feel' to it.

Start by writing the main program as a skeleton of PROCedures with REM statements to remind you of what is to happen. In a simple program this might be as follows:-

stage1.

```
 10 REM Main body of program
100 END
200 REM Start of Procedures
```

Hardly world-shaking, but it's a start.

stage2.

```
 10 REM This is the main body of the program
 20 PROC_input
 30 PROC_process
 40 PROC_output
100 END
```

```
150 :
200 REM Start of Procedures
300 DEFPROC_input
399 ENDPROC
400 DEFPROC_process
499 ENDPROC
500 DEFPROC_output
599 ENDPROC
```

At this stage the program works! It doesn't do anything, but it will run.

stage 3 Design PROC_input

```
300 DEFPROC_input
320 PRINTTAB(7,12)"Input your first name please."
330 INPUT name$
399 ENDPROC
```

Here it is, and it still works.

```
 10 REM Main body of program
 20 PROC_input
 30 PROC_process
 40 PROC_output
100 END
200 REM Start of Procedures
300 DEFPROC_input
320 PRINTTAB(7,12)"Input your first name please."
330 INPUT name$
399 ENDPROC
400 DEFPROC_process
499 ENDPROC
500 DEFPROC_output
599 ENDPROC
```

Let's do a couple of other bits.

stage 3b. Design PROC_process

```
400 DEFPROC_process
410 B$ = "Hello there " + name$
420 length = LEN(name$)
430 C$ = "Your name contains " + length + " letters"
499 ENDPROC
```

stage 3c. Design PROC_output

```
500 DEFPROC_output
510 CLS
520 PROC_centre_print(B$)
530 PROC_centre_print(C$)
599 ENDPROC
```

Notice two things:-

1.   We need to print B$ and C$ in the centre: it can be done
      as a procedure, so we don't need to worry about exactly how
      to do it at this stage.

2.   We obviously need only one new PROC because we can use the
      same one twice and just 'pass' the appropriate string to
      the Procedure.

So stage 3 ends with the program looking like this.

```
 10 REM Main body of program
 20 PROC_input
 30 PROC_process
 40 PROC_output
100 END
200 REM Start of Procedures
300 DEFPROC_input
320 PRINTTAB(7,12)"Input your first name please."
330 INPUT name$
399 ENDPROC
400 DEFPROC_process
410 B$ = "Hello there " + name$
420 length = LEN(A$)
430 C$ = "Your name contains " + length + " letters"
499 ENDPROC
500 DEFPROC_output
510 CLS
520 PROC_centre_print(B$)
530 PROC_centre_print(C$)
599 ENDPROC
600 DEFPROC_centre_print(Z$)
699 ENDPROC
```

The next stage would be to design the centre_print routine. See chapter 17 for
some real ones.

This example is trivial to the point of banality but it does illustrate some important principles.

1.   The programming is done in a manner which clearly shows
      what is happening at all stages: it is STRUCTURED in design
      and approach.

2.   You can run and test it at all stages and therefore
      eliminate errors as you go along. In fact, the errors
      ought to be few as the steps are small 'mind-sized chunks'.

3.   The first time one of the authors tried this method on a
      method on a substantial program it cut the programming time
      by three-quarters and the final program ran first time.

With anything more complex than this it is vital to sit down with a pencil and reams of paper and design the program before tapping bits and pieces onto the screen.

PROGRAMMING STYLE

1.   Programs should be meaningful to read.
2.   ...and as near to English as possible.
3.   Reduce the use of GOTO to a minimum
4.   Use single statements per line
5.   Make things clearer with spaces and a good layout
6.   Use REM's frequently
7.   Write structured programs
8.   If appropriate break a long program into several shorter ones.
9.   Use utility procedures
10.   Use defined variables rather than constants
11.   Reduce key-strokes wherever possible.
12.   Verify input.
13.   Use arrays

-oOo-

1.   Programs should be meaningful to read. Compare:

```
120 IF d > 10 AND ff$ = "diabetes" THEN PROCxz
```

with

```
120 IF blood_sugar > 10 AND diagnosis$ = "diabetes" THEN
    PROCtreatment
```

In general, use meaningful names for both variables and procedures. If you haven't done this in a program it is easy to change to more appropriate names by using the EXCHANGE facilities in ROMs such as Toolkit-Plus from Beebugsoft, BROM+ from Clares or Caretaker from Computer Concepts.

Sometimes the use of sensible variable names will make the program too long. Often the program is short enough to LIST but leaves too little calculating space to RUN. In this case it may be better to write the program with meaningful names, SAVE it, and print out a listing. Then use a crunching routine together with automatic shortening of variable names (as done by Toolkit-Plus) to produce a more compact version which leaves enough space to RUN. Thus you get the best of both worlds - a short working program, but meaningful names in the master version which you can always amend and re-crunch at any time.

2.   Try to make the program as near to English as possible. It helps to use 'flags'. In real life, we wave a flag to draw attention to a condition (there's oil on the track: storm warning: the Queen is in residence). A flag is either up or down. In computing a flag is created by using the statements TRUE and FALSE attached to a numeric variable. eg.

```
overdue% = TRUE
   short = FALSE
```

As overdue% is a numeric variable, TRUE and FALSE must be represented by numbers. The number associated with TRUE is -1 and with FALSE is 0, so you could set 'short' to FALSE by

```
short = 0
```

but this rather defeats the object of the exercise, which is to produce more readable programs which are nearer to English than to maths.

If the flag is TRUE then we say it is 'set'.

Just as any variable must be defined before it is used, so we must define a flag (ie set it to TRUE or FALSE) before testing to see whether it is 'set' or not: we also can change its state whenever we want.

Consider:-
```
IF overdue = TRUE THEN PROC_warning
```

There is an even shorter way of writing 'IF overdue=TRUE' - just write

```
IF overdue
```

To write 'IF overdue = FALSE' we could more simply say

```
IF NOT overdue
```

This makes everything much easier to read - and what is easy to read is easy to debug. eg.

```
IF overdue PROC_warning      IF NOT ready PROC_wait
```

As well as making programs more readable, flags serve another purpose - they reduce the frequency and complexity of tests to see if one or more of several conditions have been met. For example:-

```
10 out_of stock = FALSE
20 REPEAT
30   INPUT number, size, stock
40   IF number > stock THEN out_of_stock = TRUE
50   IF size > 57 THEN out_of_stock = TRUE
60 UNTIL out_of_stock
70 .....
```

This is a trivial example: but in practice it saves a lot of trouble, especially where there are complicated conditions to be met, and particularly in loops. For example, you could set a single flag if a complicated mathematical formula produces results beyond pre-defined limits: and set the same flag on another line if an alternative condition is met, and so on. At the end of a REPEAT.. UNTIL loop you do not have to repeat these complicated formulae at the 'UNTIL..' line, merely see if the flag has become set at any time during the pass through the loop.

```
eg.  10 v = 0: oversize = FALSE
     20 REPEAT
     30 v = v + 1
     40 IF weight%(v) > 16.235 * SQR(1^3 - 2.3 * h%)
        THEN oversize = TRUE
     50 IF height%(v) > inside-leg(v) - 3 / j%
        THEN oversize = TRUE
     60 IF body_mass(v) > 24 THEN oversize = TRUE
     70 UNTIL oversize
```

It doesn't matter which way round you choose to use the flag - you can test for a flag to be set or not set just as easily. It all depends upon the English! Compare:

```
IF NOT oversize THEN PROC_supply
```
with
```
IF normal_size THEN PROC_supply
```

Quite a difference, isn't there? They both do the same job, but the second example is much easier to take in - and therefore de-bug. However, the 'oversize' and 'normal_size' flags would need to be set exactly the opposite way round if they were to substitute for one another.

3.   Eliminate GOTO's wherever you can - it leads to fewer mistakes, and makes the programs easier to follow. When at first you learn to program, GOTO seems an easy and sensible command. (particularly if you have learned BASIC with a version which does not support Procedures). However, the larger your program becomes the more potentially dangerous it is and the reasons for avoiding it become more apparent.

Nevertheless, slavish avoidance of GOTO is pedantic. It is particularly useful within a REPEAT.. UNTIL loop when turning it into a pseudo-DOWHILE....ENDWHILE loop.

eg.
```
 10 REPEAT
 20    IF grade > 45 GOTO 100
 30    grade = number * 37 / position
 40    number = number + 1
100 UNTIL number > 45
```

This is really the same as:

```
WHILE number > 45 DO
grade = number * 37 etc
```

Which, if you have BASIC V (ie, the Archimedes) you should be using in preference.

If you try to write the program without using GOTO then either you have to create extra flags, or else use a lot more code, which leads to loss of readability, wastes memory, and slows down the program.

**

There are, however, some very important times NOT to use a GOTO:

1. Never GOTO a REM line or an empty line, in case you later use a crunching routine which strips out all REMs and lines with only spaces in. (Caretaker can cope with this.)

2. Never use GOTO where another construction would easily suffice. Like bull mastiffs, GOTO is dangerous if not kept under control! It is all too easy to GOTO a

line, and three weeks later redevelop that line - maybe adding a line or two before it to clear the screen and put in a heading. But your GOTO command doesn't know that the section now starts two lines earlier, and as it is not obvious that a GOTO lands there from afar you may then forget to alter the GOTO. Now, whilst losing a printed heading may not be the end of the world (it is easy to spot and correct, for a start) if on another occasion your program lands undetected in the middle of a calculation instead of at its beginning you may well end up with spurious results, and it will take an age to de-bug. You have been warned!

3. Try not to GOTO a distant line. It is harder to spot errors under these conditions.

GOTO ** and read again (!)

There are NEARLY always simple ways round using GOTO eg using the original example

```
 10 REPEAT
 20    IF grade > 45 GOTO 100            ***
 30    grade = number * 37 / position
 40    number = number + 1
100 UNTIL number > 45
```

> *** N.B. THEN does not need to be included
> after IF unless followed by a * command

Could be replaced by:-

```
 10 REPEAT
 20    IF grade <=' 45 grade = number * 37 / position
       :number = number + 1
 30 UNTIL number > 45
```

or alternatively with a procedure

```
 10 REPEAT
 20    IF grade <= 45 PROCdo
 30 UNTIL number > 45
       .
       .
1000 DEFPROCdo
1010  grade = number * 37 / position
1020  number = number + 1
1030 ENDPROC
```

Alternatively, change the whole structure of that part of the program. Using a slightly different example:

```
190 REPEAT
200   IF score > 45 number = number + 7: GOTO 220
210   number = number - 7
220 UNTIL number > 65
```

could be replaced by

```
190 REPEAT
200   IF score > 45 number = number + 7
      ELSE number=number-7
220 UNTIL
```

but when the calculations become more complex (and especially if there are further 'IF' statements, it is often easier to do a 'double test', eg.

```
190 REPEAT
200   IF score > 45 number = number + 7
210   IF score <= 45 number = number - 7
220 UNTIL number > 65
```

However, all these constructions tend to need more programming, so if you're running short of space, it may be more appropriate to retain the original GOTO construction. Just be careful, that's all!

4.   Use single statements per line, especially in areas of the program which are least like English. Short lines are quicker to alter, and less likely to be altered incorrectly because there are fewer chances of introducing errors of copying. Single-statement lines allow easy insertion of other commands without altering existing ones, because the new commands can be allocated to new line numbers instead of requiring insertion in the middle of a long line of code.

5.   Use spaces to make things clearer

   - space the line out sensibly

```
FOR J = 1 TO 10 STEP 0.5
```

is much clearer than

```
FORJ=1TO10STEP0.5
```

Similarly (and this is a genuine example, from, a crunched medical program)

```
IFWORSE=0
```

which is much easier to follow if laid out thus:-

```
IF W OR S E=0
```

If you have adequate memory space available, leave a space around all keywords and variable names: and sometimes round mathematical symbols (use your judgement on this one). There are, however, some keywords where following spaces are not permitted - eg TAB requires the bracket to follow immediately.

- use blank lines to separate sections of code. (After the line number enter a colon or a space, and then <Return>) The colon is only for decoration but it allows you to see that there is something there when you write it.

```
10 MODE 7
15 :
20 REM Set flags
30 go = FALSE: seek = TRUE: empty = FALSE
32 :
33 :
35 REPEAT
40   PROC_start
50   PROC_screen
55   FOR K = 1 TO 7
60     contents(K) = X * K + 1
65   NEXT
70 UNTIL empty
75 :
80 PROC_score
85 END
90 :
95 REM beginning of procedures....
```

- within loops insert two leading spaces on each line. It shows just where the loops are, and where they return to, and helps the readability of the program immensely. You generate leading spaces by typing in LISTO 7 <Return> and on LISTing, the spaces will be put in automatically. If you copy lines in this format don't copy the leading spaces - or you'll get four leading spaces the next time you LIST!

On the Archimedes LISTO 7 has the additional advantage that it splits up multi-statement lines, which helps enormously in reading what might otherwise be a very compacted program. (This facility is also available on the BBC-B etc with ROMs such as Caretaker, Toolkit etc.)

Unfortunately LISTO does not work correctly on the B and puts the last line of a loop in the wrong place - it should be placed so that the REPEAT and the UNTIL, or the FOR and the NEXT are vertically above one another.

6.   Use REM's frequently to remind you what is being done. You may know what

```
DEFPROC_glubfrisch
```

does when you write the program, or the exact significance of

```
IF grosl% > 65 PROCf ELSE updat = updat + als%(6)
```

but when you come to alter the program three months later you may find the subtleties escape you! However, the more your program looks like English, the less you will need REMs.

7.   As explained in the section on structured programming, the main program should be in a short early section, with the remainder of the program consisting of procedures. DATA statements should go at the end. However, a big program with a lot of DATA work may be more readable if the DATA is sited near to the READ command which uses that particular set of data -i.e. placed just after the PROC that uses it.

8.   It is sometimes safer and more legible to break a large program into several small ones, passing the results from program to program either by the use of the resident integers (A%-Z% plus @%), which don't get wiped when a new program is CHAINed, or by putting the results of a program on disc in the form of a file, which is immediately picked up by the next program. This is especially effective with discs and has the following benefits -

-      because each program only does a small amount of the whole, mistakes are easier to spot - each program is shorter, and therefore easier to de-bug

-      there is less chance of running out of memory, either because of an over-sized program, or because you have run out of calculating space with the continuous use of one program. (Each time a new program is RUN the calculating space in memory is first wiped clean.)

The problems with linking programs are:-

- it is slower in operation, especially if files have to be saved and loaded.

- there is often a lot of duplication of code - eg if you are writing in double sized letters you will need a procedure to do it in each program. For this reason the total length of the linked programs is usually larger than the original single program.

One trap for the unwary, especially those who don't use machine code, is that certain of the resident integer variables are set aside for special tasks. @% is used to set screen column widths, and X%, Y%, P% and A% all get used to pass parameters between BASIC and machine code. It is best to get into the habit of avoiding these particular resident integers.

9.   Use of utility Procedures. A utility procedure is one which may be used in many different programs (eg. to write in double-size type, to centre printing, to draw circles). Keep a library of them and eventually you will hardly need to write programs at all - just construct them from pre-defined procedures! To make them truly universal all the variables inside the procedure should be declared LOCAL. This means that you can have several procedures in a program using the same variable names, each independent of the others. (see Chapter 16)

As procedures tend to be short, if you are using the Acorn DFS it is wasteful only to be able to store 31 on each disc surface (31 is the maximum number of file names per disc with the DFS). This is where a 'Library manager' program comes in useful.

Rather than going to the trouble of merging programs each time you want to add a utility procedure, try the following ploy:-

a. When you want to store your first utility procedure, RENumber it starting at, say, 20000. Write the last line number in your note-pad.

b. Don't SAVE it, but instead

```
*SPOOL "name" <Return>
LIST <Return>
*SPOOL <Return>
```
where "name" is the filename of your utility.

c. With the next utility to be saved, RENumber it starting at the last line number of the first utility plus ten (you've lost the note-book by now, haven't you!), and save it to disc as above.

In this way your utility disc has a number of SPOOLed files on it, with no clash of line numbers.

To call up your utilities, simply

```
*EXEC "name" <Return>
```

for each and every utility you require. They will be merged into any existing program automatically. Don't worry about the error messages, they aren't errors as far as you are concerned.

10.   Avoid using numerical constants, except where defined at the top of the program. If you are writing a program to help with VAT, and you use 15 written into all equations as the constant VAT rate then you'll have an awful lot of trouble if there's a budget and the rate alters! If, on the other hand, you use vat% as the constant, and define it as vat%=15 at the top of the program, then one simple alteration to the program and all is done. What is more, there is no need to check the whole program again, in case you've left one calculation with 15 still in it.

11.   Reduce key-strokes wherever possible. Get into the habit of using GET and GET$ rather than INPUT (which requires an extra <Return>) (see Chapter 14)

12.   Trap dangerous entries So many programs can be made to crash if a letter is entered where a number should be. Your programs should be constructed so that it is impossible to enter the wrong sort of information. (See Chapter 18)

13.   Use arrays (see the section on arrays in Chapter 16). They are so much more economical of program and code space, much more legible, and much easier to debug than any other method of handling data. Take the trouble to learn to use them - they are in fact very simple and will repay dividends immediately.

16. GETTING THE BEST FROM BASIC

Some aspects of BASIC are extremely useful, yet aren't used as often as they should be, mainly because people get scared of them, and don't realise their full potential.

Equally, BASIC is a very dangerous language. It is so very 'forgiving', and you can manage to do most things with it badly (by good programming standards), yet still have a program that works. There is even a university which runs, as the introduction to its computing course, a remedial course for BASIC programmers! A lot of the fault lies with other and earlier versions of BASIC which will not support Procedures and Functions (not BBC BASIC): programmers coming to BBC BASIC from these other BASICs may well have learned some very bad habits!

There are six important areas where learning the correct way to program will make your programs better, shorter, easier to read, easier to debug, and generally better all round.

1.   The most important is to write Structured Programs, and we
      have devoted a whole chapter to this as it is a topic in itself.

2.   The next two items are connected with structured
      programming - Procedures and Functions.

3.   In terms of the internal structure of the code itself,
      Arrays make it much easier to shunt information round your
      program, or between programs. They are as easy as ABC, but
      for some reason people seem to think they're difficult.

4.   There are several different types of Loops and it is best
      to choose the most appropriate one.

5.   The use of Flags will make your programs more readable,
      more controllable, and easier to debug. (See section 2
      in Chapter 15 for a full treatment)

6.   Finally, GET and GET$ are related commands that will
      improve the quality of programming and ease of keyboard use
      of the finished program, and reduce potential program crashes.

PROCEDURES AND FUNCTIONS

Procedures and functions are useful because they behave like little GOSUB routines: but you don't have to remember the line number because you call a Procedure or Function by name:-

eg `10 PROC_draw_circle`

(How much easier to do this than to have to say `10 GOSUB 3615`)

Similarly a function is a piece of code that produces either a numerical result or a string variable result

`15 IF FN_volume > 16 THEN too_big = TRUE`

where the function FN_volume calculates the volume (having previously been given the appropriate dimensions on which to work). Functions can equally well give a string as a result

`10 IF FN_answer = "Rhubarb" THEN PROC_custard`

The coding for a procedure or a function is always placed after the main body of the program: this is to prevent the program going through the procedure unless it is specifically called to do so. The procedure or function itself is defined starting with a line with DEF in front of it

`DEFPROC_print, or DEFFN_area.`

The end of a Procedure is marked with ENDPROC: the end of a function is marked with " =" and a variable or calculation eg.

`2000 DEFFN_volume        2010 = height% * width% * depth%`

which is a Function to generate the volume of a block, given its height, width and depth.

```
1020 DEFPROC_print
1030 CLS : PRINTTAB(3,4) heading$
1040 ENDPROC
```

which is a Procedure to clear the screen and then print whatever is in the variable heading$ at position (3,4) on the screen.

In general, wherever you use the same piece of coding more than once turn it into a procedure or function. It:-

1. Saves time - you only enter it the once.

2. Saves space - ditto.

3. Reduces debugging time - once it's debugged you don't have
    to debug it again the second time it's used (as you might
    have to with duplicated code)

4. Improves the readability of your program (PROC_volume is
    so much easier to understand than GOSUB 3120!)

5. Helps debugging - you can see immediately that you meant
    PROC_volume and not PROC_area: on the other hand, GOSUB
    3120 and GOSUB 3210 are not so easy to disentangle.

There is no reason why functions and procedures shouldn't use variables from the
main program.

```
DEFFN_volume = height% * width% * depth%
```

But the real advantage of procedures and functions is that you can pass specific
amounts for the procedure to work on. These are called parameters.

```
2000 DEFFN_volume(height%, width%, depth%)
2010 = height% * width% * depth%
```

which you would call from the main program as, for example:-

```
10 PRINT FN_volume(4,5,f%)
```

Why bother with passing parameters like this?

1. It's faster - if you pass the parameters directly to the
    function then the program doesn't have to go looking around
    for the values.

2. You have more control over what you send to the function
    or procedure.

3. You can make the procedure itself more generally useful by
    passing parameters.

At the moment the version without passed parameters will only calculate for the
variables height%, width% and depth%, so you're sunk if you want to calculate the
volume of a box A% by B% by 2.345 units. If you use the version with parameters
you would simply call the function with

```
FNvolume(A%,B%,2.345)
```

Therefore, the same procedure can be called from all over the program with different variables eg.

```
PROCadd(A%, 6)
PROCadd(13, 4.347)
PROCadd(N% + 34, age% - 19)
```

If called with too many or too few parameters (which are called 'arguments') the procedure or function won't work eg. for the definition given above, calling

```
FN_volume(height%,width%)
```

won't give the function enough material to work with.

4. You can isolate all the variables used in a procedure or function by declaring them to be LOCAL, which means the procedure can be used in any program without any worries that it will cause a clash of variable names. (see below) Passed parameters are always LOCAL to the procedure.

It is worth while having a list of procedures and functions showing the parameters of each, and to use sensible names for the parameters (which are treated as LOCAL to the procedure, anyway). This helps you to remember what each procedure is for, and what parameters it needs to have passed to it.

LOCAL AND GLOBAL VARIABLES

A LOCAL variable is only attached to a particular procedure or function, and cannot be accessed by the program outside that procedure or function. A Global variable is the same whatever part of the program you are in - it can be accessed inside and outside procedures. Below you will find three programs to illustrate the principles of Global and LOCAL variables.

Here's the complicating bit - you can use the same variable name as both a Global and a LOCAL variable. The computer treats these as totally different entities, and can store different bits of information in each. (Think of this as having a letter-box at home and at work. Both have your name on them, but each contains different things.)

If you have a Global variable then you will get its contents at all times unless you are inside a Procedure or Function where the variable has previously been defined as LOCAL to that section.

The reason is very simple - if you have a bank of Procedures stored on a utility disc, then if all variables used by these procedures are defined as LOCAL, you cannot inadvertently corrupt the global variables in your main program if you happen to have picked the same name (eg J%) as a variable in both procedure and program.

The following program shows how a variable behaves as a Global. That is, the X outside is the same as the X inside the Procedure PROCadd.

```
10 X = 1
20 PRINT "LINE 20, X = "; X
30 PROCadd
40 PRINT "LINE 40, X = "; X          RUN
50 END                               LINE 20, X = 1
60 DEFPROCadd                        LINE 80, X = 4
70 X = X + 3                         LINE 40, X = 4
80 PRINT "LINE 80, X = "; X
90 ENDPROC
```

You can see what happens when you run it. Inside the Procedure, 3 is added to X: the resulting value is printed inside and again after visiting the Procedure. The value has 'come out of' the Procedure.

In this next program line 65 has been added. This says that X is to be a variable inside the Procedure only, that is, LOCAL. Line 67 is added to give this X a value.

```
10 X = 1
20 PRINT "LINE 20, X = "; X
30 PROCadd
40 PRINT "LINE 40, X = "; X
50 END
60 DEFPROCadd                        RUN
65 LOCAL X                           LINE 10, X = 1
67 X = 0                             LINE 80, X = 3
70 X = X + 3                         LINE 40, X = 1
80 PRINT "LINE 80, X = "; X
90 ENDPROC
```

Look at the Run. Notice that the X inside says 0+3=3 (correct), but the X outside has not been altered (line 40).

Sometimes we want to use the value of X from outside the Procedure, and work on it within the procedure, but yet not alter its outside value. This is called passing a variable.

152

To go back to our letter-box analogy, it's rather like taking a photostat of the contents of your in-tray at work and putting it in your in-tray at home. You can write notes and comments all over your photostats without affecting the originals in any way.

The example below is rather false for simplicity's sake, but it illustrates that all variables inside the bracket after a procedure name (eg DEFPROC_this(A$,n%,value) are treated as LOCAL.)

```
10 X=1
20 PRINT "LINE 20, X = "; X
30 PROCadd(X)                    RUN
40 PRINT "LINE 40, X = "; X         LINE 20, X = 1
50 END                              LINE 80, X = 4
60 DEFPROCadd(X)                    LINE 40, X = 1
70 X = X + 3
80 PRINT "LINE 80, X = "; X
90 ENDPROC
```

This run shows the bracket X to be LOCAL.

In all these examples, the variable name X has been used to highlight the fact that Local variables cannot be 'seen' outside the Procedure. The one drawback is that if you want to use a result calculated in a Procedure you have to store it finally in a Global variable.

LOCAL variables are very useful, especially where you want to avoid utility procedures interfering with results calculated in the main program: pass variables in through the brackets, and have all other variables defined as LOCAL and you won't interfere with the main program at all. However, take care with Procedures calling Procedures calling Procedures. LOCAL, Global and Passed Variables in these can do funny things, especially when coming out of nested procedures.

The rule is - if a variable is used in a particular procedure, whether it is Global or LOCAL, then to any procedure which it calls the variable will look global.

An example will make this easier to appreciate:-

```
PROC_A        uses X which is Global
              and y which is LOCAL
DEF PROC_A    has inside it a call to PROC_B
```

Inside PROC_B both X and y look like Global (because they are both outside PROC_B, however they may look to PROC_A). Z is declared LOCAL inside PROC_B and PROC_A is not aware of its existence.

This rule carries on however long a train of procedure calls you have.

TESTING PROCEDURES AND FUNCTIONS

It is possible to call a procedure or function directly from the keyboard. Therefore it is possible to test it separately from the main program without RUNning the whole program. This being so, it would seem that there are few excuses for putting a procedure into a program that hasn't been thoroughly de-bugged and tested (unless it relies on accessing arrays, which of course have to be DIMed outside the procedure).

ARRAYS

People get muddled over arrays, but they needn't. Do you get muddled about understanding that the occupant of Flat 2, 7 Acacia Drive is called Mr.Stubbings? No? And that if he moves you can find out the new occupant's name by going to the door and asking? Then you too can do arrays. It's that simple.

The purpose of an array is to be able to refer in a systematic and economic way to related bits of information.

For example, you could put the days of the week and the number of assistants in a shop into a program by:

```
first_day$ = "Sunday"
next_day$ = "Monday"
the_one_after_that$ = "Tuesday"
...etc...

Sunday_assistants% = 0
Monday_assistants% = 45
Tuesday_assistants% = 30
...etc...
```

but you won't have much fun trying to print out the week's requirements without going to an awful lot of fuss in the coding of your program.

```
PRINT first_day$,Sunday_assistants%,
                 next_day$,Monday_assistants%,.......
```

If, instead, you could refer to each day by number you could make life much simpler. If the first day is a Sunday, then:-

```
day$(1) = "Sunday"
day$(2) = "Monday"
...etc...
```

This clump of similar variables is called an ARRAY. Before you can use individual members of an array, you must tell the computer that you are going to use an array, and define exactly how many items there are going to be in the array. This is called 'Dimensioning' an array and is performed with the DIM command

```
10 DIM day$(7)
```

would be needed in the case above. In exactly the same way, the number of assistants on Sunday could be placed in assistants%(1), on Monday in assistants%(2), etc., having first performed DIM assistants%(7)

So to print out the day and the assistants present you would be able to do the following:-

```
FOR day = 1 TO 7
   PRINT day$(day), assistants%(day)
NEXT
```

So much neater, and so much easier to understand.

Back to the houses and flats. It will be obvious by now that there is a great similarity between flats and their owners and arrays and their contents. Let's look at it in detail:

Build a row of 7 houses	`DIM house$(7)`
Mr Smith lives at no.1	`house$(1) = "Mr.Smith"`
Mr.Jones lives at no.2	`house$(2) = "Mr Jones"`
etc etc	
Who lives at no.6?	`PRINT house$(6)`

This is called a ONE-DIMENSIONAL ARRAY. Now let's look at a more complicated version. Each house has two flats - upstairs and downstairs. So:-

Build Acacia Avenue, 7 houses each divided into two flats	`DIM Acacia$(7,2)`
Mr Hubbard lives at Flat 1, No.1 Acacia Av	`Acacia$(1,1) = "Mr.Hubbard"`
Mr.Spalding lives at	

155

Mr Trenchard lives at
Flat 1, No 2 Acacia Av   `Acacia$(2,1) = "Mr Trenchard"`
etc   etc

Who lives at Flat 2, No.6?   `PRINT Acacia$(6,2)`

This is a TWO-DIMENSIONAL ARRAY. We could have a three dimensional array if each house had two floors, each with three flats - DIM Acacia$(7,2,3) - and a four-dimensional array if each flat has six rooms - DIM Acacia$(7,2,3,6).

Arrays are at their best with linked data. Going back to the shop assistants, we could combine the day of the week and the number of assistants for each day as follows

```
DIM info$(7,2)
info$(1,1) = "Sunday" : info$(1,2) = "0"
info$(2,1) = "Monday" : info$(2,2) = "45"
..etc..
```

In this case the left hand side of the array holds the name of the day and the right hand side holds the number of assistants (as a string, because the array as a whole has to be either in string or numeric form)

This looks complicated. But it isn't - just spend a moment looking at it and you'll soon see the point.

Now - to print out the data:
```
FOR day = 1 TO 7
   FOR K = 1 TO 2
      PRINT info$(day,K);
   NEXT
   PRINT
NEXT
```

You can easily put information into arrays with the READ function. In the next case 15 different pieces of information about car no 1 is eventually contained in the first line of the array:

```
DIM car$(14,15)
FOR num = 1 TO 15
   READ car$(1,num)
NEXT
DATA Volkswagen, Golf, Blue, 1.1 Litre, 2-door, hatchback,
overhead cams, 4 cylinder,cloth, tinted, no rugs, little
swinging animal in the back window,£2045.67,10% dealer
discount,bought 12/3/86
```

And following this, similar information on cars 2 to 14 could be read in. If you want to search for 2-door models, you will have to look only at the data in car$(X,5).

The more linked information you have, the more easily it will be handled through using arrays.

If you try to DIM the same array twice you will get an error message "Bad Dim at line X" Therefore, you can't have a DIM as a line of code which could be called more than once in the program. In particular, therefore, you cannot have a DIM as a part of a procedure unless you can make sure that the line of the procedure can only be used once.(eg, by using a flag, or by calling the procedure once only). You might want to do this if you are trying to save space by not DIMing unless absolutely necessary, or setting the DIM space of several arrays depending upon variables calculated earlier in the program.

```
DIMclass_members(number%)
```

There is no need to give values to members of an array before using them - DIMming an array automatically gives a value of zero to each member, which you may then alter as you wish. (By comparison, if you try to use an ordinary variable without first defining its value you will get an error message.)

It is best to have all the DIM's together at the beginning of the program. All DIMs can be put together on one line.

```
DIM info$(7,2), Acacia$(7,2,3), mark%(15)
```

Arrays eat up memory - just DIMing an array uses two bytes for each member of the array, before you've put anything into the array itself. So make sure you use arrays efficiently. (see the section on saving memory)

Finally, computers start counting from 0, not 1. Therefore if you want 7 elements in an array, you only need

```
DIMarray$(6)
```
because you'll get it numbered 0,1,2,3,4,5 and 6

So in the shop assistants' example above, to hold all the requirements for the assistants and the days of the week you could have written DIM info$(6,1), and saved a bit of memory. However, it does require a bit of effort to think also about counting from 0, so we didn't mention it earlier on. If you're not short of space it is easier to read a program which numbers days of the week form 1-7 rather than 0-6!

LOOPS

Types of loops. It is worthwhile to look at ways of repeating an operation a number of times, seeing what we actually achieve with each and finding out how fast they are relative to one another.

1. IF this condition is met DO this operation again. (IF .... THEN GOTO) This is a 'dangerous' structure as it is not easy to deduce the structure of the program, nor to detect errors, but it has a lot of attractive features, the most notable of which is simplicity.

2. DO this operation THIS NUMBER of times.(FOR .... NEXT) A direct approach to an exact number of repetitions. No conditions are given and the operation will be carried out so long as there is no machine error.

3. REPEAT operation UNTIL this condition is met. (REPEAT .... UNTIL) A conditional repetition - the operation is done again if a certain condition is met. BUT the operation is carried out at least once, even if the condition is met before entering the loop!

4. WHILE this condition is met REPEAT this operation. Rather like the the REPEAT loop except th at the operation is not carried out even once if the condition is met before the loop begins. There is one big disadvantage to this loop - it doesn't exist in BBC BASIC earlier than Basic V (ie. other than in the Archimedes) . Other languages such as Comal and Pascal support this type of instruction - it is called a WHILE... ENDWHILE loop. A method for constructing this loop in lower than Basic V is given below)

If you study these carefully you will see that there are two types of loop structure.

Do something a set number of times.
(FOR...NEXT)

While a condition is (or isn't) met Do something.
(REPEAT...UNTIL)
(WHILE...ENDWHILE)

Which loop should be used where? IF you want to do something a set number of times use FOR....NEXT

IF you always want to do the operation at least once THEN
        use (REPEAT UNTIL)
ELSE
        use (WHILE)

WHILE boils down to:-

REPEAT
        IF condition THEN operation
UNTIL condition

or in concrete terms:-

```
100 REM WHILE
110 REPEAT
120    IF X < 6 THEN PRINT X : X = X + 1
130 UNTIL X > = 6
140 REM END WHILE .  .
```

Notice that this allows for the possibility that X may already be bigger than 6 on entry. In this case the 'Print and add' operation will be ignored and you will 'drop out' of the UNTIL first time through. The whole operation can be a procedure or function, of course, and it is here that it comes into its own.

SPEED OF LOOPS

```
10 TIME = 0
20 FOR A% = 1 TO 1000
30    X% = X% + 1
40 NEXT
50 :
60 PRINT "FOR/NEXT Time ";TIME/100;" Seconds"
70 :
80 X% = 0
90 TIME = 0
100 REPEAT
110    X% = X% + 1
120 UNTIL X% = 1000
130 PRINT "REPEAT/UNTIL Time ";TIME/100;" Seconds"
140 :
150 X% = 0
160 TIME = 0
170 REM WHILE
180 REPEAT
```

```
190    IF X% < 1000 THEN X% = X% + 1
200 UNTIL X% = 1000
210 REM END WHILE
220 PRINT "WHILE ";TIME/100;" Seconds"
230 PRINT"FOR 1000 Loops"
```

Run the program. Note the times.

The WHILE loop becomes more efficient the bigger the operation becomes.

GET AND GET$

Get into the habit of using these two related Functions which are used to take the next character from the keyboard.

```
10 J=GET
20 PRINT J
```

If you use GET the result of the function is the ASCII code for the next keyboard character being placed in the variable - eg. if you press "A" then J will have 65 in it. On the other hand, if you use GET$ and input "A" then J$ will contain the letter A. (The variable does not need to be J. It is just an ingrained habit with one of the authors!)

```
10 PRINT GET
```

will give the answer 65 if "A" was pressed as the function is evaluated when you press a key. The program waits for you. However

```
10 J=GET
20 PRINT GET
```

will give you no apparent result from pressing "A" once. If you now press "B" the computer will print "66" (the ASCII value for B). The reason is that the result of the first GET in line 10 is stored in the variable J. As there is no request to print J there is no screen output.

One useful tip. The function GET gives the ASCII code of the key pressed. As the ASCII codes for 1 and 2 are respectively 49 and 50 it is possible to get the actual number into J by:-

```
J=GET-48
```

(which will print the number input as a number) or $X = 2.79 * A\% * (GET-48) /$
1.69   A% = INSTR("@" + alternatives$, GET$)

BASIC V

Basic V is the version of BBC Basic used in the Archimedes. It has a number of very important additions and advantages over earlier Basics in loop structures and graphics amongst other things. This is covered in the special section on this machine - see Chapter 8.

17. SCREEN DISPLAYS AND GRAPHICS

VANISHING CURSOR

There are two ways of getting rid of the cursor, but they both get negated by Mode change, Break and using the Cursor keys.

The easier way to remember is:-
```
Off  ....   VDU 23, 1, 0; 0; 0; 0;
On   ....   VDU 23, 1, 1; 0; 0; 0;
```

The other way is:-
```
Off  ....   VDU 23; 8202; 0; 0; 0;
On   ....   Mode change
```

The second method gives a flashing square cursor on use of the arrow keys, and inverse video when positioned over an existing character: you may prefer this version.

To stop the cursor appearing when the cursor keys are used, disable the cursor keys by using *FX 4,1 (see User Guide).

LETTERS AND NUMBERS

CENTERED HEADINGS

Here are some straightforward Procedures for producing lines of print in a specified colour on a specified background, in single and double height, with and without a surrounding line of colour.

Call these procedures in the normal way: note the variables which have to be passed. hd$ may be passed either as, eg. (A$,.....) or ("Hello",......). Although a background colour is being called , the colour numbers 0-15 are the ones to pass - they are altered inside the routines.

DOUBLE HEIGHT WITH NO BACKGROUND.

```
100 DEFPROC_head1(hd$,Ypos)
110  Xpos = (40-LEN(hd$)) / 2 - 1
120  FOR J = 0 TO 1
130     VDU31, Xpos, Ypos + J, 141
140     PRINT hd$
150  NEXT
160 ENDPROC
```

SINGLE HEIGHT PRINT WITH A BACKGROUND COLOUR.

```
200 DEFPROC_head2(hd$,Ypos,col2)
210  Xpos = (40-LEN(hd$)) / 2 - 1
220  VDU31, Xpos - 2, Ypos, 128 + col 2, 157
230  PRINT hd$;" ";
240  VDU 156
250 ENDPROC
```

DOUBLE HEIGHT WITH COLOURED BACKGROUND.

```
300 DEFPROC_head3(hd$,Ypos,col2)
310  Xpos = (40-LEN(hd$)) / 2 - 1
320  FOR J = 0 TO 1
330     VDU 31, Xpos-3, Ypos+J, 141, 128 + col 2, 157
340     PRINT hd$; " ";
350     VDU 156
360  NEXT
370 ENDPROC
```

DOUBLE HEIGHT WITH 4 LINE COLOURED BACKGROUND.

```
400 DEFPROC_head4(hd$,Ypos,col2)
410  Xpos = (40-LEN(hd$)) / 2 - 1
420  VDU 31, Xpos - 2, Ypos, 128 + col 2, 157
430  PRINT SPC(LEN(hd$) + 2);
440  VDU 156
450  FOR J = 1 TO 2
460     VDU 31, Xpos - 3,Ypos + J, 141, 128 + col 2, 157
470     PRINT hd$; " ";
480     VDU 156
490  NEXT
500  PRINT
510  VDU 31, Xpos - 2, Ypos + 3, 128 + col 2, 157
520  PRINT SPC(LEN(hd$) + 2);   VDU 156
530 ENDPROC
```

Here is a little routine which will enable you to get double height in any Mode other than 7. The idea is to use OSWORD with a value of 10. This reads a character definition. It is stored in a memory location called 'bit' and then two characters (224 & 225) are redefined to the top and bottom halves of the letter respectively. As each half is a whole letter high the result is double height. It is quite an easy task to extend this to quadruple height by redefining 4 letters.

```
 10 REM Prints all input letters at double height in any Mode
    except 7
 20 MODE 1 : REM for example
 30 DIM bit 9 : REM This sets up a parameter block for OSWORD
 40 PROC_double("HI THERE",10,10)
 50 END
 60 :
 70 DEFPROC_double(A$,startx%,starty%)
 80  OSWORD=&FFF1
 90  A% = 10 : REM parameter for Osword call
100  FOR loop% = 1 TO  LEN(A$)
110    ?bit = ASC(MID$(A$,loop%,1))
120    X%=bit MOD &100
130    Y%=bit DIV &100
140    CALL OSWORD
150    :
160    REM Define a character as the top half of the letter
170    VDU23,224,bit?1,bit?1,bit?2,bit?2,bit?3,bit?3,bit?4,
       bit?4
180    :
190    REM Define a character as the lower half of the letter
200    VDU23,225,bit?5,bit?5,bit?6,bit?6,bit?7,bit?7,bit?8,
       bit?8
210    :
220    xpos% = startx%+loop%-1
230    REM Print top half
240    VDU31,xpos%,starty%,224
250    :
260    REM Print lower half
270    VDU31,xpos%,starty%+1,225
280  NEXT
290 ENDPROC
```

DISPLAYING COLUMNS OF FIGURES

Columns of figures are the life-blood of computer calculations and display. It is easy to make columns by using a comma between each variable to be printed.

```
PRINT X,Y,Z          gives

12          43          65
```

In order to get the column width as you want it, you have to alter @%. Just how is explained in the 'B' User Guide at about Page 70, but here is a potted explanation as there are one or two things the book leaves out.

@% is the variable used by the computer to set the number of character positions per column, how many decimal places will be shown in the output, and the 'FORMAT' of the output.

Let's look at the number as a whole. It is inserted into @% as follows:-

```
@% = &AMNXY
```

    '&' is the usual sign for a HEX number.
    'A' represents FORMAT and in this position:-
        0 = Output in the 'normal' form.
        1 = Output in Exponential form. (4.546E3)
        2 = Figures to a fixed number of decimal places.

    'MN' gives the number of digits. Now here's the rub: if
    the Format is 0, then MN means 'total number of digits
    displayed', but if format is 2, MN means 'the number of
    digits to the right of the decimal point.

So.. `If B%=1234.5678989`

```
          &AMNXY
@% = &0050D
PRINT B%
          1234.5
```

or alternatively :-

```
          &AMNXY
@%   = &2050D
PRINT B%
          1234.56789
```

From these examples notice that if Format is 0, the total number of digits excluding the decimal point is 5: if Format is 2 the number of digits after the point is 5 (if the total number of digits is less than 10!)

'XY' gives the width of the field. The last digit is printed on the right of the field. The interesting thing here is that a 'silly' entry, such as &40, is translated as 64 spaces or a line and half per column!

You need to experiment with @% to get full benefit from its use. The main thing to remember is that you are in HEX.

WINDOWS

GOT YOUR WINDOW STUCK?

Sometimes the window facility doesn't appear to work. The most common error is to have a window dimension which is too large - it is very easy to put in a wrong value for vertical height because you have muddled up horizontal and vertical dimensions. If your figure takes you outside the screen parameters in any direction the window defaults to full screen.

If you are putting windows all over the place, it is quite usual to construct a Procedure which takes the left hand side window value, then adds a width to get the right hand side. If the left hand side figure plus the width figure comes to more than the screen maximum you end up with default values again: unfortunately, looking at the program doesn't easily show up the problem.

THIN WINDOWS FOR THICK LINES AND BORDERS

It is frustration which drives us to discover new things. One such is the fact that windows are faster than plotting for drawing horizontal and vertical lines. We tend to think of a window as being a rectangle and a line as being a line. Well, a line is also a very thin rectangle.

In order to fill a screen with colour we use CLG: the same goes for filling a window. Set the colour, CLG. Therefore a way to draw a line is to set a colour, set a thin window, CLG.

As for speed, the window method is considerably faster. Don't take my word for it, try this mini-program. The screen clears for Mode 0, then starts to fill with drawn lines. When the screen is full, it clears and fills with lines generated by windows.... much more quickly!

```
10 MODE 0
20 FOR Y% = 1 TO 1000 STEP 4
30    VDU 25, 4, 0; Y%;          ( MOVE 0,Y% )
40    VDU 25, 5, 1270; Y%;       ( DRAW1270,Y% )
50 NEXT
```

```
 60 CLG
110 GCOL 0,129
120 FOR Y% = 1 TO 1000 STEP 4
130    VDU 24, 0; Y%; 1250; Y%;
140    CLG
150 NEXT
```

This is a very practical point because you can draw lines of any thickness without having to worry about triangle filling or flood filling, and without complicated programming. You only have to alter the end number in the VDU statement:-

```
VDU 24, 0; Y%; 1250; Y% + 12;
```

It makes sense to add or subtract only in multiples of 4 as this is the minimum change noticeable on the screen.

An extension of this use of windows is to make borders. A border is only a box within a box, so all we need to do is:-

```
10 MODE 2
20 GCOL0, 139                     set a colour
30 VDU24, 0; 0; 1250; 1000;       define a window
40 CLG                            clear graphics
50 GCOL0, 140                     set a different colour
60 VDU24, 100; 100; 1150; 900;    define a smaller window
70 CLG                            clear graphics
80 END
```

Why not make this into a generalised Procedure, passing position, size and colour:-

```
1000 DEF PROC_box(posnx, posny, boxlen, boxwid, col)
1010    VDU24, posnx; posny; (posnx+boxlen); (posny+boxwid);
1020    GCOL0, col
1030    CLG
1040 ENDPROC
```

WINDOWS AND CURSOR

Cursors have a habit of ending up in the wrong place at the wrong time. There is one thing certain and a little unusual. If you form a window, do some graphics, then CLG, the Graphics cursor will end up in the position it was at before the CLG. This can be useful or a menace depending on what you want to do. Just be aware of it.

USE OF COLOUR

COLOURFUL HIDDEN DELIGHTS

We hear so much about dithered colours and mixed pixels that it may come as a shock to find that there is life beyond GCOL4. Try this little program which starts at GCOL0,60. Press any key to change the number which is at the top of the screen.

What the procedure does is to show you a striped screen - this is produced by GCOL figures above 5. We are sure that there is a perfectly logical order to the effects you will find - but we haven't found it yet!

```
10 MODE2
20 FOR num% = 60 TO 250
30   CLS
40   PRINT num%
50   base% = 127
60   FOR Y% = 400 TO 100 STEP - 300
70     FOR X% = 0 TO 3
80       base% = base% + 1
90       VDU 24, (100+X%*248);Y%; ((100+X%*248)+232);Y%+250;
100      VDU 18, num%, base%
110      CLG
120    NEXT
130  NEXT
140  J = GET
150 NEXT
```

You will notice that a lot of the colours appear to be repeated but the combinations of colour tend to be different.

One thing to watch out for - if you use triangle plot to fill spaces you can end up with an ugly unfilled diagonal line across a filled space, owing to the way the machine does its plotting. The method of rectangle fill, shown earlier in this chapter, eliminates this.

(Also see the same section for a comparison of filling speeds in colour.)

WHEN RED IS RED = FALSE

If you want to change a block of colour from Red to Blue and later back to Red again there is no problem. Use VDU 19, etc. But, what happens if you have two areas of Red and only want to change one of them?

There are a few obvious possibilities:-

1.   Re-draw and re-colour one area. Good, but not always practicable.

2.   Put a window round the colour you want to change and alter
     it using VDU19 - only it doesn't work!

3.   Define one area in RED (COL1) and define the other area in
     flashing Red COL9. Now stop it flashing with *FX9,0 - this
     makes the flash rate infinity. Now alter this colour (COL9)
     using VDU 19.

This method gives us two different ways of obtaining the same colour. But it is
possible to have three reds, the third one being COL 14. Rather than breaching
copyright and putting down word for word what the User Guide says, look at *FX 9
and *FX 10 Very handy!

NOW YOU SEE IT....!

Sometimes it is nice to make something disappear once you have drawn it, but
maybe not the whole picture. To do this use EOR - in other words GCOL 3, X
where X is the colour of the 'line' you wish to rub out. Just re-draw the bit you want
to make disappear using this GCOL. This has been mentioned elsewhere, but it
bears repeating in a different manner!

NEVER WATCH AN ARTIST AT WORK

Watching a screen being formed is not always nice: it can be performed tastefully
and to advantage, but it often takes away any professional look to a program. The
normal way of getting around this on the Beeb is to use VDU19 to change all
colours to the background colour, draw the screen, and then return the colours back
to what you want. This is slightly messy, but works.

As an alternative, try this:

        VDU 23; 0; 0; 0; 0;   blanks out the screen completely.

        VDU 23; 0,X; 0; 0; 0;   brings it back again.

Where X is 127 for Modes 0-3 and 63 for the rest of the modes.

Put the first line before your drawing routine and the second one after it.

There is a problem in that the screen is blank (black) and the picture reappears rather like a startled deer. If you prefer to have a more gentle entrance for your screen and do not mind the little extra programming, try this:-

```
VDU 19, 0, 1; 0;   Turn all colours to, say, colour 1.
VDU 19, 2, 1; 0;
VDU 19, 3, 1; 0;
VDU 19, 4, 1; 0;

VDU 19, 0, 0; 0;   Turns all colours on to own palette.
VDU 19, 2, 2; 0;
VDU 19, 3, 5; 0;
VDU 19, 4, 7; 0;
```

Alternatively, form your screen and then save it as a screen dump. When you need it *LOAD from disc. Details follow.

Prepare a program to form the particular screen: then at the point where it has just been formed put the following line

```
*SAVE screen1 XXXX 8000
```

where XXXX is   3000 for Mode 0,1,2
                      5800 for Mode 5
                      7000 for Mode 7

This takes the image from the screen and saves it to disc as a file called Screen1. You should note that a Mode 0 screen needs 20K available on the disc - so you can only store five screens onto a 100K disc.

Now you can alter your main program so that instead of all the graphics commands required to form the screen, simply replace with

```
*LOAD Screen1 XXXX
```

where XXXX is the same number it was SAVEd with. Warning - do make certain you have set the Mode correctly, as otherwise results are weird!

This technique is marvellous for Mode 7 screens - they load very quickly. Mode 2 screens take 2-3 seconds.

A refinement of this method for those with a B+, Master or Archimedes, is to alternate between the main area and shadow. Build a picture in main memory, turn the screen on, meanwhile build a new screen in Shadow memory, switch the screen to shadow, meanwhile build a screen in main memory .... This method can provide very smooth movement, which works well on the Master and Archimedes but is less sophisticated on the BBC-B+.

GRAPHICS

MOVING ITEMS AROUND THE SCREEN

A slightly more mundane way than screen swapping of achieving 'animation' on the BBC-B, B+ and Master is to plot and re-plot as follows.

Shifting things around the screen is quite easy if you have a procedure to do it. This little program shifts an arrow around the screen using the cursor keys. It is the key to all simple animation - it will, of course, need modifying as all aliens are not shaped like a little arrow.....

The image flickers a little: this is because there is a time when there is no picture on the screen at all. It may make you appreciate those flicker-free games!

```
 10 VDU 23,241,248,192,160,144,136,4,2,1   Define the arrow.
 20 MOVE X%,Y%                         Move to screen position.
 30 *FX 15,1                            Clear keyboard buffer.
 40 GCOL 3,2                          Set overprinting option.
 50 VDU 241                                   Print arrow
 60 REPEAT
 70  REPEAT
 80   V%=X%                                    See text
 90   W%=Y%                                    See text
100   X%=X%+(INKEY(-26)-INKEY(-122))*4    Move right or left
110   IF (X%>1216 OR X%<64) THEN X%=V%  Check horizontal limits.
120   Y%=Y%+(INKEY(-42)-INKEY(-58))*4     Move up or down
130   IF Y%<264 OR Y%>956 Y%=W%        Check vertical limits
140  UNTIL V%<>X% OR W%<>Y% OR INKEY(-74) Until some movement.
150  MOVE V%,W%:VDU 241                 Rub out old position.
160  MOVE X%,Y%:VDU 241            Move new position, print.
170 UNTIL INKEY(-74)                          Until <CR>
180 MOVE X%,Y%:VDU 241                    Rub out arrow
210 REPEAT:UNTIL INKEY(-74)=FALSE    Until finger off <CR>
```

Explanation.

X% & Y% are the co-ordinates you set of the position for the arrow to appear when you call the procedure. They could be passed to the procedure or set globally.

*FX 15,1 gets rid of any 'muck' which may be present in the keyboard buffer. You can probably get away without it, but it does ensure that any key-strokes before the procedure are zapped.

GCOL 3,2 The number 3 indicates the EOR function - this stands for Exclusive OR. If you print on a background colour, the character 'appears'. Print the same character at the same position and it 'disappears': by this means a shape can be made to move easily. See below for a fuller explanation of how this works.

VDU 241 VDU before a character number is equivalent to PRINT.

V% & W% These variables store the position at which the character appears on the screen so that, when X% & Y% indicate that it is to be moved to a new position, these two may be used to un-plot the old position.

INKEY with negative numbers indicates a key being pressed. In this case -26 & -122 are the horizontal cursors, -42 & -58 the vertical.

IF statements These check that the arrow position will not go off screen. The figures given are for a window of a particular size for one of our programs. You will have to insert your own sizes.

UNTIL V%<>X% etc. Tests to see if the cursor keys have been used and therefore the arrow needs moving; or if <CR> indicates that you are fed up or want to stop.

150-160 Whichever option you have chosen, rub out old arrow, and print new one in new position.

170 If you have pressed <Return> earlier, this lets you out.

180 This rubs out the arrow if you are exiting the procedure. If you want to retain it, don't use this line.

210 This line is important. Unlike GET, INKEY just finds out if a finger is down, so you could slip out of the procedure before your finger was off the key and cause all sorts of havoc! This makes certain that you can't get out until you have lifted your finger.

CIRCLES AND SUCH

Drawing circles can be made quicker by a number of neat tricks.

1. Pre-calculate values of Sin and Cos which you will need
    and store them in an array. This is especially useful if
    you are doing a lot of circular graphics' work.

2. Be frugal with the number of points you plot. The
    resolution of the screen is not all that great and you may
    be able to get away with a coarser image than you think.
    (For example, it is useless to think in terms of 1280
    positions across the screen. There are only 1280/4
    available, so only mention every fourth one when plotting.)

3. Calculate a Sin/Cos combination for a certain angular
    position and then use it in each of the four quadrants.
    i.e. draw all four quarters of the circle simultaneously (well, nearly).

4. Don't draw a circle, draw a regular N-agon (an N-sided
    figure), where N is greater than 25 - then you will only be
    drawing straight lines. You won't be able to tell the
    difference at a distance. The number of sides depends upon
    the Mode you are in and the size of the circle - if small,
    you can get away with fewer sides and therefore have a quicker routine.

5. Forget it, buy the Acornsoft Graphics ROM. (GXR)

6. Throw away your BBC-B, B+ or ELECTRON and buy one of the
    later models, they all have commands like CIRCLE, ELLIPSE,
    RECTANGLE as standard.

18. GENERAL TIPS AND HINTS

INPUT ROUTINES

Often we want the computer to accept only a certain type of information at a particular point in the program - eg. only numbers: or only letters: or numbers and letters but not symbols: or only certain letters: or only certain numbers: or accept letters in upper and lower case as symbolising the same thing.

Why bother? Why not wait until the user of your program has worked out that the shift keys are set to lower case? If he is a computer newcomer, or a first-time user of your program then he may never work out what has happened - as far as he is concerned the keyboard has seized up solid against him.

Again, if you ask "Save Y/N?", and set the computer to SAVE only if upper case Y is inserted (all other entries being disregarded), your first time user will get very disillusioned when he thinks he has saved an item, only to find (too late) that he unaccountably hasn't. He won't be buying your program...

Your programs should, quite simply, be able to get out of all unexpected situations with the least interruption to its workings. This is part of making your program 'user-friendly'. It is, at heart, the difference between the amateur and professional program. More of this later.

It is really quite easy to get the computer to check at any point what is or is not permissible. There is no point in using INPUT or INPUTLINE. It is cumbersome to check for 'illegal' characters after the input has been completed and then to have to go back to ask for a complete new input if there has been an error. Instead, check each character as it is entered.

We can take a single character from the keyboard input with the GET and GET$ functions (see section 14). Thus:-

```
J = GET    or    J$ = GET$
```

This gives you the ASCII code or the actual character of the key just pressed but does no checking as to whether the entry is allowable.

```
REPEAT : J$ = GET$ : UNTIL J$ = "Z"
```

174

This gives adequate checking if you really mean that you only want an Upper case 'Z'. If you want to accept both upper and lower case then you need something like:-

```
REPEAT : J$ = CHR$(GET AND &DF): UNTIL J$ = "Z"
```

(GET AND &DF is explained later on in this chapter)

A simple input routine like this is fine if you are only having one possible input character, but is messy if there are more than a couple of allowable answers. This then develops into a more sophisticated construction:-

```
10 REPEAT
20   X = INSTR("YNP",CHR$(GET AND &DF))
30 UNTIL X>0 AND X<4
```

Here, the string in line 20 gives the range of letters which will be accepted. A more generalized Procedure might be:-

```
100 DEF PROC_in(A$)
110   REPEAT
120     X = INSTR(A$,CHR$(GET AND &DF))
130   UNTIL X>0 AND X< = LEN(A$)
140 ENDPROC
```

Here the string can be of any length and the limits in line 130 takes the length of string into account. The number returned by X could be used as an ON GOTO trigger as the position of the letter input in the string is given.

However, these are relatively unsophisticated input controllers. The next section contains some really practical answers to input vetting.

A MORE COMPLEX INPUT ROUTINE

```
10 MODE7
20 VDU 23, 1, 0; 0; 0; 0; :REM Cursor off
30 REM Set up the acceptance strings
40 alphaup$ = "-'ABCDEFGHIJKLMNOPQRSTUVWXYZ"
50 alphalow$ = "-'abcdefghijklmnopqrstuvwxyz"
60 number$="0123456789"
70 REM Just a loop to run the PROC
80 REPEAT:CLS
90   REM PROC_input (prompt$, x, y, in$, length, x1, y1)
100   REM prompt$ is printed at x,y
110   REM in$ contains 'a' for lower case
120   REM " " 'A' " upper case
```

```
130   REM " " '1' " numbers
140   REM It can contain any combination
150   REM for example
160   PROC_input("Your Surname please",6,12,"Aa",12,14,15)
170   CLS: PRINT TAB(14,20)""; name$
180   PRINT TAB(15,22)"Press any key"
190   J = GET
200 UNTIL FALSE
210 END
220   DEFPROC_input(prompt$, x, y, in$, length, x1, y1)
230   *FX 4,1
240   REM initialise working strings
250   work$ = STRING$(64," ") :work$=""
260   name$ = " " :name$=""
270   REM Select which combination for acceptance
280   IF INSTR(in$, "A") THEN work$ = work$ + alphaup$
290   IF INSTR(in$, "a") THEN work$ = work$ + alphalow$
300   IF INSTR(in$, "1") THEN work$ = work$ + number$
310   PRINTTAB(x, y)prompt$
320   PRINTTAB(x1, y1)STRING$(length, ".")
330   REPEAT
340    REPEAT
350     REPEAT
360      *FX 15,1
370      A$ = GET$
390      IF INSTR(work$,A$) = 0 VDU7
400     UNTIL (INSTR(work$, A$)) > 0
             OR A$ = CHR$13 OR A$ = CHR$127
410     IF A$ = CHR$127 THEN name$=LEFT$(name$,LEN(name$)-1)
             :PRINTTAB(x1,y1)name$;"."
420    UNTILA$<>CHR$127
430    IF A$<>CHR$13 AND LEN(name$) < > length name$=name$+A$
:PRINTTAB(x1,y1)name$
440    IF LEN(name$) = length:VDU7
450   UNTIL A$ = CHR$13 AND name$ < > ""
460   *FX 4,0
470 ENDPROC
```

Well, did you get past that one? This is a little more complicated than the last
routine and needs a little explanation.

The basic idea is that a group of strings is set up at the start of your program (lines
40-60) which contain all the characters which could be accepted by the input routine
throughout the program. In this particular case they are set up as three separate
strings for Numeric (0-9), Upper case Alpha with the usual symbols that go with

input data of names, and the same set in lower case.

There follows a short loop to illustrate the procedure in action, lines 80-210. The working Procedure forms the remainder of the program.

The following information is passed to the procedure:-

The prompt string: this is the sentence which asks for input.

X & Y, which give the position for the prompt string to be printed.

In$, which contains your choice of string from which input will be accepted: this may be any combination of the three supplied, or you can devise your own.

Length, which is the length allowed for the reply string.

X1 & Y1, which gives the position of the start of the reply string.

When called, the prompt string is printed out and dots are placed in the position of the reply string, one dot for each allowed character.

As characters are input, they are checked against the check strings: if the character is not valid, it is not accepted or printed and a beep sounds.

When a character is accepted it is printed over a dot which disappears. If a valid character is printed but you wish to change it, the Delete key will get rid of it, a beep will sound, and the dot will be replaced.

If an attempt is made to put in more than the required number of characters, a beep sounds and the character is not accepted.

Pressing <Return> tells the Procedure that the user considers his input is complete.

This is a fair skeleton from which to start. Various things can, and probably should, be done to improve it. You could, for example, leave out all VDU7 and remain in blissful silence.

GETTING NUMBERS FROM THE KEYBOARD

Use GET-48 to return the actual number rather than the ASCII code when you press a numeric key.

eg X = GET - 48

Key '3', ASCII code = 51   51 - 48 = 3

177

COUNT YOUR DIGITS

Sometimes it is nice to have a multi digit number input without having to use
<Return> (as with INPUT). GET is the answer but it only accepts one character at
a time.

This piece of code uses GET in a pre-determined loop.

```
 10 CLS
 20 PRINT TAB(6,10)"Input number of digits ( >0 )"
 30 INPUT number
 40 PROC_input(number)
 70 END
 80 :
 90 :
100 DEFPROC_input(length)
110  A$=""
115  :
120  FOR times = 1 TO length
125     :
130     REPEAT
140       J$ = CHR$(GET OR &10)
150     UNTIL J$>="0" AND J$<="9"
155     :
160     A$ = A$ + J$
166     PRINT TAB(16,12)A$
170  NEXT
175 :
180 ENDPROC
```

Notice that you cannot 'rub out' what you have input in this routine. This sort of
routine is useful when you want to input something like a telephone number with
leading zeros and a fixed length. The length would be put in automatically by the
program of course.

ALL-PURPOSE PROCEDURE FOR SINGLE-KEY VETTING WITHIN A PROGRAM

Often you want to present a set of fixed alternatives as part of your program

eg "Save Y/N"   "(A)gree, (U)nsure, (D)isagree"

It often more user-friendly not to require a <Return> after each answer, especially if
there are a lot of questions. However it is cumbersome to set up each question to

accept only its own alternative one-letter answers. A general-purpose Procedure is the answer.... (isn't it always!)

```
500 DEFPROC_answer(alternatives$)
505  *FX 15, 1
510  REPEAT
520   A% = INSTR(alternatives$, GET$)
530  UNTIL A% > 0
540  IF A% MOD 2 = 1 THENA%=A%-1
550  answer$ = MID$(alternatives$,A%,1)
560 ENDPROC
```

This will act as an all-purpose routine to allow acceptable single-key answers only to be input, and ensures that all answers are returned in upper case only, however the keyboard is set at the time. (NOTE,there is another way of handling 'Upper case only': this is dealt with later in this chapter.)

Call it with :-

```
35 PROC_answer("YyNn")
```

This means that the computer will wait until any key contained within the string "YyNn" is pressed. Therefore if you have cause to ask for a Yes/No answer on one occasion, and a (Y)es/(N)o/(D)on't know answer on another, you would call the first with

```
PROC_answer ("YyNn")
```

and the second with

```
PROC_answer("YyNnDd")
```
    etc etc.

If any key is pressed other than one contained within alternative$ the computer will ignore it. This, then, is a very useful general procedure which strictly limits the intake, but in a very adaptable way.

Note two things:-

1.   Any character entered from the keyboard goes first into
      the keyboard buffer which can store up to 32 characters in
      the order in which they were entered. Even if the
      characters are not at that minute accepted by the program
      they are still stored 'ready for off'. *FX15, 1 flushes
      (i.e. throws away the contents of) this buffer. If your
      hand is resting on the keyboard just before a question

179

comes up, it inadvertently puts characters into the
keyboard buffer (without their being written to the screen,
so you don't know they're there). If your next program
input is done with GET or GET$, then this accepts the first
character stored in the keyboard buffer - which might not
be what you wanted. Therefore, use *FX15, 1 to flush the
keyboard buffer (or alternatively *FX15 which flushes all
buffers) before ALL occasions when you use GET or GET$.

2.   The procedure will only work if the passed parameter
       (alternative$) contains all the acceptable alternatives in
       pairs of Upper case/lower case, in that order.   (eg"YyNnDd")

The number of alternative letters can be as large as you wish. This can be
expanded to provide a command mode where there are a large number of
alternatives. eg Instructions are printed on the screen:- (A)ction now (F)ile for future
reference (P)rint now Print (L)ater . . .

which can be controlled with PROCanswer("AaFfPpLl...") For a further development
of this technique, see 'CHANGING CASE in the next section.

COMMAND INTERPRETERS

Although menus are often a good way to steer the user through a program, many
programs are command-driven - i.e. they wait for specific typed commands. Also,
some programs which are menu-driven have in addition a sort of 'zip code' which
allows the experienced user to by-pass the menu system if he knows exactly where
he wants to go and issues the correct command.

Such command-driven systems use a variant on the Procedure mentioned above.
Instead of using the INSTR function to search for acceptable one-character
answers, it instead searches for allowed command words.

All keyboard entries are first assembled using an input routine (see above), put into
the appropriate case, and then put through a variant of PROC_answer in which the
INSTR function is used to seek out whole command words. For example, if the line
of input is stored in input$ then:-

```
DEFPROC_command
REPEAT
PROC_input
A%=INSTR("SAVEPRINTLOAD",input$)
IF  A% = 1 ....(saves data)
IF  A% = 5 ....(prints data)
IF  A% = 10 ....(loads data)
```

```
        .
        .
    UNTIL A%>0
    ENDPROC
```

will achieve the required results.

SEQUENCES OF SYMBOLS ON FUNCTION KEYS

Sometimes it is desirable to use function keys for an answer to a question where the options are written on a Function key strip.

*FX225 may be of help here. It allows you to reset the base value of the keys - in other words the output of the key will be the number of the key, plus the base value. If you set the base value to 65 then on pressing F0 the output from the key will be ASCII 65+0, which is the character "A": F1 gives B, F2 gives C etc. If the base value were 48 the function keys would generate these characters instead: F0 = 0, F1 = 1, etc.

To set the base value .. *FX225,base value (e.g. *FX225,65)

As well as resetting the base value for the red keys as they stand it is also possible to alter the base value for other ways of using the red keys, eg SHIFT/function key, CTRL/function key etc.

To set base numbers for:-

SHIFT/function key	use	*FX226
CTRL/function key	use	*FX227
SHIFT/CTRL/function key	use	*FX228

And on the Master, to set base numbers for the number keypad use *FX238

While we are talking about the Master keypad, if you don't want SHIFT to operate on the keypad use *FX254

CHANGING CASE

The keyboard can be set by the operator to give upper or lower case: therefore any program must make sure that answers in either case are dealt with properly. Whatever the setting of the keyboard, the following always gives an answer in UPPER CASE.

```
    J = (GET AND &DF)
```
            to store ASCII code in J

The opposite can also be done, but notice that OR is used instead of AND. These produce answers in lower case.

```
J = (GET  OR &20)
```
to store ASCII code in J

These routines work as long as the input is vetted to prevent input of anything other than alphabet characters. Outside the range of alphabet characters

```
J=GET OR &10
```

will change Sign to Numeric

```
J=GET AND &EF
```

will convert Numeric to Sign

Alternatively, from within the program, set the keyboard to whichever state you want by the following:-

```
*FX202,16  ( for SHIFT LOCK )
*FX202,32  ( for UPPER CASE )
*FX202,48  ( for LOWER CASE )
*FX202,128 ( for REVERSE SHIFT )
*FX202,144 ( for REVERSE SHIFT LOCK )
```

Reverse Shift? The keyboard is normally in Capitals and gives Lower Case when SHIFT is pressed. This can be VERY useful when programming as it allows most items (especially keywords) to be in Upper Case whilst SHIFT allows easy insertion of Variable names in Lower Case. Doing it this way is much less fiddly with the SHIFT key.

DEALING WITH DATES

Dates can be awkward things to handle. Not only do we write them in different ways (Sept.20 '86, 20th September 1986, 20/9/86, 20/09/86, 20.9.86 etc), but Americans write them in the order Month/Day/Year!

It is impossible to do orthodox arithmetic on them (1.1.87 is later than 31.12.86 but you get the opposite result if you miss out the dots). There are the hazards of leap years, not forgetting the additional oddities of years ending in 00, some of which are leap and some not.

Whatever the form in which they are input at the keyboard (American or English notation), why not store them as YYMMDD to allow numerical sorting? You can use a resident integer variable for the combined value in order to pass the date across various programs in a linked suite. Don't forget to insert zeros in the right places - the ninth month must be '09' and not '9'. Therefore, if y% contains the last two numbers of the year, m% the month and d% the day, the 'date number' is y%*10000+m%*100+d%.

Alternatively you could use three resident integers for day, month and year (but don't use Y% for the year if you are going to use machine code as it is used for other things.)

Storing a lot of dates can be wasteful of space, especially if you store them as a string: it is more efficient to store them as a single number.

There is a little trick to find the day of the week, given the date: it is called Zeller's congruence.

The day of the week

```
=INT(2.6 * M - 0.2) + d + y + INT(y/4) + INT(c/4)-2*c MOD 7
```

```
where D = day of the month
      M = month of the year
      Y = the year in the century (0-99)
      C = Century number
```

ESCAPE AND ERROR HANDLING

ALTERING THE KEY TO ESCAPE

The ESCAPE key gives a convenient and non-destructive way of exiting gracefully from the program, preserving all variable and string values for examination. It can also be used to return complex programs to a fixed starting point through error trapping.

Although 'Escape' is useful, it can also be a nuisance as the Escape key is next door to the 'TAB' and '1' keys and you may touch it by mistake. *FX 200, 1 will disable the Escape key (*FX 200,0 gets it back). This can be useful in preventing, say, children interrupting an educational program.

What happens if we want to be able to use Escape but do not want to have the chance of hitting it accidentally? In this case use *FX 220, N to change the Escape instruction to another key, or, better, to another combination of keys. With this instruction you can make any reasonable key on the keyboard act as Escape.

You could set it up to be a single key (rather silly) or a combination of 2 keys. Work out number N as follows:

Decide Key combination - (say)	CTRL/E.
Find ASCII number from this. Type	PRINT ASC(GET$) <CR>
Press CTRL/E Note number on screen.	5 is printed.
The call is therefore *FX 220,5	

There are some combinations which are more useful than others. For example, SHIFT/A is not going to be much fun if you have to put any script into the program! It is not possible to use CTRL/left-hand square bracket as this is already Escape.

The most useful would appear to be combinations with CTRL. As the normal function of the combination you choose is suspended in favour of Escape, it would be wise to choose keys which you do not normally use. Here are a couple of suggestions. CTRL/@ - normally does nothing. CTRL/G - gives a beep. Although CTRL/G and VDU 7 both cause a beep, you can still use VDU 7 in the program to give a beep and yet still Escape with CTRL/G. In other words, the two commands are not exactly equivalent. (This apparently strange effect is quite easily explained. The VDU command is a direct OUTPUT to the screen, whilst (in the unaltered form) CTRL/G is an INPUT that causes the computer to output a VDU 7 command. When you change the CTRL/G to ESCAPE you merely redirect the output of CTRL/G to Escape and not to VDU7.)

ERRORS AND ERROR TRAPPING

Errors can occur in even in the best regulated circles. Some errors are fatal, should be treated as such and allowed to do their thing. Some errors are non-fatal, can be trapped, then used intelligently to allow entry back into the program in a controlled way.

Every standard error has an error number which can be looked at and used. (see chapter 22) The program below shows a typical way of using an 'error' to start the program again. If the program detects an error it goes back to the place where 'ON ERROR PROC_error' was in the listing.

In the following demonstration we will press the Escape key to provide an 'Error'.

```
10 ON ERROR PROC_error
20:
30 REPEAT
40   PRINT "HI THERE FRIEND"
50 UNTIL FALSE
60 END
70:
```

```
 80 DEFPROC_error
 90   CLS
100   PRINTTAB(5,10)"DON'T DO THAT"
110   pause = INKEY(100)
120   PRINTTAB(7,13)"NOW PRESS A KEY!"
130   IF GET
140 ENDPROC
```

RUN the program, then press 'Escape' to get the full effect.

Although this is a trivial example it illustrates a most important principle - how to deal with an error without terminating the program. This is a very practical point with complex programs. Consider a large program, used in business. There are a number of possible errors - some predictable, some unforeseen: potential errors include unforeseen and complex bugs, discs that cannot accept any more data, insertion of the wrong disc in a drive, etc. Any of these problems could cause the program to crash, losing precious data, and, if the failure occurs whilst writing to a disc, possibly corrupting the discs to such an extent that existing data becomes garbled.

If you have full error trapping in such a program, then if an error is detected:

1.   The program does not crash

2.   The program tells you which error has occurred (which
      usually allows you to do something about it, such as
      putting the correct disc in the drive, or at least, closing
      down the system without losing information).

3.   You are then returned to a standard point in the program
      from which you can continue - such as the main menu, or a
      sub-menu.

However, no.system of trapping can ever take into account fatal errors, such as 'No room'.

As each error has a number attached to it it is possible to treat different errors in different ways. For example, the use of the Escape key gives error message number 17. If your error subroutine reads thus:-

```
10 ON ERROR GOTO 20000
20 PROC_main_menu
   .
   .
20000 REM ERROR TRAP
```

```
20010 IF ERR=17 GOTO 20 ELSE REPORT : PRINT"Press any key"
20020 REPEAT UNTIL GET
20030 GOTO 20
```

then pressing 'Escape' takes you back to the main menu without interruption. With any other error the computer will report the problem, wait until a key is pressed and then return to the main menu. It could just as easily return other errors to different part of the program, if it suited you better.

Note that the computer loses its bearings when an error occurs, so it cannot return you to the point you were at when the error occurred. In particular it cannot return you to anything other than the main part of the program.

It is possible to use error trapping intelligently to return you to various specified points in the program. In this way the Escape key can be used to guide the user around. There are two ways this can be performed:-

```
10 ON ERROR GOTO 90
20 :
30 PROCmenu
40 ON FN_answer GOTO 50, 60, 70
45 :
50 REPEAT:PROC_input: PROC_save: UNTIL FALSE
60 REPEAT:PROC_get_record: PROC_alter: UNTIL FALSE
70 REPEAT:PROC_get_record:PROC_ask: PROC_print: UNTIL FALSE
80 :
85 END
87 :
88 REM ERROR HANDLING
90 IF ERROR = 17 GOTO 30 ELSE REPORT:J=GET:GOTO 30
```

This structure generates a menu from which you are directed into one of a number of continuous loops. Each REPEAT.. UNTIL loop will never terminate: very useful if you have an indefinite number of items to process (such as adding customers' addresses into a file, or carrying out a specific calculation). To stop going round in circles you do the obvious, logical thing, and press ESCAPE.... so you go back to the menu page. Any other error is reported before returning to the main menu.

A second way of using the Escape key is by using different ON ERROR instructions in different parts of the program. eg

```
10 PROC_start_up
20   ON ERROR RUN
30 PROC_first_question
40   ON ERROR GOTO 20
```

```
50 PROC_second_question
60  ON ERROR GOTO 40
70 PROC_third_question
80  ON ERROR GOTO 60
```

What is happening here? It looks crazy - until you realise that if you are dissatisfied with your answer to question one you have only to press Escape and it takes you back to question one again. If you have answered question two and are dissatisfied with the answer to either question one or question two, one press of the escape key will allow you to re-answer question two - and two presses of the escape key will take you back to question one again... etc

GENERAL HINTS

SPEEDS OF GOSUB AND PROCEDURE

There is a lot of controversy about the relative merits and speeds of these two structures. Some say that one is faster, some, the other.

The interesting thing is that they are both right. As usual, it is a matter of circumstances altering cases.

Without going into too much detail...

GOSUBS. The computer searches from the start of the program every time one is called. This means that if the section of code is near the front, the routine is very fast: but this is not the only factor.

PROCEDURES. Once a procedure has been used, its position is put on a lookup list and the time taken to find it is independent of position, but the actual name can have an effect!

We are often told that if a Procedure name is over seven letters long it takes much longer to find. This doesn't appear to be true - the access time seems to go up by about 0.00001 second for every letter added - probably as a result of extra interpretation time.

Therefore if you are not worried about memory space as well, you can have nice long meaningful names for procedures, which greatly aids the readability of the program.

If you want absolute maximum speed from a Procedure make certain that it is called early on in the program so it goes near the head of the look-up table. It may be appropriate to make a dummy call to the procedure at the very beginning of the program in order to get it placed at the top of the list.

If you are anxious to get maximum speed out of your system using BASIC, try both methods with the coding in the intended place and with the final name. Only in this way will you get a true picture.

Mind you, if you are that worried about speed, you should be thinking of learning Assembler, or buying a Compiler!

RESIDENT INTEGER VARIABLES

The resident integer variables in the Beeb are A%, B%, C% .....Z%, and @% 27 in all. The commands RUN, CLEAR, NEW do not alter their values, whereas all other variables are cleared. In addition, CHAINing or LOADing another program does not affect them.

This means you may pass values from one program to the next. You may have a long and complicated program which can work out a series of values, and another long and complex program which uses them, but both programs together are too long to reside in memory. The answer is simple - use the first program to calculate the values, place the answers in the resident integers, and CHAIN the second program to use them.

You may want to pass date or age information down a series of programs to save repeated input - this is the way to do it! However, A% P% X% and Y% all have special functions in machine code so avoid using these particular resident integers if there are any machine code sections in your suite of programs. Similarly, in all programs @% holds information about screen layout of print, so take care over interfering with it.

EOR AND HOW TO USE IT

There are three main logic conditions which we use in computer language - AND, OR and EOR.

AND   If you AND I get into the boat it will sink (but if only
             one of us gets in - or nobody - it won't)
             ```
             IF X=1 AND Y=1 THEN PROC_sink
             ```

OR   If either you OR I get into the boat it will sink, and it
             certainly will if we both get in (but it won't if neither gets in)
             ```
             IF X=1 OR Y=1 THEN PROC_sink
             ```

EOR   (Exclusive OR) If either you EOR I get through the door we
will be able to - but if we both try it, or nobody tries
it, no-one will get through.

```
IF X=1 EOR Y=1 THEN PROC_get_through
```

EOR means Exclusive Or. It applies when either one thing is true or another, but
not both together. (The more commonly met OR applies when either one thing is
true or another thing is true, and also if they are both true.) This concept can be
confusing! If you find you don't quite grasp the idea after a couple of looks through
the next three examples, have another go after looking at the colour 'bit' below.

So if we set A=1 and B=2 then:-

```
IF A = 1 OR B = 2 THEN PRINT "Yes"
```

will print 'Yes'.

```
IF A = 1 EOR B = 2 THEN PRINT "Yes"
```

will print nothing.

However

```
IF A = 1 EOR B = 1 THEN PRINT "Yes"
```

will print 'Yes'

In the same way, if two Binary numbers are EOR'ed together, the resulting number
will contain 'ones' only where the digits are different:-

number X.	11001111
number Y.	01110011

Result of X EOR Y	10111100

Look at what happens if we EOR colour numbers. This is the way to make objects
disappear behind others in graphics modes.

Let's say the background colour is cyan (6 = 0110), character printing colour,
green (2 = 0010).

number 1.	0110	
number 2.	0010	

Result of EOR	0100	= 4 = BLUE!

So, what happens is that the character is actually printed in Blue, the result of the EOR. Now lets see what happens when we overprint the character (in Blue remember) with the green number.

number 1 .	0100	= 4	=	Blue
number 2 .	0010	= 2	=	Green
	____			
Result of EOR	0110	= 6	=	CYAN!
	____			

If you remember, the background was cyan, so having done this weird EOR print we have our character on screen but we can't see it. (The old Black cat in a coal hole on a very dark night principle). What a lot of use! Well, yes it is.

What we have done is to print in the same place twice using the same colour. The first EOR makes the shape appear but the second time makes it disappear. It 'toggles'. If you continued to print in the same place the letter would just flash on and off! This is the basis of animation. (Print . Print . Move . Print . Print . Move etc) Also we can make objects go behind objects by choosing the colours carefully.

BRACKETS?

It is not always necessary to use brackets. The prime example is after CHR$. CHR$(89) can be shortened to CHR$89 or CHR$ 89. However, certain other keywords such as TAB and LEFT$ not only demand brackets, but there must be NO space between the command and the bracket.

THE O.S. WILL FIND YOU OUT!

The Operating System is both clever and DUMB. On the one hand it can pick a KEYWORD from the front of a jumble of letters which you are using, like... INPUTASPIRIN, and correctly assume that your program is not going to get a headache this time. On the other hand it cannot tell that NOT_TONIGHT is a variable which is true and not a logical inversion. It also thinks that TOMORROW consists of TO (the keyword) and MORROW (a variable).

The moral.... use small letters for variables and CAPITAL LETTERS for keywords.

BLANKING OUT FUNCTION KEY MESSAGES!

It can be very irritating to have function key messages written all over the screen. There are several ways of getting rid of them. The obvious ways of putting CLS or backspace and delete are messy and ineffectual. The easiest way seems to be to create a window of no size! If you ain't got nowhere to write, you can't see it.

This idea is easier said than done. In general you want to use the function keys at odd times, not necessarily at a specific defined point in a program. This means that the window definition and its subsequent dissolution must be on the key. Problem... if it is on the key it will be seen before the window is defined.

There is a way round this but it calls for a small amount of devious behaviour. We are going to insert into the key definition the code that will make the screen ROM create a window of infinitely small size. We cannot use VDU28,1,1,1,1 in the key, because it will be printed onto the screen in this form before being sent to the screen ROM for action. Instead we have to substitute the characters that VDU28,1,1,1,1 gets turned into so that it is fed directly into the screen ROM, and is acted upon immediately.

You need some form of memory editor like DISC DOCTOR.

Key definitions are kept at &B00 on the B & B+. First define your key as follows:-

```
*KEY0 ABCDE ************** Z
```

The group of letters could be any symbols, and are put it solely to make space for the code we really want to put in, by replacement, later. The ******** represent what you want the key to do. The spaces are not needed (in fact they waste precious memory) but are put in here for clarity.

Having defined your key, do *MZAP B00 (or the equivalent command with your memory editor). ABCDE has to be changed to the equivalent of VDU 28, 1, 1, 1, 1 This works out to be

```
A = 1C       B = 1   C = 1   D = 1    E = 1
```

Turn your editor to HEX input and in place of the tokens for ABCDE (65 66 67 68 69) insert

```
1C  1  1  1  1
```

Now change token for Z (90) to 1A (restore default window) and the job is done.

Now when Key 0 is pressed, the window definition in token form is not displayed on the screen but translated directly by the operating system. The meat of the key command is written in visible form to a place on the screen which has no size and is therefore not seen. Finally the window is redefined to full screen by an invisible token.

This method will of course ruin any windows you have previously set up!

SOUND

Sound is a vast subject covered quite well in the User Guides. There is one aspect which is poorly understood and which is dealt with here, namely the synchronization of two or more sounds.

The ear is exceptionally sensitive to pitch change and position of high pitched sounds coming from the front. It is unfortunate that the three music channels on the BBC sound chip are out of tune with each other. There is nothing we can do easily about this. (It can be used to advantage, but we would rather put it out of tune ourselves!) It is possible to live with this out of tune sound - there is many a parlour piano which is much loved and never been in tune in its life.

A much more obvious error is the sound of two or three notes NEARLY being played together. It is quite hard to play chords on a computer as there are very small delays in setting up the sounds as they have to be read and interpreted one after the other. On the computer this error can be eliminated by using the first parameter of the sound command to synchronise the sounds.

The normal sound command is:

```
SOUND channel,loudness,pitch,length
```

The 'channel' parameter can be extended to give more control of the sound with four sections being included in the one number. The sections are:

1. H = Hold. If a note is dying away because of the way an envelope has been defined, then this parameter set to 1 will enable the envelope to 'finish' even if the length parameter of the sound has run out.

2. S = Synchronize. If this is set to 0 then the sound will play as soon as it is defined by the program. If set to 1 it will wait until there is one more channel ready and then both will sound EXACTLY together. If set to 2 it will wait until there are two more channels ready and if set to 3 will wait until all the channels are ready.

3. F = Flush. If set to 1 the note will stop any note already sounding on its channel and start to sound. (This overides any other notes HOLD.)

4. C = Channel number. As you can see, the normal channel number is these four sections with the first three set to Zero.

So, to sound a chord of three notes, getting rid of any note that may be on channel one:-

```
SOUND &0211, -12, 120, 5
SOUND 2, -12, 136, 5
SOUND 3, -12, 148, 5
```

CHANGING THE BEEP

If you want to be really nasty to someone, re-program his Beep!

*FX211 gives the channel 0 to 3 (How about Noise?).

*FX212 gives amplitude -15 to 0 as usual: now apply this formula

```
256 - ((num - 1)*,) i.e.  -12 gives
256 - (-13 * 8)
= 256 - 104
= 152
```
so the final command is *FX212, 152

*FX213 gives pitch (0 to 255).

*FX214 gives duration (0 to 255 (drive him mad with 255 .. infinity!))

If you want to do nasties with the envelope statement, use *FX212 again but this time you start off with the positive Envelope number and apply the formula (have a look in the Advanced User Guide page 215). This really is something to experiment with.

Uses include:

-       making a continuous sound which cannot be turned off (when
        a non-allowed user cannot enter a password correctly)

-       reducing the irritating beep sound in commercial programs
        where some auditory cue is helpful to indicate that
        something has happened (eg that you are attempting to enter
        non-allowed character). A sweeter noise is a good idea if
        the beep is used frequently.

RANDOM RANDOM

One of us learned quite a nice tune owing to the fact that the random function on the BBC (and most other computers) is utterly predictable as it is just a list of random numbers stored in memory. He wrote a program with a randomly generated tune as a header. It was some time before he realised that every time he switched on, the tune was the same, which was not quite what was wanted!. However, there are ways round the problem.

It is possible to start the random sequence at an unpredictable place by use of a 'seed' number which you put in. To get over the fact that humans are not as random as they should be it is necessary to use another machine function to make it really random.

When the machine is switched on, the internal clock starts ticking away. We can use this as our seed. The way to set the random generator using TIME is:-

```
this = RND(-TIME)
```

where 'this' is some variable name - it doesn't matter what. Note the minus sign in the bracket which indicates that the number following is the seed. It is quite unlikely that TIME is going to be the same every time you start your program as will never press the <Return> button at exactly the same time after the machine has ben switched on.

You should only do this once, otherwise you could make it less random. We talk about the Random Function, it is really only a pseudo random function. In reality it is virtually a list of truly random numbers, but a fixed list. The range is so large, however, that to all intents and purposes it is Random.

MERGE

Merging two bits of program is a very straightforward procedure, but in the 'Book' you can be put off from the easy and adequate way because it is described as "dirty". It works! But READ note 2!

Do it like this.
```
LOAD "prog1"       <R>
PRINT ~TOP-2       <R>    this gives xxxx needed in next line.
*LOAD prog2 xxxx   <R>    loads prog2 straight after prog1.
END                <R>    this tidies up internal pointers.
```

Note 1. The ~ sign is actually the 'Tilde' or wriggle symbol to the right of the equals sign. It means 'What is to follow is to be printed in HEX'.

Note 2. You are told in most of the literature to make certain that line numbers in the two programs don't overlap. You can sometimes get away with it. Just renumber the thing after you have typed END. As an experiment try joining a program to itself, RENumber and you ought to find the thing is neatly sorted out. HOWEVER, it is wise to renumber the second program so that its LOWEST line number is higher than the first programs Highest number BEFORE merging. The problems which make this necessary arise if you use GOTO, GOSUB, RESTORE, that is, where line numbers are referred to directly.

RE-NUMBERING STORED 'RESTORE' NUMBERS

If you store a list of line numbers for the RESTORE function in a DATA statement, (eg DATA names,1230,sizes,3450 etc etc) these will not RENUMBER. Try this dodge: have a dummy line which is not used by the program. Begin it with ON p% GOTO.... and copy in all the line numbers from the DATA statement, in order. When you RENUMBER, the line with ON p% will be re-numbered, and you can copy the values from this new line back into the DATA lines.

eg.

```
2300 DATA names, 1230, sizes, 3450, heights, 7000
2310 ON p% GOTO 1230, 3450, 7000
```

After RE-Numbering you might have

```
1200 DATA names, 1230, sizes, 3450, heights, 7000
1210 ON p% GOTO 760, 1400, 1550
```

Now copy the numbers in the lower line to the appropriate places in in the upper line.

BREAK MAKES THINGS EASY

Frequently, when we are doing a programming sessions there is a sequence of key-strokes which happen again and again.

Mistake .. Escape .. MODE 7 .. list .. SWEAR .. (forgot to change CAPS LOCK) .. LIST .. SWEAR .. (forgot to put into PAGE Mode) .. CTRL N .. LIST .. Sigh with relief .. try to find the correct line.

A lot of this can be avoided by re-defining the BREAK key.

```
*KEY 10  OLD |M  |N  LIST |M
```

When BREAK is pressed OLD .. PAGE MODE ON .. LIST

This may be improved if you are doing a lot of work on a particular section by putting in the start line in the LIST command ie LIST 120, or LIST 120, 170

Remember, if this is put into a program (which is the best way to do it) then you have to run it before the key will work. However, a major disadvantage of using the BREAK key is that all the variable values are lost, which is not helpful at certain stages of debugging a listing. Under these circumstances, program a Function key with *KEY X |N LIST |M so that you can ESCAPE then press the Function key X. Alternatively, put all this in the program itself in the error trapping routine activated only when ESCAPE is pressed. (see above)

19. INCREASE THE SPEED OF YOUR PROGRAMS

A. THROUGH SOFTWARE

1.   By efficient programming.

-   avoid GOTO's entirely (they take ages to execute)

-   leave out REM's - the computer has to read them before
    going to the next instruction. Never put a REM inside a
    loop, as the computer then has to read the REM each time
    the loop is executed.

Obviously, a reduction in REMs goes against the principles of good programming
style. Therefore, have a master program with REMs included, and use a crunching
routine (taking the REMs out) to create your working program.

2.   Reduce the number of lines used by the program - avoid
     going through a lot of useless IF's eg. instead of:-

```
100 DEFPROC_select
120 IF loud% > 45 decibel% = 78
130 IF loud% > 65 decibel% = 85
140 IF loud% > 100 decibel% = 103
150 IF loud% > 150 decibel% = 120
160 ENDPROC
```

you could have

```
100 DEFPROC_select
120 IF loud% <= 45 decibel% = 0 :ENDPROC
130 IF loud% <= 65 decibel% = 78 :ENDPROC
140 IF loud% <= 100 decibel% = 85 :ENDPROC
150 IF loud% <= 150 decibel% = 103 :ENDPROC
160 decibel% = 120 :ENDPROC
```

In this way the program goes through the shortest possible path.

3. Multiple statement lines are faster (but less clear).

4. Spread out variable names through the alphabet

5. Where you can, use integer variables, and especially the
    resident integers (A% to Z% plus @%). This applies
    particularly to loops, where any change in speed is
    multiplied by the number of times the loop operates.
    Integer work is much faster than that using 'real' numbers.
    Integer division with DIV is much faster than normal
    division with integers.

If you don't understand the difference between Integer variables and Real variables,
read on.

An Integer variable is a storage box in the machine which will only accept whole
numbers (positive and negative) such as 3, -32154 etc. '%' after the variable name
designates the variable as Integer - eg. V%, total%, batsmen_out%.

A Real variable is a storage box which will accept a number with a fractional part
(eg.13.564). Any variable name such as V, total, batsmen_out etc (note the
absence of the '%') will accept numbers with or without fractional parts.

There are good reasons for having different variable types, the main two being
speed and storage space. As you might expect, a Real variable takes up more
storage space because it contains more information and therefore takes a little
longer to process. This difference is significant and very worthwhile pursuing.

So, if you want to speed things up a bit try not to use fractional numbers. (Dealing
with Sine and Cosine is awkward for this reason.)

You can enter a non-whole number into an Integer Variable (e.g. X%), but it
knocks off the bit to the right of the decimal point i.e. V% = 3.14 when printed gives
3.

Oh dear? No: it saves truncating using INT, is about 10% faster, and saves a little
bit of memory. Against it is the fact that it is not obvious what is happening.

If you deal with a mixture of integer and real arithmetic then put the integer
arithmetic first in any calculation - in this way the first part of the calculation
continues to deal with integers - once real numbers are introduced all the remaining
answers must be assumed to take real values, and therefore will be dealt with in a
slower fashion.

Sometimes you can eliminate the need for real variables, by multiplying all values by a fixed amount. eg if instead of working with pounds and pence you work throughout in pence (ie multiplying by 100 so that £13.56 becomes 1356p) you can use the speed of integer variable work without losing accuracy.

6.   Omit the variable name after NEXT - the computer knows which it is anyway.

7.   It is faster to pass parameters to a procedure than to use global variables.

8.   See Chapter 18 for a discussion on the relative speeds of Procedures and GOSUBs.

9.   When procedures are used the computer assembles a reference list which it uses to look up the address of each PROC. When a procedure is called for the first time it is added to the bottom of the list. Therefore, for speed make sure your most frequently used procedure is first in the list. You can do this by making a 'Dummy call' on the procedure to place it first in the queue, where it is most quickly accessible.

10.   Assembly language programming bypasses the BASIC interpreter and so is much faster.
      However, it is surprising just how many things can be done just as quickly with VDU statements. They require less work to set up and can frequently be more understandable. Again, although machine code routines are very fast calling them isn't and you may get very little extra speed by going into machine code for short sections only.

      If you cannot write assembly language, you may be able to compile your program (i.e. change it into its machine code form, ready to run). Accelerator by Computer Concepts, among others, will do this for you. However, there are limitations on the BASIC instructions that can be compiled.

      If you are a newcomer to Assembly language get R.B.Coats' book on the subject, published by Arnold. Read it, do what it says and you can hardly fail to come out a better programmer. The book has a unique approach which is very refreshing. It explains a difficult subject lucidly and will turn you into a faster programmer, faster!

11. Reduce the time spent accessing discs. A physical disc has to get up to speed before disc access can take place: therefore reduce the number of disc accesses as much as possible.

    a. If there is space, store disc files in memory, in arrays: they are much quicker to get at in this form.

    b. Solid state discs are vastly quicker than physical discs, and access is about as quick as RAM.

    c. Hard discs are the next most speedy method, about ten times faster than a floppy.

    d. Floppy discs are slowest.

If you have to access two files at the same time, try to put them on different drives (not on the opposite side of the same disc) Thus the head has less shuttling about to do.

The fewer clunks which come out of your drive the better, both for the wellbeing of your drive and because it means a faster access time.

B. THROUGH HARDWARE

Surprisingly, there is a lot that you can do to make programs run faster through use/choice of hardware, some valuable, some less so.

1. Increase the clock rate. The CPU of the BBC-B works at 2 MHz. By using the 4 MHz board from Solidisc you can double the speed of some portions of your work. You may get some timing problems but most are avoidable.

2. Speed up your disc access time to the maximum possible. You can experiment with the *FX255 or by altering the links on your keyboard. If you are at all uncertain as to what *FX255 means you should not be attempting this.

3. Use the Archimedes - it runs BASIC faster than most machines run machine code.

20. SAVING SPACE

Many of the Acorn computers do not have that much memory available. The standard BBC-B is a 64K machine, but much of this is taken up with its own internal workings. It is referred to as a 32K machine, meaning it theoretically has about 32,000 character spaces in memory available to the user. Unfortunately the user is anyone using it, and the machine itself is one such user! It slices out chunks to use for storing the screen picture, envelope definitions, Function key definitions, for the cassette filing system, for the ROM filing system, for doing its own calculations and yours and before you know it a lot has disappeared. The actual figure is about 28,000 character spaces if you have cassette, or 24,000 with the DFS fitted. All this if you are in the basic screen MODE 7 - any other mode and the memory goes like cash at a funfair.

The B+ has more room because 'Shadow Ram' takes care of the screen memory (the same applies to the Master), but even at a nominal 128K, the Master still has only about 30K of memory available for the user unless a special program is run which releases up to 64K. The big difference is, that in the case of the B model, and the Electron, the amount of RAM available to the user alters with the screen mode, whereas for the other models it stays the same whatever the mode.

At first this may all seem a lot of space - 24000 characters occupy a good many pages of printed paper. But you will soon find that this seems limited, especially if you are using your machine for business (where files and data eat up available memory), doing a lot of graphics, or using a mode with eighty characters per screen width.

There are a number of ways of maximising the memory space available.

HARDWARE METHOD

If you have a 2nd processor on board, use it. With this add-on the main machine merely becomes an input and output device for the 2nd processor itself. Now, although the add-on only has the same amount of memory as the parent machine, it can all be used for 'calculation'. There are other gains because it does not have to worry about the screen or any other input and output buffers except for its link to the parent: it is therefore faster as well. This is a bit of a cheat as the title is Saving Space and this is really a case of Adding Space, at quite a considerable extra cost.

REDUCE THE SIZE OF THE PROGRAM

Remove all REM's

Remove unnecessary spaces - but some have to be kept, eg after most variables eg IF x=bigANDy=tall will set the computer looking for the variable bigANDy .

Reduce the number of lines in the program by having multiple statements on each line.

Reduce variable names to as small a length as possible

The above items can all be performed automatically with the use of a 'crunching' routine, as available on TOOLKIT PLUS, BROM+ etc. (However, their use can create problems so please take note of the information on crunching routines).

Use integer variables (eg space%) wherever possible, especially where using arrays. However, referring to integer numbers takes up more room in the program (an extra character is required to store 'F%' as opposed to 'F')

Arrays eat up memory, so use them carefully.
1.   Arrays start at number 0 (so that DIM array%(1) actually
       has two elements in it - array%(0) and array%(1)). Don't
       DIMension bigger arrays than you need. This can really
       save space, especially in multi-dimensional arrays. eg
       Using A(5,6,4) instead of A(6,7,5) saves about 75 Bytes.

2.   When using arrays of numbers, remember that integer
       variables take up less space than real variables. If all
       the numbers are going to be integers, then an integer array
       will save a lot of space by comparison with a real array
       (ie.DIM buses%(6) is 20% more economical than DIM buses(6))

3.   String arrays are even more dangerous. (For explanation,
       see below about string handling and rubbishing of space.)

4.   Contrary to what you might expect, a two-dimensional
       array is not that much smaller than a pair of
       one-dimensional arrays (ie DIM friends$(4,1) is not much
       better than DIM males$(4),females$(4) except that referring
       to just one array in the program itself may make the
       program neater and shorter.

Data held within the program in DATA statements can occupy large quantities of space. This is particularly true in programs for commercial use where parts numbers, customer details, salesmen's information and the like has all to be recorded. In these cases, reduce the amount of data where possible by holding it on disc as an index file.

You can reduce the size of data even more by a coding and decoding routine which strips out common pairs and triplets of letter combinations and replaces them with a single character - eg replacing all occurrences of 'ing' with, say, CHR$(152). Text compression techniques such as this are frequently used in adventure games. They can be used on data held within the program in DATA statements, or on text files, or indexes on disc.

SCREEN MEMORY USAGE

Changing to an alternative screen mode may help (on the B but not with the other models, nor if shadow RAM is present). In the BBC-B main memory is available for user programs but is also used to a greater or lesser extent for the screen display. Some screen modes (especially those which support graphics) are especially greedy of memory. The following are the requirements of each mode:-

Mode 7	1K
Mode 6	8K
Mode 5	10K
Mode 4	10K
Mode 3	16K
Mode 2	20K
Mode 1	20K
Mode 0	20k

The essential difference between modes is in how much, and how detailed graphics they support. If your program does not require graphics then switch to an appropriate non-graphics mode - exactly which may depend upon the size and style of screen printing you require. Note that Mode 7 is especially economical on memory, and you can do limited graphics in it - admittedly, rather chunky. (Look at the Ceefax or Oracle pages on television - these are the same as Mode 7)

Shadow RAM is one way of getting round the extra memory requirements of graphics modes. It consists of a RAM board which is inserted in the CPU ROM socket. The CPU is plugged into the add-on board which has on it a series of memory chips and controlling circuitry. Instead of requiring main memory, screen memory now resides entirely in the shadow RAM so that graphics modes do not intrude upon main memory space. (Some boards leave the screen memory in the main machine and divert the program memory into sideways RAM.) In effect, you retain the same amount of available memory whichever mode you are in. This increases the power of the BBC-B immensely, as there is otherwise so little memory space available in graphics modes.

It may be possible to split a long program into two or more sections. When one complete module has been finished, the next is loaded. The only difficulty with this is the transfer of information from first to second. (see section 8, Chapter 15)

When using assembly language, memory is addressed directly, so you can re-use memory locations time and again. Additionally, assembled machine code is very compact compared with an equivalent program in BASIC.

OVERLAYING PROCEDURES

It is possible to have a number of procedures stored on disc: each is read into memory as required, overwriting what was previously there (ie, a previous procedure) In this way a program may make extensive use of procedures without increasing its use of memory. This needs careful programming to achieve.

REDUCING CALCULATING SPACE

The BBC has certain quirky habits regarding its use of memory: one of these is that, in BASIC programs, memory once discarded cannot be re-used unless positive action is taken by the programmer (see strings and rubbishing, below). This means that after some time of running a program it may run out of space for calculation and variable storage - this is more likely to happen with database work than games programs.

There are two neat ways out:
1.	The command CLEAR (which can be used within a program) wipes all variables, both string and numeric, with the exception of the resident integer variables (A%-Z% plus @%). In this way all variable memory space is restored for use: but you will have to 'pick up' all variables again. If you only have integer variables, it's easy - pass all values you want to keep into the resident integer variables. Alternatively (and especially if you need to retain string variables), store the information you want to keep as a disc file, use CLEAR to wipe the memory, then read in the disc file again. This does, of course, take a little time to carry out. WARNING .. Don't do it inside a PROC, the program tends to forget where it is!

2.	Each time the program is RUN the non-program memory is cleared: if you are able to toggle between two programs then each time you start a new program the memory is clean. For example, you could use one program to enter and vet inputs of names, addresses, part numbers etc: then store this information as a disc file: then program 2 is CHAINed. This picks up the disc file and then uses its information to amend a database of parts. Then program 1 is CHAINed again......

SHIFTING PAGE

Of the memory available in the BBC machines, the first few kilobytes are taken up with the memory the machine requires to keep itself sorted out and running. After this comes the memory completely available to the programmer. PAGE is a variable which indicates where the start of the next program will be fed in. Normally this is the first free position in memory above the memory the computer needs for its own internal workings. In the ordinary Beeb it is &E00: with a disc drive, and therefore a DFS fitted, space is required for the machine to organise its reading and writing to the discs, so PAGE goes up to &1900. With other disc systems and some ROMs it may go even higher. With some networks PAGE is also higher (Econet), with some it is lower (ENET). The newer machines use 'hidden' space to store filing systems and so PAGE stays at &E00.

The value of PAGE can be altered by the programmer, up or down.

   eg `PAGE=&1300`

The only constraints on the new value of PAGE is that it must not be below memory space that is actively used by the machine. Although the DFS has about 2.5K of memory allocated to it, this memory is not always used, and as the position of this memory is just below memory available for programming it is possible to 'borrow' some of it. For example, if you only require one disc file open at a time you can bring PAGE down to &1300 and if, having loaded your program from disc, you are not going to read or write to your discs again, you can then bring PAGE down further to &E00 (as for the tape system). In this way you can make more space available for calculation or program. But you must do a *TAPE if PAGE is to remain at &E00: if you leave the disc system operative then even if it is not used it tends to scribble all over the lower end of your program.

To bring PAGE down to &1300 in order to save space and run a long program, but still retain the ability to read and write to discs, do this:-

   `PAGE=&1300:CHAIN"program"`

and the program loads itself in, starting at &1300.

Once this has been done, you can still LOAD and SAVE programs, and write to disc, but only one file may be open at a time. Any attempt to open two files together will cause the early part of the program to be overwritten and you will get a 'Bad Program' error message. If you need to read or write to more than one file during the course of the program it is quite easy to do so - provided it is done sequentially, never having more than one file open at once. As long as you attend carefully to this, working with PAGE at &1300 should present no great difficulties. A little more programming will be needed - opening and closing files more frequently will need extra code, and you may well need to use a number of variables to hold PTR# for each file. In this way you may treat your disc files almost as if several were open together - the computer can OPENUP a file, go to the position in the file as determined by the variable holding PTR#, extract or write information, and CLOSE the file, then do the same for the next file, and so on. It is slower, because opening and closing files takes time.

The golden rule for programming with lowered values of PAGE is -   CLOSE disc files as soon as you are able.

Note that pressing BREAK resets PAGE to its usual value. If you try to RUN the program again, you will get a 'Bad Program' message.

To reduce PAGE still further (to &E00) in order to use all the DFS workspace you will have to make the change after the program is loaded in. The program originally goes in at &1300 or higher and then has to be transferred down in memory to start at &E00. This is not quite so simple: use the program below. It does two things: when the program is loaded from disc it is re-located to a new position (usually &E00, the value for tape machines); then it commits honourable suicide to get rid of itself, thus making even more room.

```
1  IF PAGE=&E00 THEN      (If cassette Machine)
       (*KEY0 *TAPE M     (Turn to Tape system)
          DEL.1,3 M       (Delete this bit of program)
             END |M       (End of this bit of program)
             RUN |M)      (Run Main bit of program)
     ELSE                 (If PAGE does not indicate cassette)
       (*KEY0 *TAPE |M
          DEL.1,3 |M
          FORI% = 0 TO TOP-PAGE STEP4:
            I%!&E00 = I%!PAGE:  (take 4 Bytes down in memory)
          NEXT |M
          PAGE = &E00 |M   ( Change to new PAGE value)
          END |M
          RUN |M)
2  *FX138,0,128            ( Cause Key 0 to operate)
3  END
```

206

This in more compact form is:-

```
1 IF PAGE = &E00 THEN *KEY0 *TAPE |M DEL.1,3 |MEND |MRUN |M
  ELSE *KEY0 *TAPE |MDEL.1,3 |MFOR S% = 0TO TOP-PAGE STEP4:
  S%!&E00=S%!PAGE:NEXT |MPAGE=&E00 MEND |MRUN |M)
2 *FX138,0,128
3 END
```

*FX138 enters the number of a key in the keyboard buffer, causing it to operate (in this case F0). So Key 0 is set up with the program, the first command on it deletes the lines which set it up. If the memory is to be moved, 4 Bytes at a time are shifted. The form... S%!&E00 ..means 'the 4 Bytes starting at address (&E00+S%)' If you don't want to shift to &E00 but &1200, for example, just substitute this figure.

As a rider to this, if you are trying to run cassette programs on a disc system you may run into trouble as many commercial programs address memory directly, and if PAGE is changed the direct addressing will not work. Therefore it may be necessary to relocate the program at &E00 before it will run, even if it doesn't make great demands on memory usage.

STRING HANDLING AND RUBBISHING OF MEMORY

Strings can waste a lot of memory if you are not careful. If you store a new string that is bigger than the old one you will waste memory each time - and the computer has no way of re-using this rubbished space.

What happens in effect is this:-

```
ENTER          Computer Thinks              Computer does

A$="AB"        Hi! lets store you           Stores A$ at,say, &2000
B$="LM"          A new face, Hi!            Stores B$ after A$
A$="ABC"       You again, you've grown,     Stores A$ after B$,leaving
               can't put you in the same      old A$ store unusable.
               place, rot it.
B$="LMNO"      Agh!! done it again          Stores B$ after new A$.
```

To re-use the wasted space you could use the command CLEAR in your program, which gets rid of everything except the program and the resident integer variables (A%-Z% plus @%), but this is a bit violent as it also gets rid of the string variables you want to keep!

There is a solution. Just as we dimension arrays, so we can do a sort of dimensioning of strings. Luckily this is quite straightforward. At the start of the program enter a dummy string of the largest size the string is going to be.

eg. A$=STRING$(25,"*")

This fills A$ with 25 '*'s. As long as A$ in the program never becomes longer than the figure you chose (25 in this case), no extra memory is used in storing the variables contained in A$, however frequently the program uses and re-uses A$. Make certain that the length of the dummy string is accurate - err on the generous side if you are uncertain.

As a horrible warning, consider this - if A$ is originally 200 characters long and you enter an item of 201 characters you will immediately rubbish 200 bytes of memory. Merely increasing the dummy value by 1 character would save 199 bytes!

If single strings can rubbish space, arrays can do it more quickly, because each mistake could be multiplied by the numbers in the array! The solution is simple - before using an array, load each member of the array with dummy strings using STRING$(X,"*") where X is the length of the longest string that the particular section of the array will ever be asked to hold.

STORAGE OF NUMBERS IN A VARIABLE

It is possible to store quite a few small numbers in one variable .... here's how.

'Quarter to three in the afternoon of the twenty seventh day of June in the year 1985 A.D.' can be compressed into:-

2:45PM   27:6:85

If we now write it like this :-

02:45:27:06:85

you can still decipher it and if you saw it in future written in a special place and having been told to expect a date and time you would be able to unravel even this without too much bother:-

0245270685

You might take a pencil to it and take a few seconds to work it out, but it is quite straightforward.

In a similar way we decipher £34.42 to mean 34 Pounds and 42 Pence rather than 'point 4 2'. The position of the numbers has a special meaning through familiarity.

The biggest possible number you can store in one of the integer variables available on the Beeb is &FFFFFFFF (if you don't understand hex notation, see Chapter 18 first as it is crucial to what follows). Each of those F's represents 16 digits, or oranges or items. Each position of an 'F' represents a box in which we can deposit information, in exactly the same manner that the '6' in the number sequence representing date and time means 'the sixth month', rather than '600'

So we have the potential of storing up to 8 numbers in this one variable, so long as none of them is bigger than can be held in one column, i.e.15, as it's in hex.

Alternatively, we could use 2 positions and be able to store up to 255 - remember, we're talking in HEX. (This is exactly similar to the date/time number where the '27' represents 'the 27th day', and not'270,000'.

So, in one 8-bit hex number you can store :-

8	1-bit numbers
4	2-bit numbers
4	1-bit numbers and 2 2-bit numbers
	..etc.etc.

As you can see it is a trade off - size of number v Number of numbers stored.

How do we put an individual item in its own slot?

Think about a good old decimal number, say 1200. If we start off with 1000, how could we insert the 2? The 2 in the number actually represents 200, that is, 2*100. So we get the 2 into the number by multiplying it by 100 and adding it to the 1000. The same is the principle with the HEX storage.

It is somewhat easier to see how to extract a number from its position first..so

```
Number = &00FE62FF
```

If you want to find out what digit is in the 5th position from the right.

1. Number MOD &100000 gives the right-most 5 digits ie.
    &E62FF (note the number of zeros gives the number of
    places retained)

2. New Answer DIV &10000 gives the left-most digit ie. &E
    which is the number we want. (note the number of zeros
    gives the number of places discarded)

This can be written as

```
answer% = number% MOD &100000 DIV &10000
```

To change a digit at a certain position we have to change tactics a little. Let's say our original number is:-

```
number% = &FC45A69B
```

We want to insert &F into the 5th position from the right.

1.   change% = &10000 * &F (note, the 1 lands on the digit we want to change)

2.   answer% = (number% OR change%)

(For those who understand assembly language the logic OR function puts the number in position without generating a carry)

```
P.&answer% gives FC4'F'A69B
```

Which is just what we want.

As an example, this technique was used used by one of us for storing sound parameters, as follows.

Position 1.	Octave number
Position 2.	Envelope number
Position 3/4.	Pitch number/4
Position 5/8.	Time from start of tune in centi-seconds.

Experiment a little, it's quite easy once you have had a go!

21. DEBUGGING

There are four general rules about debugging:-

1.   If you write structured programs, with sensible variable
     names you will make fewer mistakes, and those you do make
     will be much easier to find.

2.   Enter small sections of code at a time, and debug
     immediately. If you have only altered a few lines then you
     know where to begin looking for any problems. Don't forget
     that individual procedures can be called by name when in
     command mode (i.e. with the program in memory, but not
     running) This helps the debugging process as Procedures can
     therefore easily be tested on their own. The Archimedes
     has rudimentary line syntax checking in its Editor, but
     this still leaves logic errors and run time arithmetic
     overflow errors to be dealt with by you.

3.   When debugging check the line you are on, and the previous
     line used by the program: in the case of printing, check
     the subsequent line also.

4.   The fault may well not lie within the line mentioned in an error message.

a.   An error at a line with a PROC call may be directly
     because of the PROC call itself, or through an error in the
     Procedure being called. If the first Procedure calls
     another Procedure then you may have to go even deeper.

b.   Printing defects may occur because of what has happened in
     the line before: eg you expect to see something printed at
     the beginning of a line; whereas on running the program it
     turns up half-way across the page. If your previous piece
     of printing had a semicolon after it, this will 'drag back'
     the next bit of printing to where the cursor stopped.

c.   "No such variable at line ...." might mean that earlier in
     the program you have erased or bypassed the line which
     assigned a value to the variable.

d.   If you have a comma after your last item of DATA you will
     get the wrong line mentioned in the error message "Out of
     DATA at line..." because the computer is scanning down the
     program for further DATA lines without finding any.

If the cause of a bug is not immediately obvious then the quickest way to find it is by
working methodically through all the possibilities. Resist the temptation to try this,
or that, or the other, without any logical pattern to your actions. There must be a
reason why the program has gone wrong. Sometimes it can take several hours to
find out what has happened, and if you are having difficulty, a methodical and
ordered approach is all the more appropriate.

One of the most elusive bugs we ever had to find was when a program appeared to
take absolutely no notice of an instruction at all. The line in question read

```
IF answer$="A" THEN ....
```

We knew that answer$ contained "A" because PRINT A$ gave the result

```
A
```

After two hours we discovered that answer$ didn't contain just A
- answer$ held "A " (i.e.a space after the A) and we only found it by

```
PRINT answer$;CHR$255
```

It took the two of us a whole evening to find it! So if in difficulties, check everything,
even the apparently obvious.

In looking for a bug it often helpful try the effects of other instructions. To lose a line
on a temporary basis, put REM at its head, then if you want it back again delete the
REM! It can save having to re-type the line. This is also a way of having several
different versions of a line on view at the same time but only using one of them.

CHECKING WHAT IS HAPPENING

1. Examining the contents of variables.

When a program is not RUNning you are in command mode. In this state you can
enter instructions directly from the keyboard

```
eg FOR loop = 1 TO 10: PRINT "Hello": NEXT <Return>
```

which will print "Hello" ten times down the screen.

In command mode you can access all variables 'known' to the machine. For example, if in your program the contents of city$ were last defined as "Manchester" then once the program has been RUN, in command mode you can confirm what city$ contains simply by typing in

```
PRINT city$
```

and the computer will print "Manchester". This works provided that the computer has actually got to a part of the program where the variable is defined.

It is also possible to print out the contents of an array in command mode

eg FOR X = 1 TO 9: PRINT array$(X): NEXT

All variables are wiped when any alteration is made to the program itself, eg by inserting, deleting or altering a line, and by RUNning the program. The only exceptions are the resident integer variables (see Chapter 15), whose contents remain until the next hard break (i.e. CTRL/BREAK or its equivalent).

An essential part of debugging is using command mode instructions to investigate the contents of variables at the point in the program where errors are occurring.

If the program isn't stopped by the error, you can make it stop (so as to find the current variable contents) by putting STOP at the appropriate place in the program. You could use END, but STOP displays the line number - and usefully, demonstrates that the code has been read up to that part of the line: if you have an error in a very long line you can dissect out which part of the line is not working by putting STOP at various points along the line and seeing whether the program STOPs before the error message is generated. You can STOP at a particular point in a loop: put in a counter which increments each time round, and insert a STOP line in the following form

```
IF count%=...   THEN STOP
```

2. Checking which part of the program you are in.

Understanding your program may help(!) (This is where structured programming is so important). If your program is clearly written, with correct nesting of loops, then mistakes are more obvious. If you type LISTO7 in command mode, then the next time you LIST the program all loops will be indented by two spaces - a great help in sorting out complex nested loops. LISTO0 cancels it. The indentation with LISTO is not done quite correctly - the last line in the loop (containing NEXT, or UNTIL) is indented by two spaces, and it shouldn't be. (Why not do the job manually yourself, when writing the program.)

Use the command TRACE. This displays all line numbers as they are reached, and helps to work out which lines the program was using when it entered the problem area. TRACE is activated by typing TRACE ON - either in command mode, in which case the whole program will be TRACEd, or else adding TRACE ON to a line of the program, in which case the program will only be TRACEd from the moment the command is encountered.

TRACE OFF will turn TRACE off, but in any case it turns off automatically when the program has finished its run. If you are using page mode (VDU14 or CTRL/N) then you may have to press the SHIFT key to keep the program running with TRACE working. There is so much extra material written to the screen that what previously took up a screenful of space now occupies twice or three times that amount when line numbers are added.

Finally, you may find that your program has landed up in a most strange place indeed, apparently unrelated to the program logic. There are three possible causes:-

1. There are too many nested loops of one particular type and the computer has lost its bearings within the program. (see the next section)

2. You have jumped out of a loop and when the computer encounters the next NEXT/UNTIL goes back to the start (the FOR.. or REPEAT...) of its original loop. (This type of error illustrates the danger of using GOTO.)

3. You have a multi-statement line with an IF somewhere in it yet you intended that the end of the line be used in all circumstances. This leads to an error whenever the IF condition is not met.

Just occasionally things happen within the memory - perhaps a mains spike - which causes strange errors to occur. CTRL/BREAK may clear things - but if not, turning everything off for 10 seconds may rectify the problem.

AN INSTRUCTION ISN'T OBEYED.

Is the computer reading the line at all? - there may be a GOTO, or an IF bypassing it.

Is all the line being used? - it may have an IF which causes the program to drop through to the next line. Test this by inserting STOP at appropriate places and re-running the program.

Is a limiting factor too exact? For example, consider this loop:-

```
10 TIME=0
20 REPEAT
30   PRINT "LESS THAN 3 SECONDS"
40 UNTIL TIME=300
50 PRINT "END"
```

This program was designed to wait for 3 seconds and then drop through to line 50 - but if you run it, almost certainly it will stay inside the loop for ever - because TIME will not be exactly 300 when line 40 is reached - perhaps being 298 on one pass and 304 on the next. The cure is obvious - change line 40 to read

```
UNTIL TIME>=300
```

If a keyboard instruction isn't obeyed (particularly where you are taking keyboard input using GET or GET$) is SHIFT LOCK, or CAPS LOCK set incorrectly? Either alter your program to accept upper/lower case, etc., or set the keyboard to the correct case within the program (see Chapter 18).

Do the variables and flags hold what you think they do? Print them out in command mode - or print them out from within the program so you can see what they are contain at the moment when the program crashes. (This is useful when the bug appears to depend upon a combination of circumstances rather than on a recognisable event.)

Are there two ELSE's in the line? If there are, check the logic of what should happen with a dummy program. This is one you have to do yourself otherwise you will never learn it!

Bizarre effects sometimes happen when there is too great a nesting of loops. There are limits on the number of each type of loop allowed at any one time - ten FOR/NEXT loops, twenty REPEAT/UNTILs, and twenty-six GOSUBs. If these are exceeded you may get an error message - but sometimes you don't: under these circumstances the program usually does very strange things indeed.

The first remedy is not to nest so deeply. The second is to turn an active FOR ... NEXT loop into a REPEAT ... UNTIL loop (or vice versa) and see if the error still occurs.

This can also happen in a recursive procedure. As the program proceeds any local variables and the return address stack start filling up. Even though the procedure may return to the same line 1000 times during recursion, 1000 addresses have to be stored, possibly new variables (x1000). It eats up space and can be a common and hidden cause for error.

Is the computer carrying out arithmetic or logical operations in the order you want it to? There is a great difference between

```
2 * 3 - 2 / 3      and      2 * (3 - 2) / 3
```

also between

```
IF big AND tall OR thin     and     IF big AND (tall OR thin)
```

The order of precedence of arithmetic and logical operators are given in the User Guides. If in doubt, brackets will always sort things out.

PROBLEMS WITH COMPACTED PROGRAMS

Compacting ('crunching') routines save space by removing REM statements, spaces and unnecessary keywords, shortening variable names, and running lines together wherever possible. They can give rise to three types of problems:-

Errors can arise from copying 'crunched' program lines. If you try to alter the line - or even copy it without alteration you may end up with error messages. This sounds odd, until you work out how a crunching routine works.

BASIC commands are stored as a 2 HEX digit TOKEN. Any spaces you may put on the line are stored as tokens as well. If you WROTE your program without spaces the interpreter would have an initial hard time of sorting the lines out eg

```
FORTUNE=LOVETODEAR
```

may make sense to you, but not to the interpreter! However, once 'tokenised' the interpreter has no trouble in sorting out the mess. Thus all the Space tokens may be removed. There are no spaces in the line, and the line runs correctly because the tokens are correctly understood.

But if you copy (ie. re-enter) that line, it won't run because the BASIC interpreter cannot make sense of the un-spaced, re-entered line.

For example, consider a crunching routine getting to work on this line:

```
IF X=Z AND Y=7 THEN LET P=Q
```

The routine will say

```
IF           Hello 'IF'! - I recognise you. You're a Keyword.
             I will tokenise you to &E7
(space)      Go away, you're redundant
```

```
X               You're a variable, I've met you before
(space)         get lost
=               equals, out with the tokens!
(space)         ..yawn...
Z               Oh, another variable
etc etc
```

This line then gets memorised as :-

```
E7    58    3D    5A    80    59    3D    37   8C    50    3D    51
IF    X     =     Z     AND   Y     =     7    THEN  P     =     Q
(token)     (token)     (token)     (token)    (token)     (token)
```

which the BASIC interpreter understands: the line has no spaces, and this is how it is stored in memory or on disc.

If the line is printed on the screen it first goes through the BASIC interpreter, where the tokens are translated back in interpreted form:-

```
IFX=ZANDY=7THENP=Q
```

It still runs because the BASIC interpreter RUNs the tokenised version, not the screen version. But try to copy the line, and the BASIC interpreter will deal with it letter by letter, re-entering it back into memory:-

```
IF              keyword
X               the variable X
=               equals
ZANDY           HOLD IT - WHO ARE YOU???? Quick, deliver
                error message....
```

If you have crunched a program, be very careful about the way you copy lines, in order to avoid this trap. You may need to enter spaces in certain places.

Incorrect running together of lines may produce errors. Here is an example:-

```
REPEAT: IF X > Y THEN PROC_long: UNTIL P = 6
```

What happens if X is not greater than Y? ...not a lot at present. The program continues having dropped out of the line before 'THEN'.

Now here's the problem - the machine has stored the address for the UNTIL part and has not been told it is not needed. It is stored on a stack in the machine and more than likely has a list of other return addresses underneath it. So everything is now out of order and chaos will ensue.

This can all come about when trying to save space, either by hand or with a compacting utility program. One method of compacting is to join several lines together to save a couple of bytes each time, and this is the one which can do the damage. Different commercial utilities handle this problem with varying success. (TOOLKIT-Plus does the job well)

Moral - be greedy, but examine your program carefully afterwards.

It is well-known that in programs * commands must be the last command on a line. Additionally, if you are using an IF ... THEN structure in your program, the 'THEN' is optional and is frequently left out. However 'THEN' is not optional for * commands.

```
10 X=1
20 IF X-1 PRINT"YES"
30 IF X=1 *CAT
```

Try it like this, then try with THEN before the *CAT

Some crunching routines may not recognise the need to include THEN in such lines.

GENERAL POINTS

1. Typing errors.

Is the line exactly what you intended? eg PTR#X or PTRX# ?

Are brackets in the right places?

Have you mixed up similar looking characters eg-

```
; , . : ;
L  l  1  i I !      (especially those who type and are
                     accustomed to  using lower case
                     L as a 1)
$ S s 5
? 7
B 8
O o 0 Q D           (it is useful to program in modes
                     other than 7 ( especially  mode 4
                     or 6 ) to avoid mix-up with O and 0)
_ _
                    (again, use other modes)
: ;                 (except in MODE 7)
] > )                ditto
```

```
[ < (              ditto
6 b
F P
Z 2
```

Have you used an incorrect abbreviation? (a full stop missed out or a keyword abbreviated too much)

    eg `REN instead of REN.`

or an asterisk been missed off or added

    eg `DEL. and *DEL`

or an abbreviated * command that expands in two ROMs to become different commands

    eg `*FORM`

where you have more than one ROM capable of carrying out formatting instructions. Exactly what which ROM deals with it depends upon the physical order of the ROMs resident inside your machine. If you have problems, use the non-abbreviated instruction name. Some ROMs have additional letters to place before the instruction to avoid problems of clashing names.

It is possible to get error messages occurring from this source, if your two ROMs have commands which differ in the arguments they take. For example, imagine you have two ROMs with formatting routines, both called with *FORM. ROM A requires the drive number first and the number of tracks second whereas ROM B requires them the other way round. If you issue the command *FORM 80 0, then if ROM B is in the higher ROM socket it will take the command and act on it. If ROM A is in the higher priority slot it will accept the command, then give an error message as the numbers given are outside its limits.

Are there spaces in the line where they are needed? If you run certain words together the computer won't know what you mean.

    eg `IFtotal=yAND X=20`

generates an error ("No such variable") because the computer will be searching for the variable yAND. Re-enter the line with spaces. If you are running short of space 'crunch' the program later, removing unnecessary spaces automatically.

Does a variable name begin with a BASIC command? The interpreter will look for, and tokenise first, all keywords it recognises. Thus any keyword at the beginning of a variable name will get tokenised: TOTAL% will be read by the BASIC interpreter as

TO	Keyword - tokenise to &B8
TAL%	Who?

This is why it is worthwhile using lower case for all variable names - it avoids unnecessary mistakes of this nature, as all keywords are in upper case.

Are your spaces spaces? Sometimes a line just will not run. Everything looks right, syntax correct, DIM statements done etc. Before you start questioning your sanity, try replacing all the spaces with spaces! Non-printing characters can appear in lines from NOWHERE! They do nasty things In a BASIC line! Sometimes re-typing (not copying) the line will be needed.

Are the line numbers in the right order? It is easy to muddle them up when altering occasional ones - LIST to see.

When trying to copy a line to another part of the program, did you copy the original line number as well?

2. General programming errors

Are there quotation marks round all strings? - particularly in DATA statements where the string contains a comma: also in PROCedure calls where eg PROC_size(large) means quite different things from PROC_size("large"). The first will send the computer looking for the variable large, the second will pass the string "large" to the Procedure.

Use of / and \. In BASIC you divide either with DIV, for integer division, or the symbol /. The symbol \ (on the key next to the left arrow) is not the divide sign: it is written as % only in MODE 7.

Have you arranged brackets in the right order? - there is a special order with which the computer deals with + - / *, and with AND, NOT, OR and EOR. Refer to the User Guide for operator precedence.

Do you mean EOR or OR? 'OR' means 'either...or....or both together'. 'EOR' means 'either... or...but not both together'

Don't jump out of loops - the computer will get itself lost. (in other words never use GOTO from within a loop structure unless the target line is also within the loop and also not the start line of the loop.)

SCREEN PRINTING DEFECTS

Everything sticks at the bottom of the page.
Page mode is on (as VDU14 or CTRL/N). Either press <SHIFT> to continue; or VDU 15 in program to turn it off, CTRL/O from keyboard.

Printing stops in mid-screen, or only scrolls up a bit, then sticks, or even doesn't do anything at all and the program 'hangs'.
The computer is trying to send information to a printer (i.e.VDU 2 or CTRL/B has been used) which is not on-line. If it is supposed to be working - plug the printer in; switch it on; switch it on-line. If it is not supposed to be on, use CTRL/C to switch it off at keyboard, or VDU 3 from the program. Alternatively (particularly when testing a program which normally would print, but when you are not hooked up to a printer, or don't want to have printed output whilst testing the program) use *FX5,0 prior to the instruction to turn the printer on. This acts as a printer sink, and causes output to the printer to vanish into thin air instead of causing a blockage.

The printing scrolls up when trying to print on the bottom line of page
Use ; at end of last print line; or put page mode on - VDU14 in program, CTRL-N from keyboard.

It is not normally possible to print in the bottom right hand character position of the page without either the printing scrolling up or the machine jamming up until SHIFT is pressed. There are two possible cures:
1.   In screen Modes other than 7(teletext) print using the Graphics cursor
2.   If you have a Master alter the configuration of Scroll.

Columns of numbers and words are not aligned.

Numbers are justified right, words are justified left. Use ; and , appropriately in the PRINT statement. You may need to alter @% which sets up column width - (see Chapter 17).

In printing, anything to the left of the new printing is wiped.
You're using PRINT TAB(X). Use PRINT TAB(X,Y) instead.

Double height characters only have the top half of the characters.
Double height printing requires you to print the same item again one line below the first. Avoid the problem by printing double height characters with a procedure containing a FOR ... NEXT loop: (see Chapter 17)

In mode 7, text unexpectedly prints a few places to the right
You've forgotten to allow for the spaces required to print the control codes for colour, background and flash etc., or else you are using a window.

When using coloured backgrounds you get a blank strip instead of characters.

You're either printing a null string (a string with nothing in it) or trying to print in the same colour as the background.

The TAB command doesn't work

The numbers are too great for the screen size

A window doesn't work

You have tried to create a window with dimensions greater than the screen. Check that you haven't muddled up height and width parameters: especially with calculated window sizes check that you haven't gone oversize, and if you have, put in limiters to prevent the problem happening again.

Spurious answers keep appearing on the screen, or the computer doesn't pause at GET or GET$.

The computer takes the next item from the keyboard buffer. If keys have been pressed prior to the GET or GET$ they will be waiting in the keyboard buffer for the program to accept them - so they will enter as unwanted input. Use *FX15,1 immediately before GET or GET$ to flush the keyboard buffer.

Only part of your answer is accepted by INPUT.

Your input contains a comma (a frequent happening with addresses.) INPUT strips off leading and trailing spaces, and stops at the first comma. Use INPUTLINE instead - this will accept commas and leading and trailing spaces up to the position of the <Return>.

PRINTING DEFECTS

Everything is printed out in double spacing.

There are various ways of sending print information to the printer. You can set the printer to scroll up a line at the end of each printed line (i.e.line feed), or you can set it not to scroll. Equally, you can set your computer to print out a line feed or not.

Obviously, if you set both of them to issue a line feed, then after each full line of word-processing your computer issues a line feed - and so does the printer. Result - instant (and unwanted) double-spacing.

There are three possible ways to cure the situation - firstly, stop your printer scrolling up at the end of a line. You can do this by setting the dip-switches appropriately - you will need to consult the printer manual.

The second method is to leave the printer with its line feed on and instead suppress your computer from issuing line feeds - with either the *FX6,10 command, or, for the

Master, Compact, or Archimedes, use the CONFIGURE routine to do the same. This latter method has the advantage that you don't need to put a *FX call in every single !BOOT file on every single disc.

Which method you use is up to you.

The *FX6 call defines a 'printer ignore' character - i.e. when this character is issued it is suppressed and not sent to the printer, even if it is sent to the screen. *FX6,10 prevents character 10 (line-feed) going to the printer. You can still send line feeds to the printer, if you want to, by preceding them with VDU 1 (eg VDU1,10)

Your printer doesn't scroll up at all and prints everything on the same line, leaving a long splodge of ever-increasing density.
See above. You've managed to suppress both the printer's line-feed and the computer's! Either alter the dip-switches, change the configuration or issue *FX6.

22. SPECIFIC ERRORS

Although the User Guide contains a complete list of error messages they are mentioned in outline form only. This chapter gives further information about the possible causes of each error.

Be wary of error messages - they are not necessarily as specific as you might expect. For example, mistyping a variable name can give rise to "Mistake", "Syntax error", "Array", or "No such variable", depending upon precisely what has been typed.

There are a number of cassette system errors which have much the same cause, and the same cure - they are all related to errors in reading data or programs stored on tape. There is no great advantage in knowing precisely which aspect of the checking mechanism has gone wrong - so we have lumped them all together under "Block?".

The same is true for disc faults, and they are treated all together in one section.

The numbers allocated to each error enable error trapping routines to be devised to deal with specific errors in different ways. (see Chapter 18)

ACCURACY LOST   No.23

If you use an angle outside the range +/- PI Radians you stand the chance of getting this error. The algorithm reduces angles until they fit within this range. However, it takes a few thousand degrees to get this error. Moral - do a calculation to reduce to within the range before using in (say) SIN ( ).

ARGUMENTS   No.31

PROCEDURES and FUNCTIONS are made more useful when the material on which they are going to work can be passed to them directly. This is called passing parameters.

```
eg. DEFFN_volume(height, width, depth)
       = height * width * depth
```

is a function to obtain the volume of a block, given its height, width and depth. In the main program you would call the function as

```
eg 100 IF FN_volume(A%, X, 33.6) > 4900 THEN PROC_too_big
```

There is no reason why a Procedure or function shouldn't use variables from the main program, but passed parameters are faster, and make the procedure more generally useful.

If called with too many or too few parameters (which are called 'arguments'), or if the string and numeric arguments are passed in the wrong order, the procedure or function won't work

```
eg FN_volume(height%, width%)
```

won't give the function enough material to work with as it requires three parameters to be passed to it.

Again, a Procedure

```
PROC_strike("Active",2)    and    DEFPROC_strike(X%,A$)
```

will produce this error message, it expects a numeric variable followed by a string, and gets instead a string followed by a variable.

When you get the error message, check with the calling (PROC) and the called (DEFPROC) for a dissimilarity between the numbers of parameters passed and required. Also check that you haven't inadvertently ended up with two procedures of the same name, one with, and one without parameters! (This is very easy to do, especially if you have a disc of utilities)

It is worthwhile having a list of procedures and functions showing the parameters of each, and using sensible names for the parameters (which are treated as LOCAL to the procedure, anyway.)

(See Chapter 16 for a fuller treatment of this subject)

ARRAY   No.14

Before using an array, you must tell the computer that it must create space for one, with the command DIM

```
eg DIM passengers%(15)
```

Trying to access an element of an array, either to read to or write from it,

```
eg height%(14) = 67
```

will produce an error unless the array has been DIMensioned earlier in the program.

Therefore, all you have to do is to dimension the array earlier in the program.

Alternatively, you have mis-typed a variable in such a manner that the computer thinks it is part of an array

```
eg Ar($="car"
```

For further information on arrays, see Chapter 16)

BAD CALL   No.30

This occurs when an illegal character appears in a Procedure or Function name

```
eg PROC.fido
```

Characters for Procedure and Function names are the same as for variables - all alphanumeric characters are acceptable plus the underline character.

BAD DIM   No.10

Arrays can only be DIMensioned using positive integers. Therefore a negative, or non-integer number in the dimension statement will produce this error. This is of particular importance if you are using a variable to define your array

```
eg DIM managers$(total)
```

when you must make sure that the variable says 'within bounds'.

You can also get this error message if you try to DIMension the same array twice. For this reason it is best to have all arrays DIMensioned together at the start of the program. Do not DIMension an array in a procedure if the procedure can be called more than once.

BAD KEY   No.251

You have attempted to load a key in an illegal manner, such as:-

1.   Trying to re-define a key while it is still in use.

2.   Running out of space for the string you are
       inputting. The total space for all key messages is
       256 Bytes (1 Page) on the BBC-B and four times as much
       on the Master. If necessary, delete key definitions to
       save space. Remember, the key stores messages as a
       string not as tokens. It is possible, with the help

of a memory editor to pack quite a lot into the key by
editing in tokens, but it is a lot of hard work.

BAD HEX   No.28

Hexadecimal counting works to the base 16, and is written

'Normal'	Hex	'Normal'	Hex
1	1	17	11
2	2	18	12
3	3	19	13
4	4	20	14
5	5	21	15
6	6	22	16
7	7	23	17
8	8	24	18
9	9	25	19
10	A	26	1A
11	B	27	1B
12	C	28	1C
13	D	29	1D
14	E	30	1E
15	F	31	1F
16	10	32	20

If any character is used other than 0-9 and A-F you will get a BAD HEX message.

Hex numbers are preceded by an &, (eg &1A) to tell the computer that the next
number is to be read as a hex number. If an '&' gets in the wrong place, the
computer will read the symbols following as a hex number and get muddled.

Don't use & instead of AND. Unless you are specifically referring to a hex number,
use '&' only inside double inverted commas (i.e. as part of a string) .

BAD MODE   No 25

1.   You may not change to a mode where your program is too
     large to allow enough memory for the screen display.

2.   You may not change mode inside a procedure or function -
     but you can do so inside a GOSUB.

A. Where there is not enough room for the particular mode:-

1. Change to a different mode using less screen space, as different screen modes take up different amounts of memory. Modes which support graphics gobble up memory, so if you're only using words you can choose the same appearance on-screen using much less screen memory by using a non-graphics mode displaying the same type size.

2. Save space within the program itself (see Chapter 20)

3. When CHAINing a new program the screen mode stays the same. Therefore a program which runs in, say, MODE 7 may produce a "Bad Mode" message if CHAINed from, say, a MODE 3 program. (There is much less memory available for program and calculations in Mode 3.) Therefore get into the habit of defining the screen mode at the beginning of every program you create, to avoid future errors.

If you get 'Bad mode' before you run the program change the mode inside the old program, before CHAINing the new program. And if the old program is too big to allow this to happen, CHAIN an intermediate program whose sole function is to change Modes!

B. When the error is generated in trying to change mode in a procedure:-

1. Change mode just before entering the procedure.

2. Change the procedure into the main part of the program.

3. Change the PROCedure into a GOSUB.

4. It is possible to change Mode with VDU22,n where n is the new Mode. This is not quite the same as MODE n, however, as the value of HIMEM remains unchanged. It is possible to change mode within a procedure using VDU22,n but it is wise to go from a mode using more screen memory to a mode using less screen memory, to avoid trouble with the unaltered HIMEM.

BAD PROGRAM

This is an un-trappable error - in other words, you cannot filter it out through an ON ERROR routine (see Chapter 21).

There are many reasons why this error message appears:-

1. The memory has become corrupted, either by errors arising within the machine, or by a mistake in writing directly to memory. The internal checking messages indicate that something has been added or left out.

2. A program is loaded or running, with PAGE set to a value other than default. Pressing BREAK will now produce this response, as it re-sets PAGE to default, and places &FF in the byte at position PAGE+1.

A cure which can work and is worth a try. - reset PAGE to the running value. (Then LIST to check that the program is still there.)

BLOCK?   No 218

(Also ......Data? Header?...) These only occur when using the tape filing system when part of the recorded program or file fails to load properly.

BLOCK?   means that the computer has found a non-consecutive block number.

DATA?   means that some of the data from within the block is missing or corrupt.

HEADER? means that the file header can't be read.

Rewind the tape and read that part in again. There is no need to touch the keyboard or stop loading the program. If the problem is persistent:-

1. Check that all leads between computer and cassette are pushed in firmly.

2. Increase the output volume on the tape recorder in case the signal volume is too low.

3. Is the treble control turned down, or Dolby noise reduction system switched in? They shouldn't be.

4. Do the heads on your tape recorder need adjusting? If the read head needs adjusting it is quite easy to do the job. The way to tell is to listen to the sound of the recording. If the sound is dull it needs a tweak, if a very sharp sound grates through your head it most likely should be left alone. There is usually a small hole (about 1mm

diameter) above the record/playback head in the casing at the front of the recorder. Underneath, when the tape is playing, is a small adjusting screw. Make certain you know which way it is pointing and adjust until the sound of the 'WELCOME' tape is at its sharpest. That usually works. Ears are better than a battery of test instrments here!

5. If other tapes load well, the recorder on which the troublesome tape was recorded may have misaligned heads.

6. If none of the above apply, you have a duff tape, or a corrupted recording. Has the tape been stored near to a magnet, or in heat?

7. Some tapes have a kink in them for the first few turns at each end. This can cause problems at the start of a tape. Cure - start at least a count of 10 in from the front.

BYTE   No.2

This is 6502 assembly language program error. Registers can only hold a single-byte number, and you have just attempted to load a larger number. (ie. 256 or more)

Can't match FOR   No.33

See "No FOR"

Channel at line ...   No.222

You have attempted to read or write to cassette or disc without having a channel to do so. This usually means there is no file of the appropriate name on the disc, and the error message occurs not when you try to OPENUP a non-existent file, but when you subsequently try to read or write from that file.

1. Use OPENUP, OPENIN or OPENOUT to open the channel.

2. You have tried to OPENIN or OPENUP a non-existent file on the disc - check that the file exists, and that you haven't inadvertently changed drives, or inserted a new disc.

3. Have you used the wrong variable name for the channel? or the wrong case? (You are more likely to get "No such variable" if you have.)

Data?   No.216

This is a cassette filing system message. See under 'Block?'

DIM space   No.11

You have tried to DIMension an array for which there is insufficient room free in the memory.

1.   Arrays eat up memory. See Chapter 12 for ways of saving array space by not DIMensioning more than you have to.

2.   See all in Chapter 20 (!) on saving space.

Division by zero   No.18

You can't do it! The answer would be Infinity and the computer cannot represent this number.

1.   If you are dividing by a variable (including a loop variable) which might become zero, you will have either to insert code in the program to test if the variable is zero, and to deal with the problem if it is or arrange an error trap using ON ERROR (see Chapter 18).

2.   This error could be generated inside a Procedure or function when dividing by a variable which is defined as LOCAL. On defining a variable as LOCAL it is set to zero, and if not re-defined in the procedure will cause this error if used as a divisor.

$ range   No.8

This can be generated when you are trying to write directly to memory if you get the address wrong. You may not write to zero page - ie addresses below &100. Therefore

```
$70="item"
```

is illegal.

Eof   **No.223**

This error is generated by the cassette filing system when the end of a stored file is reached during a read operation. It gives information which is useful and then leaves you to close the file in the normal way.

Escape at line...   **No.17**

The escape key was pressed. (Note the line number : if your program has stuck and you have to ESCAPE to regain control, it helps to find what's gone wrong) To disable escape, or change the escape key see Chapter 18

Exp range   **No.24**

The EXP function (which raises a number to the power stated in the brackets) has an upper limit of 88.

Therefore within your program set limits on the input to any exponential function.

FAILED AT ...

When re-numbering with the RENUMBER command, the computer checks to see if any referred line number is present

```
eg     GOTO 450

       RESTORE 3450

       ON P% GOTO 30,456,75
```

- if the line referred to is missing it prints 'Failed at (line number)' and the line number mentioned in the error message is the one which contains the instruction: this instruction remains as it originally was before the line numbers were changed. All the rest of the program will be re-numbered correctly, including the rest of the line.

Note that with the ON... GOTO construction, a failed line number will be replaced by zero, rather than remaining as it was before.

(Note that calculated line numbers will not be re-numbered at all by the RENUMBER command.)

File?

The cassette filing system has been given an unexpected file name. The polite equivalent of 'Yer Wot??'

FOR variable

The variable in a FOR... NEXT loop must be a numeric variable.

```
eg FOR  X = 0 TO 5
```

A constant or a string is not allowed, for obvious reasons.

```
     eg FOR  7 = 0 TO 5
 or
        FOR X$ = 0 TO 5
```

are both wrong.

Header?   No.217

Another message from the cassette system. See under 'Block?'.

Index

This is an Assembler error indicating that a wrong mode of indexed addressing has been used.

LINE space

There is no room left to insert into memory the line you are trying to enter.

You will have to reduce the amount of memory taken up by the rest of the program: see Chapter 20 on 'Saving Space'

Log range   No.22

You cannot calculate the log of a negative number, or of zero.

Missing ,   No.5

There is a comma missing from an instruction in the line. Commas are very important because they tell the computer where one piece of information ends and another starts. For example, if you type

```
A$="Hello":PRINT LEFT$(A$3)
```

the computer doesn't know what to make of it - there should be a string immediately after the brackets, followed by a comma, whereas as it stands the computer is sent to hunt for A$ and then doesn't know what to do next.

Missing "   No.9

As for " Missing , " this shows that the computer has become confused because it doesn't know where the string ends.

Inverted commas must surround all strings, and any DATA statement which contains a comma in the string itself.

To put inverted commas inside a string you have to use them doubled.

```
A$ = "This is a ""ball"" of string"
P.  A$
This is a "ball" of string
```

Missing)   No.27

As for all the "Missing - " group, the computer doesn't know where the instruction ends. It has to evaluate the innermost brackets first, then the next-to-innermost, etc etc.

But note that a pair of brackets is not always required - notably in the statement CHR$n.

Mistake   No.4

The computer cannot understand the line: this is a general error message - if the line is almost correct the more specific 'Missing ...' may be given. 'Mistake' means that the computer was unable to sort out even the beginnings of the structure of at least one of the commands.

This message will also be given if an illegal character is used in a variable name.

Some characters or character sequences are not allowed in variable names.

1.   You cannot use the space - instead, use the underline
     character to_give_the_feel_of_a_space.

2.   A variable must start with a letter, but numbers may be used after this
     eg A3% is acceptable   3A% is not

234

3. You may not use punctuation marks, except for the underline character.

4. You may not start with a BASIC keyword (watch 'TO' especially) To prevent inadvertent use of BASIC keywords, it is better to use lower case for variables, or at least always start variables with lower case letters.

-ve root   No.21

You cannot calculate the square root of a negative number. This error message can also occur with ACS and ASN.

No GOSUB   No.38

The end of a GOSUB routine is marked by the command RETURN. If this is met without first entering a GOSUB this error message will be given.

Causes:-
1. There is no END on the main program, and it has dropped through to the sub-routine immediately following.

2. You have used GOTO in error and landed on a line inside a sub-routine - then the computer encounters the RETURN as the program drops through.

No FN   No.7

As for 'No GOSUB', but in this case the computer has reached the end line of a function (the one beginning with a equals sign) without having called one.

The causes and cures are exactly the same as for 'No GOSUB'.

No FOR   No.32

The computer has come to a line containing NEXT without their being a corresponding FOR statement.

1. The FOR part of the loop is missing
    - perhaps deleted in error
    - or inaccessible eg
    ```
    120 IF A = 90 THEN FOR X = 1 TO 5
    130    PRINT"Hello"
    140 NEXT
    ```
    will produce this error if A is not equal to 90

2.   You have jumped into a FOR..NEXT loop with GOTO

No PROC   No.13

As for 'No GOSUB', except that the computer has now found itself at the end line of a Procedure (ENDPROC) without knowing how it got there.

Causes and cures as for 'No GOSUB'

No REPEAT   No.43

As for 'Can't match FOR', except that the computer has found itself at the line UNTIL, of a REPEAT...UNTIL loop without having first encountered a REPEAT statement.

Causes and cures as in 'Can't match FOR'

NO ROOM   No.0

Causes:-

1.   Too long a program
2.   Not enough calculating space left.

There are so many ways to make more memory available that we have devoted a whole chapter to it - see 'Saving space'(Ch.20)

No such FN/PROC   No.29

You have called a procedure or function with a name that does not match with any procedures or functions defined in the program.

```
eg PROC_square
```

when the procedure has actually been defined as

```
DEFPROC_squares
```

When using a longish name for a procedure definition, it is just as well to use the copy key to make certain that the spelling is correct.

If the procedure name is correct, but there is a disparity in the number of parameters that are being passed, you will get the error message 'Arguments': however, if by mistake you have defined two procedures with the same name, one with parameters and one without then you could get either message (depending upon which is first in the computer's internal lookup table of procedures or functions): so have a good look. (This mistake is easier to do than you might think, especially if you have a Utility disc of procedures.)

No such line   No.41

The computer has been asked to GOTO, GOSUB, or ON....GOTO a line which does not exist.

1.   You mistook the line number.

2.   You deleted the 'arrival' line when altering that part of the program.

3.   You RENUMBERED, got an error message, and failed to follow it up.

4.   You calculated a RESTORE number incorrectly or 'out of limits'.

Either way this illustrates the grave dangers that can lurk when you use GOTO. It is very difficult to 'see' potential errors in the GOTO construction, and the further away the new line is, the harder it is to check.

NO SUCH VARIABLE   No.26

You cannot PRINT the contents of a variable, nor do anything with it, if you haven't told the computer what its contents are! It can also occur if you forget to OPENUP a channel, and then try to PRINT# through the variable that you thought had been allocated to that channel.

This error occurs more often than not through mis-typing a legitimate variable name, putting it in the wrong case, or running it together with another variable, keyword or expression.

It is good practice to have all variables in lower case, to differentiate them from the keywords (which have to be in upper case, of course), and to leave spaces round all variable names.

Avoid similar or confusing names for variables, if possible. (See Chapter 21 for a list of characters that can easily be mistaken for one another.)

Sometimes this error occurs when there is a general procedure to do something (eg print out a screen display) and a particular variable has not been defined at the beginning of the program, but instead is defined and given a value at a variable position during the program, in the form

```
IF... THEN var% = .....
```

If the condition is not met the variable remains undefined. When the screen display is reached this error message will occur.

Cures:
1. Type the variable accurately
2. Surround variables with spaces.
3. Define all variables at the head of the program with a value, if you are able to, (eg vat% = 15), or give it a nil value to start off with (eg vat% = 0 answer$ = "")

(Defining a variable in a procedure or function as LOCAL automatically gives a value of zero, also that DIMensioning a string array (but not a numeric array) zero's it.

String variables always have to have a $ sign following (eg variable$). Only integers can be stored in numeric variables followed by a % (eg variable%); real variables and integer variables can both be stored in numeric variables without a '%' sign after (eg variable).

No TO   No.36

A FOR .. NEXT loop has been set up without the TO present in the FOR.... line.

NOT LOCAL   No.12

This means that LOCAL has appeared outside a Procedure or Function. LOCAL is a way of making a variable apply only to its own procedure (it means the variable cannot get muddled with a different variable of the same name within the main program. - See the section on Procedures in 'Getting the best from BASIC', Chapter 16. Thus, inside a specified procedure, stating 'LOCAL F' creates an entirely different variable to F, and an entirely different variable to 'LOCAL F' in a different Procedure.

The most common reason for this error message is that the computer has ended up inside a function or procedure without knowing how it got there. Alternatively, you have written LOCAL in the main program thinking that the section you were writing was inside a procedure.

For causes and cures see 'No GOSUB'

ON range   No.40

The X in the following line is referred to as the control variable
```
ON X GOTO 300, 350, 460
```

This error message will be given if the control variable is less than 1, or greater than the number of entries in the ON list.

1. You may have made a mistake in the number of entries

2. When the control variable is a calculated one, it may be that you have forgotten that the control variable may only take the numbers 1 to the size of the ON list. If you are calculating the number and it ends up in multiples of, say, ten, you cannot use this for the ON... GOTO function. If the control variable is a real number (eg 6.4) and not an integer, it is truncated (not rounded) to its control value. eg In the example above, if X=6.99 it will be truncated to 6.

To get X to a proper range for ON (1,2,3,4 etc) use a secondary variable

```
( eg. IF height < 6.4 AND height > 3.7 X = 2 )
```

ON SYNTAX   No.39

ON must have a numeric variable, then GOTO or GOSUB followed by line numbers separated by commas. Therefore

```
ON p% GOTO 200, 400, PROCread, 550
```

is not allowed.

OUT OF DATA   No.42

An attempt has been made to read more items of DATA than there are in the DATA list.

Causes:-

1. You have not arranged how the READ command should be stopped. Therefore, either:

```
REPEAT: READ car$.....  UNTIL car$ = "ZZ"
```
or
```
FOR J = 0 TO 7: READ car$: NEXT
```

2. You are attempting to match a variable with material in DATA but the matching condition has not been met and the loop has run out of DATA. Therefore:-

```
match = FALSE
REPEAT
   READ car$
   IF car$ = "Volvo" match = TRUE
UNTIL match OR car$ = "ZZ"
```

3.   You have grouped DATA eg

```
REPEAT
   READ car$, colour$, cost
UNTIL car$ = "ZZ"
DATA Renault, Sand, 5600, Rover, Blue, 2300, ZZ
```

but you haven't given any DATA to be entered in colour$ or cost% on the last time round the loop. Alter the DATA line to end

```
..ZZ,end,999
```

(or any other string and number you fancy).

4.   There is not enough DATA.

6.   READ has begun in the wrong place - easily done by reading on from where the last READ ended. Use RESTORE n to return to the head of the DATA set (at line number n) that you want to read in. n can be a calculated line number if you   want.

If READ...DATA statements don't work properly, and end up with the wrong contents (but without generating error messages) consider if:-

a.   You have started READing at the correct line (use RESTORE)

b.   You have added extra commas, either at the beginning, or more commonly at the end of a DATA line.

c.   One of the DATA strings contains a comma. In this case, surround the string with double inverted commas

```
eg  DATA Grommets,"Nuts,metric",Bolts
```

Out of range   No.1

In an assembler program there are too many instructions between where you are and where you are trying to Branch to. The maximum distance is 127 Bytes forward and 128 Bytes backward.

SILLY   No.0

A typically useless error message, big on impact, small on information. It might just as well read 'Tut Tut!' This occurs if an attempt is made to RENUMBER or use AUTO with a step size of 0 or more than 255.

STRING TOO LONG   No.19

The maximum length of a string in BASIC is 255 characters. This message gets it right!

SUBSCRIPT   No.15

You have tried to access part of an array which is greater than the size of the array (rather like trying to post a letter to 14 Acacia Avenue when Acacia Avenue stops at No.13). Alternatively you have tried a use a subscript of less than 0.

```
eg DIM places(10)
      .
   places(11) = 16
```

Either reDIMension your array to include the higher elements, or correct your mistake!

SYNTAX   No.220

This is a cassette filing system error indicating a failure whilst loading or saving.

SYNTAX ERROR   No.16

Much more usual! A command was issued incorrectly -

```
eg RENUMBER LIST
```

This message also occurs if you call a procedure using arguments when the called procedure has none

```
eg PROC_square(side, colour%)
   .
   .
   DEFPROC_square
```

It can also occur under some circumstances if you write a string incorrectly.

```
eg A.$ = "big"
```

TOO BIG   No.20

A number was entered, or an answer was calculated, which was too big for the computer to handle.

Deal with this by dividing by powers of ten and storing the two parts of the number separately, or alternatively divide, and discount the remainder, which will not be a very significant proportion of the original amount.

If you MUST have very large numbers and MUST have high precision then you are into the realms of multi-precision arithmetic. It is possible to calculate any sized number with any sized answer completely correctly. This involves splitting the numbers up into small parcels, working on them and rejoining. This is outside the scope of this book.

TOO MANY FOR'S   N0.35

You can only nest FOR..NEXT loops to a depth of 10.

Possible causes:-

1.   You have tried to construct 11 or more FOR..NEXT loops.
      If you run out of one type of loop, convert some of the
      loops to work in another manner - eg convert FOR..NEXT
      loops to REPEAT...UNTIL loops by putting a counting
      mechanism in which adds one to the total each time the loop
      is circled. In desperation construct your own loops with
      IF... THEN GOTO...

2.   You have jumped out of a FOR ..NEXT loop with GOTO,
      without jumping back in again. If you have to jump out of
      a loop you MUST jump back in again, otherwise the 11th time
      round you'll get an error message (earlier if you have
      other FOR...NEXT loops in operation at the same time). If
      you need to terminate a loop without knowing exactly when
      it will need to happen, use REPEAT....UNTIL.

3.   If you return by a GOTO to the FOR line without
      encountering NEXT the computer thinks it is starting
      another loop, and gets its internal counters muddled. eg

```
20 FOR J = 1 TO 11
30   IF house$(J) = "empty" GOTO 20
40   PRINT house$(J)
50 NEXT
```

will generate the error before the loop ends.

Bizarre effects sometimes happen when there is too great a nesting of loops, and if this sort of event occurs, try changing a loop or two to see if the problem still happens. When the computer runs out of a particular type of loop, it gets its internal pointers mixed up and doesn't know where it is - hence the jumps to odd areas of the program.

TOO MANY GOSUBS　　No.37

There is a maximum nesting of 26 GOSUBs.

Causes:-

1.　You have nested more than 26 GOSUBS

2.　This is sometimes generated by jumping out of a GOSUB
　　without using RETURN - and is very similar to the problems
　　of "Too many FOR's" - see this section for details of what
　　may have gone wrong.

By contrast, you can use nesting of Procedures infinitely, including a most interesting variant called recursion, whereby a procedure calls itself. This is quite legitimate (and very useful in certain mathematical constructions).

TOO MANY REPEATS　　No.44

The maximum nesting of REPEAT.. UNTIL loops is 20 This error can be caused by returning to a REPEAT statement (by GOTO) without encountering the UNTIL. (See "TOO MANY FOR's") for details.

If you want to use more REPEAT.. UNTIL loops you can convert FOR.. NEXT loops, but you must avoid jumping out of them when the condition is met. You can terminate a loop artificially by increasing the loop variable to its maximum, in this manner:

```
10 FOR X = 1 TO 100
20   IF array$(X) = "culprit" PRINT "ARREST HIM!": X = 100
30 NEXT
```

This is the exact equivalent of:

```
 5 X = 1: arrest = FALSE
10 REPEAT
20   IF array$(X)="culprit" PRINT "ARREST HIM!":arrest=TRUE
```

```
30  X = X + 1
40 UNTIL X = 101 OR arrest
```

TYPE MISMATCH   No.6

Where the computer is looking for a string and gets a numeric variable, or vice versa. (They are stored in different ways).

Causes:-

1.   Mis-typing a string for a numeric variable

2.   Reading in from a disc file where the wrong type of information is next off the file eg. You stored the information with

```
PRINT#X,number,string$,number%
```

and you have tried to access this file with

```
INPUT#X,number,number%,string$
```

DISC ERROR MESSAGES

On the Acorn DFS Disc errors are reported as numbers only. There are really only two important types of error - those beginning 'Disc fault' and those beginning 'Drive fault'.

Of the two, drive fault is the more serious, indicating that something is possibly wrong within the hardware: but you will also get this message if you try to access a non-existent drive - eg CH.":2.$.PROGRAM" when you possess only a single sided disc drive. This is easier to do than you might think, especially if you are working with a suite of programs that is designed for a bigger system than you possess.

'Disc fault' means a problem has occurred in reading or writing to the disc itself. When the error message appears it will say at which track the problem has occurred: you can use *DZAP from DISC DOCTOR or similar to try to read the offending track and confirm that one sector is 'down' - or else use *VERIFY.

'Disc fault' means one of three things:-

1.   You are trying to read the wrong type of disc - ie the disc is 80-track and your drive is set to 40-track working, or vice versa. Re-set the drive (or your software if appropriate) for the correct number of tracks

2. The disc has not been formatted on that side. (Before you can store information on a disc it has to be formatted - in other words, has to have guide tracks laid down. On blank discs you must do this yourself beforehand.)

If the track number in the error message is greater than 00 then the disc is at least partially formatted as the catalogue has been read.

*VERIFY on DISC DOCTOR or similar ROMs allows you to verify the formatting of each track without damaging or overwriting it. The error messages will tell you which track has developed an error.

If none of that side of the disc has been formatted then format it! But be careful - if it has been formatted in the past but became corrupted then the disc may still contain mostly intact information which you can recover with the techniques described in Chapter 12. If you re-format a disc you will wipe off everything previously stored on it. (It is possible to re-format selectively only the corrupted tracks.) As some formatting programs use main memory to work in, be sure to save your program to another disc before you try to format the target disc.

3. There has been some form of corruption of the stored information on the disc. Illegal alteration of a single character can prevent a whole program from loading, and can prevent the disc being copied. Sometimes the cause is a piece of dust on the disc getting in between the disc drive head and the disc. Taking the disc out, putting your fingers through the central hole and rotating the disc backwards and forwards a few times may clear the obstruction. Be warned, if it is dirt, grit, or some other offensive body on the disc surface, copy the data and throw the disc away. Data is precious, discs are cheap (unless you rate your time at less than £1/week)

If 'Disc Fault' occurs during *COPY or *BACKUP, make sure you find out which of the two discs is at fault - if possible see which drive light is on when the fault appears.

A disc that has a fault on it cannot be copied in its entirety: but if the catalogue is intact you can read off all programs except the one with the fault in using *COPY <filename>. *BACKUP will not work. A long file will still work for random access, except for the portion with the fault in.

If *BACKUP is the first sign of a disc fault you may be lucky and be able to *COPY all the files. If this is the case then the fault is in a portion of the disc so far unused. (*BACKUP copies the WHOLE disc, empty tracks as well as full ones)

For methods of retrieving information off a corrupted disc, see Chapter 12

DISC ERRORS CAUSED THROUGH SOFTWARE HANDLING

CAN'T EXTEND   No 191

A DFS error message, indicating that you have tried to extend an existing file but it has either come up against the start of another file/program or has come to the end of the disc. When you get this message, it is important to close down the file. (CLOSE#0 <RETURN> will do it.) If you have good error trapping you can also do this from within a program.

Unfortunately you may now have an unusable file, depending on just where it runs out of space. For example, if you are using a disc file index, filing the code first and the full name later:-

        eg. PRINT#X, code$, name$

then if the point where the file couldn't be extended occurred just after you had put down code$, then when the program came to pick up the pair of strings with

        INPUT#X, code$, name$

there would be an error message - 'END OF FILE' as the second item is not there to be read.

Under these circumstances, clever work with your disc editor (if you know just what to do) is indicated. More likely you will have to use your backup copy to re-run the program having first rearranged your disc files so as to make more room available. (see below)

DISC FULL   No 192

This message occurs when there is not enough room left on the disc to save the current program. We all know that 'the Law is an Ass' and frequently the DFS don't know Nuthin'. What has usually happened is that your files have got spaced out all over the disc due to deletion and resaving leaving gaps all over the place. Unfortunately no one gap may be big enough to save your program in. Say you had a 5K file, a 24k gap, a 2K program, a 24k gap, a 6K program, a 24K gap, a 1k program. You have 86k of spare space but you cannot squeeze a 25K program in anywhere! This may seem to be an extreme example, true, but it can happen.

You can avoid this problem in several ways, all of which require forethought.

Make sure all redundant space between files is eliminated by *COMPACTING your discs on a regular basis, making sure that:

a.   you have nothing important in the machine as it will be wiped out

b.   you have a backup of the disc. Power failures do occur
      and the middle of a backup leaves a nasty mess on your disc
      which is almost certainly irretrievable.

Arrange your discs so that any files which are growing are not 'hemmed in'. This means that you take one of two actions.

1.   Only have one active file on a disc and make certain it is
      at the end. (Copy it to another disc, Compact the
      original after deleting that file, copy the file back again
      and it will be at the end.)

2.   The other way is more crafty and means that you have to
      think quite carefully about exactly what you need to do.

First decide how many files really have to grow on the disc. Empty the disc completely. Save the first one. Save another large file, doesn't matter what, then save your second file. Save another large file and then your third file. Continue like this until you have all your growing files on the disc. Now delete all the padding files and each of your own files now has breathing space around it. Remember not to *COMPACT the disc at any time otherwise you are back at square one! And don't SAVE any other programs or files to this disc as they may get slotted into spaces you want to keep as spaces

'COMPACTION REQUIRED'

This is an ADFS message. The ADFS is a lot more intelligent than the DFS. Any file that is growing too large and jamming up against the next file is quietly copied to a bigger space - if there is one. Only when there is no bigger space available do you get the 'CAN'T EXTEND' message.

In practice, the occurrence of this message may mean that you have an unusable file for the reasons outlined above in CAN'T EXTEND. If you *COMPACT your disc you may make enough room available, but you may have to do it several times as it does not do the whole disc at one go. If all else fails, make the file in question the last file on a compacted disc.

Drive fault   No 197

This implies that something physical is wrong with the drive.

Disc fault   No 199

This occurs for a number of reasons all of which mean that the expected data was not where it should have been. Two numbers are given with this fault, the fault number and the track location.

NOT ENABLED   No 189

Certain 'dangerous' commands need to trapped prior to execution to prevent their unintentional use, because unintentional use can have disastrous consequences (such as wiping your discs!). There are two ways of trapping - the first is to ask a subsidiary question ("Are you sure you want to format Y/N"). The second is to require the 'dangerous' command to be preceded by an enabling command - eg *ENABLE (there may be parameters attached)

If you don't issue a *ENABLE prior to a 'dangerous' command you will get the 'Not enabled' error message and the command will not be carried out.

Precisely which of your commands require enabling depends upon which type of DFS and other ROMs you have in your machine, but typically FORMAT, DESTROY and BACKUP require enabling first.

CATALOGUE FULL   No 190

The DFS can only cope with 31 titles in a catalogue: the ADFS can have up to 45 in EACH directory. So 'Catalogue full' is only a problem with the DFS. It becomes more of a problem with 80-track discs: if you have a number of short programs or files the disc can be only a quarter full of data, but have no room left for further file names.

There are three main ways of dealing with this:

1.   DISC DOCTOR has a *FORMAT command which makes each disc face into two separate faces - the *SWAP command allows you to select which of the two faces you are using. Someone without DISC DOCTOR can read the face you last used on the disc, but cannot access the second part.

2.   Get the ADFS !

3.   Make sure you use your discs more effectively - don't use any one disc for a lot of short files.

TOO MANY FILES OPEN   No 192

You can only have 5 files open at any one time with the DFS. If you try to open any more you will get this message.

Close unwanted files. (In any case it is good practice to close files as soon as you can after accessing them, though this can slow things down somewhat)

FILE READ ONLY   No 193

If you have used OPENUP for reading your file you will not be able to write to that file.

Use OPENIN instead.

FILE OPEN   No 194

In order to prevent corruption of file contents, a file must be opened before accessing, and then properly closed down afterwards - this is because when a file is written to, it is not written to directly but the input goes into a buffer within the machine's memory, and the disc is only written to when the buffer is full. When you close a file, anything left in the buffer is put onto disc. If you don't close a file properly, you may get data left in the machine.

Therefore, you are not allowed to re-access an open file by another channel.

If you get this error message, either issue CLOSE#<file-variable> or else CLOSE#0 which closes all files. Now you can access the file.

FILE LOCKED   No 195

Locking a file is a precaution against accidentally deleting it. If you try to delete, rename, or write to a locked file you will get this error message.

Unlock the file with *ACCESS <filename> <Return>

FILE EXISTS   No 196

If you try to use RENAME with the name of a file which already exists this error is given. Trying to change say g.edward to G.EDWARD would give this error.

DISC CHANGED   No 200

This error message is self evident - you have started accessing a file on a disc but have changed the disc so that the original file is no longer present.

DISC READ ONLY   No 201

As a further precaution against the accidental deletion of valuable files you may protect a disc against any kind of over-writing or deletion of files by covering up the write-protect notch, which is the small square cut-out portion on the left side of the disc (as you put the disc in the drive). If this notch is covered up the disc drive will not write to the disc at all.

If you've received this message then presumably you're trying to use a disc that would be better left alone, so put another disc in. If you are SURE you want to write to the disc then remove the small plastic cover to the write-protect notch (carefully! - don't bend or scrape the disc cover in the process, you may damage the disc itself).

BAD SUM   No 202

The check sum (an internal data count to minimise un-noticed data transfer errors) does not add up because there is some form of corruption in memory.

BAD OPTION   No 203

When using *OPT you have put in a number outside the acceptable range (1-4)

BAD FILENAME   No 204

On the DFS filenames can be up to seven characters long: on the ADFS up to ten. Neither of these figures includes the directory.

With the ADFS it is common to use directory titles that are greater than the single character directories of the DFS. Mistakes can arise when using a filename like this on the DFS.

eg `aco.fle` on the ADFS means 'Directory `aco`, file-name `fle`'

On the DFS the same filename means 'Current directory, filename aco.fle'

BAD DRIVE   No 205

You are trying to access a drive NUMBER that doesn't exist, either because you have given a number above the maximum for your filing system (which for most systems is 0-3 inclusive): alternatively you have used a variable as the parameter

```
eg *DR.N%
```
which isn't allowed. If you want to write to a drive which is delineated by a variable, then use the OSCLI command

```
eg    G$="*DR. "+STR$(N%)
      OSCLI G$
```

which passes the contents of the string variable G$ to the command line interpreter.

Note that trying to access a drive which doesn't physically exist in your set-up will give a 'Drive fault' error message, not 'Bad drive'.

BAD DIRECTORY   No 206

With the DFS the directory is only one character long: the ADFS can have up to 10 letters. Most characters are acceptable in directory names except for the 'wildcards' * and #, full stop etc.

This error message means that you have tried to change the directory (using *DIR) to one of either an unacceptale length, or one containing unacceptable characters.

As with 'bad drive' you cannot use *DIR with a variable eg *DIR new_directory$ is not allowed (*DIR new_dir$ WOULD be allowed in the ADFS because the $ would be treated as an ordinary character, not a variable name)

If you want to change to a variable directory, use the OSCLI comand, as outlined in 'Bad Drive'

BAD ATTRIBUTE   No 207

You have tried to alter the ACCESS value of a file using a letter other than 'L'.

FILE NOT FOUND   No 214

The file you tried to access is not found in the current directory. On the Archimedes system there is a way to avoid this error if you are trying to delete a file. Use *REMOVE rather than *DELETE: the result is the same but if the file does not exist then no error message is issued.

BAD COMMAND   No 254

You have attempted to issue a command which the computer did not understand. *DR or *COT would give this error.

23. STANDARD PROGRAMS

There are a number of standard programs on the market - standard, that is, in the overall plan of what they set out to do, but by no means standard in the way they do it.

WORD PROCESSORS

Word processors are one of the 'big three' general computer programs, and arguably the most useful. They have aptly been described as programs which allows you to "paint with words".

The basic idea is to allow manipulation of text - writing onto the screen, then altering one word for another, changing the position of a word or phrase (and maybe changing it back again); inserting a paragraph, deleting another: merging with another document stored on disc and saving the final composition to disc for review on another occasion - or else printing out a copy or two. You never need type anything twice again! Store paragraphs of frequently used text on disc and call them up into your main text when required, or put frequently used words or phrases onto the function keys so that you can call up whole phrases with a couple of key-presses.

Word processors are excellent for creative writing - if you don't like what you've written you can alter it: change words, alter the order of words in a sentence, change the type-face, underline, quickly change whole sections from lower-case to capitals, and vice versa, alter the order of sentences or paragraphs - until you are satisfied. You don't have to re-type sentences in other positions - just put markers round the part you want to move, press a button and the whole section is transposed to its new site.

In business standard letters can be prepared and quickly customised. You can replace a particular word throughout the whole document (so that "Mr.Smith" becomes "Mr.Jones" or possibly "Ken") - or replace some of the occurrences with "Mr. Jones", and others with "Ken". You can even make this automatic, by preparing a skeleton letter, and a file of names to be inserted in it. Load your printer with paper and sit back to watch each personalised letter printing out - or better, do something more constructive, like play golf.

There are basically two types of word-processor on the market:-

1.   Those which show you exactly (or very nearly exactly) on
      screen what you will get on the paper. This is known as
      WYSIWYG (pronounced "Whizzywig"), and stands for "What you
      see is what you get". If actual layout of text on the page
      is very important to you, then you will want a WYSIWYG
      word-processor: if the ideas matter,and the layout is
      unimportant then it doesn't matter if it's a WYSIWYG or
      not. However, a word of warning - if you do a lot of
      column and figure work, get a WYSIWYG - it is very
      difficult to do this on the other variety.

      The WYSIWYG brigade is a slightly mixed bag and each
      has its loyal supporters.

2.   Those which insert various print commands, etc in the
      text: this alters the look of the page - so editing is done
      in Mode 7, and you can preview the final layout in Mode 3.

A second important distinction is between those which hold the text entirely in
memory and those in which the text is actually on the disc, with the memory of the
computer acting as a window onto it. This latter method is called 'virtual memory'.
Its great advantage is that it can produce gigantic documents, limited only by the
size of the disc. The disadvantage of the virtual memory technique is that it slows
down the workings of the program to some extent. As far as we know, of the
wordprocessors available for the Acorn group, only Scribe uses this technique.

The choice of a Word Processor package is so important that you really must
spend a long time deciding.   Questions to ask yourself are:-

1.   Is it a WYSIWYG (and does it matter)

2.   Does it have all of the facilities you need now?

3.   Can the Word Processor handle the size of document
      you will be creating?

4.   Can you understand the manual?!

5.   Once you have used it for a week or so, will you be able
      to abandon the manual almost completely?

WYSIWYG WORD PROCESSORS

VIEW is one of the older ROM word-processors available, but has been well updated and provides a fairly accurate version on-screen of what is about to be printed on paper - but there are one or two instances where 'Highlight' commands (which give bold print, etc) disturb the formal picture on screen. Its facilities are comprehensive and has the advantage of being part of a well established set of programs with limited common handling of data (View, Viewsheet, Viewstore, Viewspell, Viewindex etc). The documentation is excellent.

VIEW allows you to do almost anything you wish but can be quite difficult to get into. However, it is easy to use with the VIEWSTORE database in order to produce automated letter writing. The big plus with View is that it is free with the Master series!

VIEW PROFESSIONAL is an integrated Word Processor, Spreadsheet and Database which takes a lot of getting used to and is not at all easy to operate satisfactorily as a Word Processor. However, the wealth of facilities provided makes it a very attractive package at the price.

INTER-WORD is the WP component of the highly successful INTER series. The three main programs, Word Processor, Spreadsheet and Chart are available separately but are now also available on one Rom, Mega Three, at a very competitive price. Mail-merge is possible and the sophisticated set of controls is easy to use. However, the on-screen presentation can look a little cluttered with Rulers etc but it is VERY powerful and easy to use.

INTER-WORD is from the same stable as Wordwise plus and is very nearly WYSIWYG. You still have to preview to see what a page of text is going to look like because in edit mode the text is interrupted by big rulers for every change in format or column width. Having said that, most people use very few 'ruler' changes and one soon gets used to the format.

Shadow RAM is a must if you wish to produce documents of any length as the best screen presentation for text uses a large amount of memory. (This applies to ALL of the Word Processors, not just INTER-WORD.) It will not work with some Shadow Ram boards, but Aries and Watford boards are compatible and recommended. If you have a board which is not one of these, check directly with Computer Concepts. This of course only applies to the BBC-B or upgraded A model.

INTER-WORD is designed to be part of an integrated suite of programs (INTER-WORD, Interchart and Intersheet (excellent) and INTER-BASE) and as such must be able to handle transferred data. The transfer of data is easier in this system than in any other we have come across at this level of sophistication. INTER-WORD looks like becoming another industry standard like Wordwise.

PROWORD seems to have the best of all worlds and is the cheapest. - it has a rudimentary database attached, but this does not have the sophistication of the VIEW family although adequate for Mail Merge etc. The screen is totally un-cluttered and all commands are visible on a comprehensive Key strip.

Really WYSIWYG. A delightful program which deserves more publicity and much wider recognition. It is menu-driven with a wealth of features, including the ability to display double height letters on-screen, and all the main functions are accessible from a comprehensive key-strip. It also has the advantage also of being the cheapest Word Processing package. Its disadvantage is that it is not one of a suite of programs. As extra features it has its own mail-merge database in the chip, multiple size screen dump, multi-column printing, designer fonts etc on disc. VERY impressive. Separate ROMS for Master and B models (Direct from D.Hall, 31 Wethersfield Road, Noctorum, Wirral, Mersyside.)

SCRIBE is totally disc based, the programs being loaded from disc rather than being resident in ROM, and the disc containing the files being used as 'virtual memory'. If you need very large documents this is the one to investigate, as it can handle the whole disc as though it were one long document. An advantage of the disc approach is that it is possible to have longer, and therefore more sophisticated, utility routines than it is possible to cram into a ROM (this advantage is slipping away with the very large chips now becoming available).

Non - WYSIWYG WORD PROCESSORS

WORDWISE and **WORDWISE PLUS** have much the same way of presenting and editing text, but Wordwise Plus has improved safety features, more commands and a comprehensive programming language built into it which allows you to create a wealth of facilities. It comes with a number of useful programs already written - for sorting names and addresses, to mail-merge from a database (which you have to create yourself in Wordwise Plus itself so it might not necessarily work with other databases), printing text in two columns, and continuous processing which attempts to treat the whole of all your disc sides as one big document. The language allows you to set up programs of your own to fill in blank forms etc.

A big disadvantage is that you cannot easily see what your main document will look like as you edit in Mode 7 - previewing its final form in Mode 3 is easy, but you can't edit text in this mode, having to go back to edit mode to do so - this is irritating. There is a new ROM available which is said to turn Wordwise into a true WYSIWYG. We haven't seen this in action, but if it does what it says without problems it should get round the only real objection to the Wordwise group - that they are not WYSIWYG.

The final choice is very much a matter of what you need the Word-processor to do: plus your personal preferences. (One of us is a WORDWISE PLUS addict, the other a PROWORD/VIEW nut!) If you want a complete suite of programs go for VIEW - it is long established and works well. In business it is important to have the ability to merge word - processed letters with information from a database. Therefore in assessing a Word Processing package it is necessary to assess the associated database as well. (INTER-BASE in the Inter series takes a lot of programming experience to get the best out of it, then it is one of the best, but VIEWSTORE is a Database for mere mortals) If you need to create your own wordprocessing programs as well as conventional WP, go for WORDWISE PLUS. If you just want a standalone word-processor, try PRO-WORD.

As a sub-heading we must mention...

PRINTER DRIVERS

Good word-processors come with the ability to run nearly every printer under the sun. However, beware. There appears to be no such thing as a standard set of printer codes, (though a lot of manufacturers say they are EPSON compatible, and in the main they are) However, it can be quite traumatic setting up your package to work with your particular printer.

There are two approaches. Wordwise (and WW+) give you the ability to run a basic printer without a driver and when you need to do special things you insert the code for it in the text (as green commands). This has the advantage of flexibility but can be very irritating if you indent, change font, underline and emphasize a lot. It is possible to get over this by re-defining your function keys, but it can still be a bit awkward and require a lot of characters.

View has a printer driver program which you set up once only, by going through a set of questions and then storing the result. Before a printing session you simply load in this short program and the printer is set up. The various features are then called by Highlight codes with a considerable saving on key-strokes. Unfortunately these codes are visible in the text as blocks. There is also a series of 'margin' commands which are used to do things like Centre text, Page eject etc. It is a good workable system but a little difficult to come to grips with.

Proword has a printer driver program like View which also has to be loaded by your !BOOT file. The advantage here is that the commands do not appear on screen to disturb your text. The method of entry (Function keys) is extremely economical in key-strokes (3 to set Bold, underline a heading and centre!)

MAIL-MERGE AND LABEL PRINTING

Mail-merge is another way of saying .. standard letter .. different details such as name. This involves having some form of database incorporated in the package. Proword has a simple database integral with the chip. View does the same thing with files on disc from which it calls details (MACRO's). Wordwise+ has a programming language built in which allows very sophisticated programming of such things as mail-merge. Inter-Word has a routine using two 'segments' of memory to do the same thing.

There are a number of specialist programs to do label printing (on rolls of labels) for any WP package on the market but if you have a little ability and time it is easy to set up your own program.

SPELLING CHECKERS

These are programs which search through your word-processed files, checking the contents against their own dictionary. If the come up against a word they haven't met they ask you whether you meant to spell it like that. There are three possible answers

- yes, it's correct: enter it into the dictionary so that it won't be queried again

- yes, it's correct, but it's a one-off (such as a surname), so don't bother putting it in the dictionary

- no, it's wrong. Mark it for later correction, or in Spellmaster do it there and then.

A point to remember with spell-checkers, though, is the vast number of disc accesses required per document - so it is worthwhile getting one which fits into Sideways RAM. A ROM chip alone won't do quite the same job, because your own personalized dictionary will have to be on disc, so the number of disc accesses will increase again. The larger chip sizes are now coming onto the market and so this situation is changing. Spellmaster is one of the first of the large-chip checkers.

The VIEWSPELL spelling checker is good and fast, but there are a number of alternatives on the market. The one bundled with Solidisc enables all work to be done entirely on the solid state disc, but an irritating feature of the program is the inability to catalogue the disc to check what file you next want to put through the checking routine.

There is really no competition, however, for SPELLMASTER by Computer Concepts. This really has everything, speed, facilities and a reasonable price. The dictionary size is nearly 60,000 words and you may fill up any sideways RAM banks with your own dictionary files. It really is a delight to find your personalized articles going through the checker with hardly a new word in sight. Until you realise that this must mean that your vocabulary is BORING! This is the one totally indispensable Utility ROM for anyone doing any writing.

ACCOUNTING

Accountancy packages are still generally a disappointment. The real aim should be to get a set of programs to fit your peculiar circumstances which are INTEGRATED. This means that you should only ever have to type in a piece of information once and it then becomes usable from all the programs in the package. This is rarely the case. There are a few good reasons for this. One is that you, the customer, are unique! It is difficult to design generalised packages to suit all 'tastes'. The other and more difficult problem is the lack of space in the BBC-B memory. Unless you are sure of what you are doing in terms of memory usage, or are able to break up your commercial work into self-contained units (such as word processing, database, mailing)then for commercial use, especially in accountancy, you probably shouldn't start below the Master and preferably the Archimedes, because the memory requirements aren't there. Read the business section of magazines like The Acorn User: there are excellent reviews and articles for the small business user. No punches are pulled!

Two which can be recommended:

Micro Trader by Meadow Computers. This is not from personal knowledge but by recommendation from those who use it.

Minerva Systems, Personal Accounts Package. A misnomer, we feel, as it is really for the small business. In discussion with Minerva they admit to the dilemma of the name. This firm has a backlog of good programs based on their Database language ROM. Good stuff. Different versions for Archimedes and the rest. (See also Bank Manager under Household Budget, below)

GRAPHICS

Even with the limited memory and resolution of the screen on the Beeb, this is possibly the most exciting area of operation. There are some stunning packages available both to the amateur, and for a lot more money, the professional. Computer aided design (CAD) is possible using the very up-market BITSTICK or NOVOCAD. At the lower end of the price structure the advertising pages of magazines are bulging. Free art packages, either Joystick, Mouse, Tracker ball,

Graphics pad, light pen or Cursor driven proliferate. Good ones come from Homerton College (IMAGE), AMX (SuperArt) and Wigmore (ARTIST).

Every so often, however, there is a program which is so good for its time that it takes the breath away. In the field of art packages the Quest Mouse (Watford Electronics) system is one such, way ahead of its rivals. There are two ROMs which may be bought separately. The first gives all the basic functions and this ROM by itself is more comprehensive that any other available. The second ROM adds many extra features! There are several clever points about the system which make it a joy to use. The first is so simple that you wonder why it has not been done before: the whole screen is available for the picture! When a menu is required it appears over the top or the bottom of your work, you make your choice, and it can then be made to disappear. Any description of the system would merely be a page and a half of features. Suffice it to say - ignore it and you won't get the best. Look at the adverts for a full description.

Try to establish what you want to do with the package. No one program does everything - although Quest comes close - in fact there is almost no overlap in some cases. It is impossible to give specific advice. Some of the better ones are associated with particular types of hardware. Find out which sort you prefer to use - look around and try them out.

DATABASES ARE A 'GOOD THING'

It is difficult to show enthusiasm for something which isn't there until you have done something about it. A database is effectively a set of empty boxes which you fill with information. The good bit comes when you start interrogating the database - you can fiddle with the information in a variety of ways - searching for particular items, listing things in alphabetical order, or by order of price etc. Unfortunately, it's not easy to understand the virtues of a database if you haven't actually seen one in action, but when you have the effect on your concept of computing is electrifying. It is as if your your black-and-white television has just become full-colour! You suddenly see whole new areas where your computer can be a useful and effective tool. The whole field of databases is fascinating and the range of tasks limited only by your imagination.

The underlying basis for a database is that it is not the information you put that is important - its what you get out that counts. The idea of setting uo a database is so that you can interrogate it - and the better the interrogation, the better the database.

For example, you have a database of customers and their purchases. You can extract a list of all customers who purchased a certain item within a certain period, so that you can automatically send a circular letter (personalised for each customer) about a further offer that they may find of interest. If you are a stamp dealer,and have a lot of Spanish stamps to sell, think of the advantages of being able to contact only those customers who have bought Spanish stamps in the past; or for a medical clinic being able to search through its list of patients to find all children who have not attended for their various booster jabs in the last three years

You could list all articles and books relevant to your particular interests, with a short note about their contents. When you want information of a specific nature, ask the database for all entries containing a specific word or words. So if you have a reference file on computer articles and you wanted to see if there was anything about databases available on ROM chips you would just ask for all references containing those two words. The more sophisticated the database the more you can set up complex search routines, such as "Print in order of date of issue any reference to (DATABASE, FILING SYSTEMS, OR INDEXES) AND (ROM OR BUNDLED SOFTWARE) BUT NOT IF WITH (LIBRARIES, OR ROMs if dated earlier than November 1983)"

In many ways, databases are just electronic card indexes. Unfortunately, card indexes can only be arranged in one way at once - usually alphabetically, date order, or numerically. Once a card index is in one sequence it is very difficult to convert it to a different primary sequence and then back again. It can be done - preferably with only small numbers of cards - but it is a fiddly job, and things frequently end up in the incorrect place.

To search a manual database for information is difficult when that information is not the primary order of the database - i.e. if a card index is organised alphabetically, then to get a list of people born before 1900 requires you to look at every card. (Had the cards been in order of birth it would have been easy.)

The singular advantage of electronic databases is that you can search easily on topics outside the primary order of the index. It also takes far less time than a manual search of a card index would: if you want, you can re-order the database electronically without any possibility of the equivalent in the physical system of getting a card out of place.

What databases could you use? Names and addresses (Christmas labels will never be the same), phone numbers, etc are within a few seconds of inserting a disc. If you can't remember the correct spelling of a surname, just put in as much of it as you can remember and anything containing that combination of letters comes up.

One idea which seems to be popular for some weird reason is that a database needs to be large to be useful. Rubbish! If you are into using them, a number of small individualized bases are very nearly essential. Keep your discs and their programs catalogued. Where is that stamp in the collection? What track is that particular song on? How many short stories by that author do I have? How much did I pay for that toaster last year, where did I buy it, and what was the guarantee number? How on earth did I make Mealy Loaf, what bits and pieces do I need? How many rolls of paper to do the hallway, how much did it cost last time? You can even archive your main bills to enable prediction.

On the business front, databases could contain
- customers' names and addresses
- particulars of each order
- details of stock items, parts numbers etc

Teachers and databases should not be parted: pupil details, marks etc. (Mind you, spreadsheets are also very useful here!) But watch the legality of anything you keep. Check with your local Computer Education Centre. You may need to register under the Data Protection Act (see chapter 27).

If you haven't tried a database yet, there are several ways to make a start. Two programs which will get you off the ground are:-

Mini Office II by Database Publications (this also includes a wordprocessor and spreadsheet, all for about £20.00!). However, it is not all that sophisticated.

Magscan by Beebugsoft, a super 'bung it in and search' type base. No sorting, just a look-up card index type, but easy to use, create and maintain. We both use Magscan for filing articles. We used to take ages to find an article in our piles of computer magazines, with half a dozen titles spreading over three years. After a week of evenings with Magscan typing in article titles, a few keywords and sometimes a comment, the whole lot was entered. To keep it up to date, when a new magazine arrives all relevant articles are entered straightaway. Then to find an article, just pop in the disc and in literally seconds you have the titles of all articles with the keywords you were asking for, together with details of magazine title, date and page. Invaluable!

Other more complex and sophisticated systems include:

MASTERFILE 2 from Beebugsoft, very comprehensive and Menu driven. A little limited by the use of Mode 7 screens throughout but very powerful for most applications.

KEY marketed by ITV (The Television ITV) this is an astounding piece of software for about £5 -£6. Aimed at schools it also deals with graphics and statistics.

INTERBASE at the time of writing still had various teething troubles. It is a database programming language, rather like dBASE for PCs. It has all the commands of BASIC plus some astoundingly easy to use array and string handling features. The book that goes with it at present is abysmal but there is another being written which will be up to the normal Computer Concepts standard. We understand that even if you have this system with the old book the new ones will be sent to you on publication. That's good customer relations.

MINERVA SYSTEM DELTA is another database language, very comprehensive but a little more finicky than Interbase. However, Minerva produce ready-made database management packages using this system, which saves you the problems.

VIEWSTORE is a delightful database - very comprehensive and one of the best single-file databases available (although 'SUPASTORE' comes a very close second). In particular, the ability to pass database information across to a VIEW 'macro' (i.e. a skeleton letter, to be filled with specific details from selected database entries) is a powerful tool, especially for business use. (A friend's son uses it for Christmas thank you letters...)

Example use!....

```
        Dear ...@1...

        Thank you for my   ...@2...    I had a good Christmas
        using it ...@3...


                         Love

                         Arthur
```

DATA   `Uncle James,cricket bat,in the garden`
            `Auntie Flo,stamp album,to file all my Colonial stamps`
            `Freda,money, to buy this book`

SPREADSHEETS

A simple spreadsheet is a useful tool for manipulating columns of figures even if the calculating function is not used. It can act as a sort of word-processor for figures.

Spreadsheets have a curious way of growing on you. The basic ethos is "What if...?" and sure enough, this is just what happens when you start getting involved in them.

Much of what we said about Databases is also valid here. Most of the spreadsheet packages we have come across are friendly - in particular we very much like Ultracalc and Inter-Sheet. The remarks about Mini Office are also true here - cheap, cheerful and remarkably sophisticated: even if you go on to another program at a later date you would not regret having had a close encounter with this. (You might even find that you stay with it.)

Teachers can use the sheet for mark collection and manipulation. It is useful for applying formulae to a whole year group and coming up with a 'faked' spread, a skew or some such. You can do averages, maximum and minimum, etc.

One thing to find out before you buy - some sheets calculate a column at a time (top to bottom), whereas some calculate a row at a time (left to right). This can make a considerable difference to the way the sheet looks both when printed and on screen. You have also to be aware of this so that you don't make silly mistakes when setting up calculations.

VIEWSHEET has many excellent features but one irritating one - it is not possible to alter the width of individual columns. Otherwise it is extremely easy to use.

INTER-SHEET is a particularly good spread-sheet, having all the good characteristics of Wordwise in its input system. The display is unique in allowing 106 columns on-screen at once. It is very easy to get to grips with and even quite advanced levels are simple to implement.

ULTRACALC 2 by the BBC is a lovely program with a lot of features but some people find the command structure complex. It really only takes a little work to release the power of this package.

QUICKCALC by Beebugsoft has one of the easiest entry systems of the lot, but it is severely limited by only working in 40 column mode. It is superb as an introduction to spreadsheets and may even serve all your purposes.

DON'T BUY A HOUSEHOLD BUDGET PROGRAM

If you are the sort of person who could use it properly, you are probably already doing the job well in any case! A general spreadsheet program and/or database program would probably be of more use in the long run. If you are the sort of disorganised person who makes a muck of your budget and imagine a household budget program might be your salvation, think again. In all probability it will only make you a few quid poorer and in a few days' time you will be wondering where this money went as you'd forgotten to enter it into the database!

Having said this there are excellent programs about which, if you are prepared to spend the time to really learn them, will certainly deal efficiently with your home accounts and beyond. We used to say that there was no point in buying a home accounts program - the size of the BBC-B's memory means that there is really not enough room both for the program and the data files that need to go with it. In turn, this limits the usefulness of the program, firstly by reducing the number of records that can be dealt with, and secondly, reducing the effectiveness of the program because lack of memory reduces the ability to do the internal checking, searching and cross-referencing that is the difference between a good program and an indifferent one. Such is the case with many of the cassette-based programs, some of which can handle only one month's accounts at a time.

The Bank Manager from Contex computing is a welcome change from this - it is entirely disc-based and has a wealth of internal cross-references and checks: it can handle data on up to 36 different 'bank' accounts (including credit card accounts, building societies, etc), can analyse the results under 100 different headings, can deal with standing orders, has full bank reconciliation etc. It is ideal for keeping track of ALL your home accounts, mortgage and credit cards.

It is also applicable to small business accounts, with the proviso that dealing with VAT is not a standard item. You CAN do it, but you lose some of the powerful analytical ability in the process. There is a Master and Archimedes version which gets over this problem and provides extra (and useful!) facilities. It has also been specifically designed so that it can also interface to Winchesters thus widening its potential.

One small word of warning. If you are dealing with large quantities of data expect to wait a little while whilst processing is done. The disadvantage of a small memory and disc-based rather than memory-based data is the access time to the disc. This of course applies to all programs which are ambitious on the earlier Acorn machines.

INTEGRATED SUITES

A suite of programs (word-processor, spreadsheet, database, graphics package) is said to be integrated when all data is transportable between programs (though each program can work on its own). Thus information created on the spreadsheet may be transferred to the graphics package or the word-processor: or a mail-shot may be prepared, as detailed above, to groups of customers selected from the database.

Two particular integrated suites of note are:

-       **Acornsoft's VIEW series (VIEW, VIEWSTORE, VIEWSHEET)** The
        details have been given above in relation to the individual
        programs. These transfer files via the disc. The theory
        of file transfer is fine, but actually doing it is somewhat more difficult.
-       **Computer Concept's INTER- series (INTER-WORD, INTER-BASE,
        INTER-CHART and INTER-SHEET)** - again, mostly mentioned
        above. INTERCHART is efficient and does its job wall as a
        provider of graphical output. INTER-BASE is the database
        element of the suite but is an entirely different animal to
        the rest. The others are child's play to use, Interbase
        needs a programmer. Transfer of data on a small scale can
        be done actually in the machine.

COMMUNICATIONS

Without a doubt, communication between computers is going to become a major part of life in the next ten years. Why? Because it is so much more efficient. If you compose a letter on your word-processor to your bank, requesting a transfer of money from account A to account B, you have to print it out, find an envelope and stamp, and walk to the post-box. The letter has to be collected, sorted, delivered, opened and read. Then the contents are entered into the database of the bank's computer, by hand, so that the sum of money may be transferred.

How much easier if you connect your computer through the telephone system to the bank's computer and put in the request directly.

This:-
- reduces human error, such as the letter being sent to the wrong address or the bank clerk misreading your letter and transferring the money from account B to account A.
- is much quicker and more reliable
- you can get instant acknowledgement from the bank's computer that the transaction has been completed to your satisfaction.
- is cheaper, as it cuts out all the expense of moving and sorting mail, and reduces the number of bank clerks needed to open, sort, and act upon the day's mail.

Equally, if you hadn't wanted to do anything to your account but just wanted to find out how much you had (or owed!), or whether a cheque had been paid in, you could call up the bank and get a direct reply immediately - even at midnight. (And let's face it, most of us 'do' our personal accounts out of banking hours, don't we?)(We may even be able to prevent by early action the type of letter which goes..
Dear Mr +++, Please try not to spend our money faster than you can earn it. Yours sincerely ...)

In the future we will all be doing a lot of business in this way. As well as direct banking from home (which is here already, with some banks) there will be direct computer booking of holidays, of mail order items, and eventually of groceries, ordered like this from the local supermarket, gathered automatically by the supermarket computer-controlled stocking robot, and paid for automatically by direct computer access to your bank account. Your only involvement, apart from ordering, will be to pick up the groceries in the car... and eat them! This degree of sophistication is not quite with us yet, but it's not far off.

By linking computers you can send information and acquire knowledge. Knowledge is power, and the best-informed person usually makes the most effective decisions. Whether you want to know the weather forecast, the latest Financial Times Index, the exchange rate against the Lira, the side-effects of a drug, or the runners in the 2.30 at Sandown, extra information will allow you to make better decisions. The man who does not have information is always at a disadvantage compared to the man who has. How many times do you hear "Oh, if only I'd known"?

There are two main types of information you can get from other computers.

1. Database information - general information that applies to anybody (if they're interested). All the items we mentioned earlier fall in this section - financial, sporting, weather forecasts, together with specialised information for doctors, lawyers, chemists, engineers and the like. This allows access to a wide range of information that either changes very swiftly (so electronic dissemination of information is the only way for outsiders to keep up to date) or else is not normally worth keeping in sufficient detail against the remote possibility of being needed in the future. For example, a pharmacist may only once in his career need to look up the interactions of an infrequently-used drug - but when he looks it up his information must be accurate and up-to-date.

The advantages of accessing databases such as these are
- up-to-date information
- well-ordered information
- no need to hold massive files locally, with all the problems of storage, up-dating, and retrieving the right piece of information.

A variant of this is the keeping of personal records such as medical information on one database accessible to others with computers and the correct passwords. This enables centralized data to be collected, which is generally more accurate and easier to keep up to date than records distributed all over the country.

2. Mailboxes. A mailbox is the term used to describe a way of sending information from one person to another by storing it in a central computer. When the intended recipient dials the computer he is told if there are any messages waiting for him. There could be any number of documents or messages, and the documents can be long. It is like telephoning someone, without having to wait until they are found, or until their line is free. The advantages are:-

speed - the message is instantly there, even if you are in Lands End and they are in John O'Groats.

- there is no need to know where the recipient is at the time you send the message, because he can dial into the central computer from wherever he happens to be. If you're still in Land's End, your recipient might be in John O'Groats or New York (or Land's End!) He can still get your message.

- you can send a complex document to him and he does not have to re-type it at the other end. The document, being electronic, can be transferred from the mailbox in the central computer to his own word-processor. (incidentally this is one way of making "incompatible" computers talk to one another.)

- the recipient does not have to return to a central base to get his messages. Nor is he limited by time (or time difference, if he's in another continent).

- the recipient can finish off a job before 'taking his calls'. This is an instant blessing to those of us for whom the telephone is a constant interruption, lengthening our work because of the need to re-collect our thoughts after every call. In some types of mailbox (especially those using in-house computers in large firms) it is possible to flash a message on the recipient's screen when an urgent call is waiting.

- the same message can be sent to a number of people, with little extra effort. You have a team of salesmen working for you up and down the country and you want to tell them of the new pricing structure following budget changes? One message can be prepared, then sent to each salesman's mailbox automatically.

The whole world of communications is expanding rapidly: the hardware is becoming cheaper and facilities more numerous.

The hardware needed is fairly simple, just a computer and a MODEM. The modem (it stands for MODulator DEModulator) attaches your computer to the telephone system and turns both incoming and outgoing signals into a readable form. It can AUTODIAL, automatically disconnect when communication has finished and manage the flow of information in between.

For up-to-date information on this exciting world you must keep an eye on the main Micro magazines. They are courting the user with attractive offers at present to encourage usage of Bulletin boards etc. 'There has never been a better time to buy!'

24. ASSESSING COMMERCIAL PROGRAMS.

Before describing how to assess the software itself, may we make one general point? Normally, in selecting important software (especially for business use) the rule is:-

"First find the right software. Then buy the hardware."

However, as you have chosen to read this book, you have probably bought a computer already - possibly from the Acorn group, or alternatively one of the other machines capable of running BBC BASIC.

We are about to describe the best ways of assessing software: please be aware that that is in some ways not the right place to begin your search. If you haven't yet bought your hardware then maybe you ought to look around more widely, at least at the beginning.

For instance, if you are looking for a commercial system running the 'big' commercial accountancy systems then you need a machine with a lot of RAM: Only the Archimedes has the memory capability to run the industry standard programs like dBASE III PLUS, LOTUS 1-2-3, JAZZ, SYMPHONY etc. The machine has an IBM emulator program available and should be able to run most IBM software(at the time of writing this had not yet been released officially: its release coincided with our publication date). If you want lots of speed in computing, then maybe a 16-bit machine won't be appropriate: if you want compatibility with other commercial personal computers then you will need to think of different operating systems, such as MS-DOS or CP/M: you can achieve this with the Archimedes, or a BBC with a 2nd processor but you may need hardware compatibility (size of drive etc). Therefore, consider first what you want to do: choose the right software. Then choose the hardware that this software will run on. If you have a number of possibilities at this stage, remember that compatibility with existing systems may be more important than you might at first think.

Having said this, don't dismiss the BBC-B out of hand. One of us has recently installed a network in a school: the RM Nimbus with MS-DOS, BBC BASIC, built-in networking and masses of memory fitted the bill very nicely, price included. The other author has just extended his office equipment - and has chosen to go for second-hand BBC-B's, even though he had the option of going for 'professional' machines. Rather than choosing a big network, a number of small stand-alone systems (which can be connected together if needed) has proved the most appropriate use of computers in that office. The BBC-B fits in well with the particular office environment, has lots of relevant software, and is compatible with the existing office and home machines, so that in the event of hardware failure the office is not left stranded. All the plugs are compatible (easy to forget this!): if part of one system fails it is possible to effect a temporary repair by cannibalising a less important part of the system.

The small size of memory is no problem, because the type of work done depends mainly on large disc files and less on computational requirements. Amazingly, the BBC-B out-performs some professional machines in computation and speed of file handling: and BBC BASIC is streets ahead of many other BASICs.

Commercial software for the Beeb is cheap - about a tenth of the price of equivalent commercial software. The secretaries already know how to work the BBC, so there is no time taken up in learning how to operate a new machine.

So - the humble Beeb has a lot going for it, and may fit your particular requirements very well. But do be aware that other systems may be more appropriate.

It may be that the answer to most questions in this section will be 'buy an Archimedes', as this machine:

-       out-performs most commercial PCs, being a 32 bit machine as
        opposed to a 16-bit and also being made speedier by its RISC technology.

-       has adequate memory requirements for most commercial
        programs. (although the 305 model is inadequate in this
        respect, only having 500K)

-       can run an IBM emulator program, which opens up a vast
        range of top-class commercial software.

-       can draw on all the existing Acorn-compatible software
        which has been correctly written. This, of course, includes
        a vast amount of educational software. In addition, most
        of this software is vastly cheaper than its IBM-type rivals
        and a lot of it is remarkably sophisticated. BUT, it is
        early days yet and there is no definitive list of which
        software will or will not run on it. TRY BEFORE YOU BUY ..
        you have been warned.

ASSESSING SOFTWARE

How do you assess commercial software?

Does it do what you want it to?
No, this is not a daft question! An otherwise excellent and comprehensive database package may not be right for your particular purposes. For example, if a particular package won't print address labels, or can't print non-English characters, then if your business does a lot of mailing to Sweden, think again!

Equally, many packages are used for purposes the creators never dreamed of, and very effectively too!

Is it convenient to use?
Look particularly at those parts of the package that you will be using frequently. Do they need lots of key-strokes to enter information? Do you have to enter the same information more than once? Is it easy to slip from one module to another, or have you to go through several menus and sub-menus in the process?

Can it cope with the quantity of information?
(Bear in mind that most computer databases end up double or treble the intended size.) Quantify your intended use and see if it will fit - eg, will the database hold the amount of information you need - are the field sizes big enough: can you put enough records into the system? Can you use it where you want to - can you integrate it within your existing system? ie. if you want to be able to use the program within a suite of programs that you have written for your business, will it let you do this, or must it function as a stand-alone system?

What are the hardware requirements?
Do you need more memory, more storage space, shadow RAM, ADFS instead of DFS, a hard disc instead of floppies?

Is it compatible with your existing hardware?
Some systems will not work together as they compete for the same workspace. Problems can occur with non-standard DFS chips, ROMs and sideways ROM boards.

How quickly does it work?
You would be surprised at the difference in speed between some commercial database systems. There is one system on the market that takes two hours to sort information that another database will do in two minutes. Don't be fooled by a salesman's demonstration program on a database containing only a small amount of data. Searching and sorting a small database cannot help but be fast, but will a full database match up to this initial promise of speed? It may - but on the other hand.....

There are standard tests (called benchmarks) for performing certain operations - this allows a direct comparison on speed under laboratory conditions. Results are published in reviews in the journals (see below). However, benchmarks may not necessarily be a good indication of how a micro is going to behave with your software in your circumstances. If this seems a strange statement, think of the problems involved with filing Scottish surnames: standard tests on surnames spread randomly through the alphabet may not be all that helpful in assessing software for use in Aberdeen!

How 'safe' is it?
(This applies particularly to business-oriented programs) Do you lose a lot of information if you press BREAK or ESCAPE, or has the package been adequately protected again this sort of thing? Test it out.

Is it easy to rub off important information with one key-stroke (if you touch the wrong one by mistake)? Or are there checks to make sure that this is what you really intended? (such as a second question saying "Are you sure you want to ...(whatever it is)". Can you overwrite a disc file easily? Or will the computer tell you that you have already got a file of that name, and is overwriting really what you intended?

If the wrong disc is inserted, or a mistake is made, does the system tell you and guide you over what to do next, or does it crash, or lock up solid with no indication of what's wrong?

If a business package asks for a date, try putting in a silly one (like February 29th 1987). If it rejects it as invalid, fine: if it goes happily on, think on this - date checking is easy. If the programmers haven't thought to check the date entry properly, what does it promise for the rest of the program?

Do lots of silly things - enter numbers where it expects letters, and vice versa. Put the discs in the wrong drives. Give silly answers and see if decent verification of data entry has been done. Does it matter whether you enter information in upper or lower case?

When the mistake is made, does it tell you what you've done wrong, give an audible warning that an incorrect button has been pressed, or just lock up solid?

Obviously, the bigger the system, the more these items should be dealt with correctly. In fairness, it is not always possible in a relatively small computer such as the BBC-B to put in as much error-checking as you might like to see. But at least these principles will give you an idea of how easy or difficult it is to foul up the whole system. Murphy's law says that if a thing can go wrong it will. Pure pragmatism says that, given time, every possible mistake will be made. If the system crashes with a lot of important information locked inside it then you will be the loser.

Having said all this, no system is proof against hardware failure, and few will withstand mains failure without losing some data. All systems fail for one reason or another, sooner or later - the most common problem being disc failure. However good your system, don't neglect the important matter of backing up data, especially if you are in business.

How easy is it to use?
For example - there are many database programs on the market. They all do much the same thing - store information in a number of related fields; search for specific information; and sort the stored information. With some packages you can search for information in a matter of a few seconds and as many key-presses - in others you get an unnecessary third-degree interrogation! This takes time and in the end becomes extremely off-putting. In general, the smaller the number of key-presses to take you from section to section, the better the system. However, there should be adequate checks to prevent you doing silly things, and supplementary questions such as 'Are you sure?' may be very necessary.

The method of input can often be revealing. The computer is well suited to providing long answers at the cost of one key press (eg 'Hard copy required (Y/N)'). If you find yourself answering 'Yes' <Return> 'No'<Return> 'No' <Return>..... then you haven't got an efficient program. All those Returns will eventually drive you mad! The same goes for menus - they can be a very efficient way of reducing key-presses in inputting information - but if the menus are stacked tortuously so that you cannot get to the nitty-gritty without first negotiating an obstacle course you will soon be put off from using the system.

Is there adequate instruction?
Have a look at the manual. If it appears to have been written by a Ph.D in computer science who failed GCSE English then think again. (Some manuals are amazing!)

There may in fact be no need for a manual - especially if the program contains a lot of HELP screens, or if the possible commands are permanently displayed at the top or bottom of the screen. In many ways, the smaller the manual the better - it implies that the program is self-explanatory... they hope!

Comparing software.
Read the reviews! O.K. - but inevitably the thing is not in the magazines when you want it. There are two courses of action. Go to your local library and ask them to find out when reviews on your package were published. Then either ask to look at copies (they should have them on file somewhere in the county) or ask if they can get photostats for you, at a small charge. The second method is quicker. Ring up the top magazines' editorial office, and ask the editor's assistant when they published a review. They are invariably courteous and helpful and may be able to give more help than you expected.

A final word.
We have concentrated talking on programs for Acorn machines. For the BBC-B programs may be up to 30K long - wow! Take a look at some professional programs on office micros and personal computers - you can find that a "Help" file may be 140K long and part of the main program 312K long. The 8-bit micros really do perform miracles but it is only possible to get 10 pints into a 1 quart pot (.....thinking in binary, of course!).

25. MAKING THE MOST OF COMMERCIAL SOFTWARE

If you try to write your own business software it will take you a very long time indeed. It is much more cost-effective to buy a ready-made program 'off the shelf' and adapt it to your own needs, if you can.

This is not easy, nor necessarily possible with some packages, so if you are buying software, make sure that it can do what you want - have it demonstrated before you buy.

ADAPTING EXISTING SOFTWARE

Good packages are adaptable and by looking around you should be able to find one that suits your purposes. But how do you adapt software that you can't break into, and that provides nowhere in the package for permanent customer changes (as is the case with all packages supplied only on ROM chip)? It can be surprisingly easy. Many packages allow you to adapt the red keys to your own needs. In addition you can create your own programs, parts of programs, and files that fit around, or are used in, the commercial program.

The most convenient method creates disc files that can be routinely read into the machine on starting up, or called up en bloc within the program.

Here is an example of how to adapt and tailor a piece of standard commercial software to your own needs. Most well- written programs are sufficiently open-ended and adaptible to allow this sort of manipulation.

WORDWISE AND WORDWISE PLUS

When you are on the Menu page you can enter material into the user-defined keys with the command *KEY followed by the number of the key and then the material you want in that key.

What to put in them? Things like the commands for heavy type and underline, or standard (complicated) printer settings such as italic type, double size type,(and their cancelling instructions), and temporary indent (for starting off paragraphs). Equally, you might prefer to have your pet phrases, or awkward long words, on some of the keys.

When you want to use a user-defined key hold down SHIFT and CONTROL together and dab the Function Key (as in SHIFT/BREAK). Don't forget that Wordwise and Wordwise-Plus use the normal function keys for the word-processing itself and Wordwise-Plus uses SHIFT-function key to start off a segment program, so watch what your left hand is doing when your right is going towards a function key!

As an example of the sorts of items that we use, try the following:-

```
*KEY 0 |!!DS|!!US|!"       (F1 Double strike F1 Underline F2)
*KEY 1 |!!UE|!!DE|!"       (F1 Underline end F1 DS end F2)
*KEY 2 |!!DS|!"            (Double-strike begin)
*KEY 3 |!!DE|!"            (Double-strike end)
*KEY 4 |!!LL60|!!OC27,33,55|!" (set heavy large type)
*KEY 5 |!!LL68|!!OC27,33,8|!"  (reset to normal size type)
*KEY 6 |!!TI5|!"           (Temporary indent of 5 spaces)
*KEY 7 computer            (frequently used words )
*KEY 8 disc drive          (    "        "      "    )
```

The commands above for double strike and underline only work in this format with Wordwise-Plus. If you only have Wordwise you will have to do things in a slightly more long-winded fashion - refer to the manual.

Note, '|' is the symbol generated by SHIFT\. You will obviously think up your own set of commands.

Setting the red keys for the inserted commands is a pain in the neck - all those exclamation marks and quotes! All too easy to make a mistake - so - have a separate disc for Word-processing. Then build a !BOOT file which sets all the red keys with your choice of useful commands, and finally calls Wordwise itself. In this way you can start wordprocessing simply by inserting the disc and pressing SHIFT/BREAK. This immediately sets the function keys and calls Wordwise. It saves hours.

Next, set up blank files with all the printer settings (line length, margins etc) for your standard formats. eg type your usual letter-heading on it, with 'Yours sincerely,' etc at the bottom, and SAVE it as "LETTER".

Now, to write a letter you insert the disc, press SHIFT/BREAK - this sets the red keys and calls Wordwise. Now LOAD "LETTER", and you're ready to start typing - the red keys are set to your most frequently used commands and phrases, the formatting of the page has already been done for you, and all you have to do is insert the text.

This is what is meant by "making the micro work for you". It takes a little time to set up the !BOOT and BLANK files, but the savings in stress and time are ultimately enormous.

This is only a small example. WORDWISE-PLUS now has its own programming language, and it is possible to do very many more subtle things using it. One of us has the Micro at work set up so that on starting word-processing the secretary can call up any of a number of forms and automatically fill in names, addresses and other details before going on to the typing of the message proper.

IF YOU WANT EXTRA SPACE, GET CLOSER.

This is a silly one which fools some of the people all of the time and all of the people some of the time.

If you have a wordprocessor, such as Wordwise, which uses control codes actually in the text, beware of spaces. What happens is this:

You look at what you have written and decide that an extra space is needed before a word. There is a control code before the word so you put the space between the word and code.

Problem... When you look again you find that no extra space has been added. The fault is that you have put the space before the end code which is invisible. It is good policy to add any extra spaces tight up against a word if there are control codes around.

While on the subject of W.P., a lot of people with Wordwise Plus don't seem to have read the instruction book again once they are familiar with the package. It is remarkable what you can glean from the book once you know how the thing works. One particular feature is CTRL/F. This releases the word wrap feature and enables you to line up columns of figures easily. However, use CTRL/F again before printing as some printers don't like it.

ZIP CODES FOR RAM BOARDS.

The principle of adapting Wordwise apply in much the same way to RAM boards. With these there is usually some form of software which loads the ROM from disc, settles it comfortably in its new home and then gracefully bows out.

Usually there are a few ROMs which are in use most of the time, or at least more frequently than others. It is always irritating to have to go through a situation like this...

Load Disc.
Type in the title of the loading program.
Choose which ROM was to be loaded.
Choose where the ROM was to be loaded.
Decide if another ROM is to be loaded.
Choose where.
Choose to Exit.
Fire up the appropriate ROM.
Collapse exhausted.

Most people have standard ROM's they want to put into the machine prior to a programming session, so... Why not use the !BOOT option to load the loading program, and make it all automatic?

For example, using the excellent RAMAMP board (which is fairly typical of the way the menu program works):

Type in Menu name. <RETURN>
"Which ROM?" (a letter has to be input)
"Which Slot?" (a letter has to be input)
"Do you wish to add a 7K printer buffer?" (If the first
ROM was 8K and the board may use the rest of the 16k for
a printer buffer, a letter has to be input).
"Do you wish to load another ROM? Y/N" (Another letter)
"Which ROM?" (Another letter)
"If write protect switch fitted, operate now." (operate
switch, press space)

Now most of this can be put into the !BOOT file. But there are still a couple of problems. The first is that the options are all accepted by the GET function and do not require a <RETURN>. Therefore all the answers have to be put on the same line without a <Return>.

If the option answers happen to be:-
Which ROM C
WHICH slot ..... A
Print Buffer.... N
Another ROM..... Y
Which ROM....... D
Don't want write protect switch.

Then write the !BOOT file as follows:-

```
*BUILD!BOOT
001 *FX15,0          (Clears all buffers)
002 CH."RMEN32K"     (Loads Loader program)
003 CANYD-           (Where '-' represents a space
                      NOT the minus sign!)
004 <ESCAPE>
```

(If you want to operate the Write protect switch do not put the space symbol in after the last letter. The space is recognized as a key press.)

*OPT4,3 <CR>(which makes the computer seek the file !BOOT when SHIFT/BREAK is pressed.)

All is now ready. Put the disc in, SHIFT/BREAK and everything is loaded into the RAM board automatically.

You my well find it easier to create and amend the !BOOT files on your wordprocessor (see Chapter 12). It is far easier and if your disc is fairly full sometimes the only way to do it. (The *BUILD command tries initially to reserve enough space on the disc for a small novel even if you only want a one liner!)

It is always a good idea to have a working disc for each ROM or pair of ROMs, so that if there is any damage to the disc you can easily use the back-up and not lose too much in the way of working files and time.

26. INTRODUCING COMPUTERS TO THE OFFICE

Computers can be a boon to a business - or in extreme cases they can ruin it.

There is a definite art in introducing computers into the office environment. There are eight distinct aspects to the problem:

1. What aspects of the business are to be computerised.
2. Who arranges for it to be done.
3. Choosing the system
4. Choosing the software
5. Cost
6. Fitting in the computerised with the non-computerised   office work
7. Introducing the equipment
8. Staff training
9. In-service training, software and hardware servicing.

It is not within the scope of this book to deal with these in anything other than the broadest approach, but if we can convince you of the underlying principles behind successful computerisation you will be able to work everything else out for yourself.

1. WHAT IS TO BE COMPUTERISED?

First, refer to Chapters 1 and 23 on what goes well, and what does not go well on a computer.

Second, ask yourself why you want to computerise. If you can't answer the question, don't do it! Above all, don't do it just because everyone else is. Computerisation takes money - it also takes time (lots of it - especially at the beginning). The benefits are only seen after the system has been working for months, if not years.

You should be thinking of computerisation if:-

1.   You can devote more time to the actual production of whatever you make or do if the drudgery of paperwork is taken away. This applies especially to the small or one-man business, where a good photographer / dress designer / handyman / shop-keeper / etc is weighed down with accounts, invoices, VAT, letters, mail-shots and

advertising, staff wages, National Insurance, PAYE, stock
control and customer records. There are standard programs
which may help in each of these cases.

2.   You can advertise more quickly / more appropriately with
      customised mail-shots that might otherwise never get done
      by hand, or might get done badly.

Computerisation should give you more time for your business in the end. Don't
expect to save time immediately or you'll get in a mess. In fact, allow a lot of extra
time to sort out the teething troubles of the system, and train your staff well. It will
repay you in the long run.

2. WHO ARRANGES FOR IT TO BE DONE?

You, if you're a one-man business! Otherwise make one competent member of
staff responsible for the whole show, and let him get on with it. Don't poke your
nose in too often. The first law of computerisation is that everything takes ten times
as long as you thought it would. The best way to get duff results is to push too hard
too soon.

Your designated staff member may, or may not, know a lot about computers. It
doesn't matter. He must know a lot about your business. It will be up to your man
to assess whether the computer hard- and soft-ware will do the job you want it to,
because the computer salesman won't know the ins and outs of your business.

If your man knows enough about computers then he may be able to make decisions
without outside help. Otherwise, don't be afraid to ask for specialist advice.
(Remember, computerisation might take your company to the wall if you get it
wrong, so a lot hangs on the decisions....) However, beware of computer
specialists. Some get a discount for selling particular hard- or soft-ware. Others
have a vested interest in writing custom-built software, when an off-the-shelf
package might have suited you just about as well.

If in doubt about the quality of your advisers, try this approach - find a
recommended computer advisor, preferably through friends who have computerised
successfully. Go to him and make it quite clear that whatever he says you are not
going to purchase a system through him, but that you wish to buy his advice. Under
these conditions you'll probably get a relatively impartial opinion, with the proviso
that if he is working particularly for one particular supplier his knowledge of other
suppliers may be limited.

3. CHOOSING THE SYSTEM

Don't assume that one big computer will satisfy all your needs. A computer with only one terminal may create a huge bottleneck. Distributed computing may be better - either using a number of small, standalone systems, or else a network of computers all tied together to the same database and printer.

When a system gets bigger, problems increase in geometric progression! It takes much longer to devise and debug a big integrated system. You also end up with all your eggs in one basket - consider what happens if the hard disc develops a fault. If you are able to develop several little systems, then do - it will be much cheaper (because small systems usually require only small amounts of memory), will save time, will reduce bottlenecks, and if you use the same hardware throughout, will give you automatic back up of hardware if one part of the total system fails. However, the development of lots of little systems may mean that you have problems entering the same piece of information several times over, and there are difficulties in keeping several different databases in step with each other.

But if the office work of your business can be broken up into sections which don't really interlink, then you will be better going for a number of small computers rather than one big one. Does letter-writing require constant access to your list of customers, or can you get by without? If you can, your word-processing can be done on a small systems such as the BBC with VIEW, WORDWISE-PLUS, SCRIBE, INTER-WORD, PRO-WORD etc. (If it can't you may need a bigger system altogether.)

The same goes for your staff wages (which can probably be handled by a program working on the same micro).

Your main customer accounts, invoicing, and stock control are all interlinked, so these will almost certainly need to go together - but if nothing else is required from the particular computer handling these items you may well be able to get away with something small and relatively cheap, like the BBC-B.

And so it goes on....

Beware of one hidden danger - the all-singing, all-dancing program on one machine. Great for access to all aspects of your business. Rotten when a customer rings up with a query and you're in the middle of a mail-shot which has your computer tied up for the next two hours.

Finally, data entry takes time - lots of it. Don't assume because you are going to be computerised that the basic processes of entry of information will be speeded up - they won't. Customers' names, addresses and telephone numbers will still have to be taken down, even if the stock control on items they order is done automatically.

Log-jams of information can occur if you do not take care in calculating how much access to the machine each employee really needs - and when..

If this area proves to be a problem consider two alternatives - several standalone systems, or else a networked system. The BBC can be networked with the Econet or E-Net system, but this is rather expensive and it may be better if you think of alternative hardware, some of which (like the RM-Nimbus) runs BBC-BASIC.

4. CHOOSING THE SOFTWARE

The second law of computing is always to choose the software before the hardware. The software is the most important item in the system. It determines whether your computer really will help your business, or whether it will merely replace one out-moded and inefficient system with another. We have dealt with the assessment of software in Chapter 24.

5. COST

If you are choosing a system for a small company you may well find that the BBC and its associated software fits the bill neatly - if so,you will be saving yourself a lot of money. "Professional" systems may be no more effective, but up to ten times the price, especially the software. When manufacturers think that they are aiming at the 'professional' market, they tend to stick another nought at the end of the price tag. (This does, however, cover the cost of having an efficient advice and training system coupled with an ongoing update service.)

The BBC should definitely be a front runner for many office computing functions as far as cost is concerned. The hardware is amazingly good value for money - it is quick, versatile, has an excellent BASIC and accesses the disc quickly. Commercial machines often do not have these advantages. Some are clumsy to use: you sometimes have to load in the operating system from disc, then the language and the finally the program. By the time you have finished your 512K machine may have 30K for programs!

6. FITTING COMPUTERISED AND NON-COMPUTERISED WORK TOGETHER

In many ways what counts is not whether the computer system works properly, but how well the computer and the manual office system integrate together. The ideal system would be a completely "paperless office" where all transactions, notes, memoranda, appointments, information etc are noted on the computer alone. In practice, even the most sophisticated office system does not do away with paperwork, and for most people the concept of the paperless office is an un-realizable myth.

Although it may not appear necessary to have a printout from the computerised records, nevertheless, a physical backup is often both comforting and useful - particularly in a power cut! Additionally, there are often times when you will want to look up odd items of information (such as the telephone number of a customer with a problem) without interrupting what the computer is doing, or in the evening when you don't want to power-up the computer just to find out an address. It is easy to think you will computerise everything - but in practice, notebooks and small card-index files are often faster than the computer, bearing in mind the time taken to start up the program, load in the files and search them.

If you have some information on computer and some on paper you will have to ensure that the two formats keep in step. It is no use having a good computerised system if the manual records are hopelessly out of date, and vice versa. Where there is duplication of data between both systems, the computerised system must have built in to it some method of keeping the physical files up-to-date, preferably automatically. And the keepers of the manual side of the system must inform the computer of what they are doing.

In practice, it is best if the manual and computerised system deal with entirely different parts of the business, with as little overlap as possible. In this way problems of duplication of information, or of the two systems getting out of step, are minimised.

7. INTRODUCING THE EQUIPMENT

There is often a lot of resistance to the introduction of computers. It falls into two main areas - fear of redundancy and fear of the computer itself.

Computers may in some cases make people redundant, but more often change the nature of their work. It should remove a lot of the drudgery and set staff free to do things that require humans - such as person-to-person contact,the use of judgement, wisdom, initiative, kindness and sympathy. Computers, properly used, should make you and your staff freer to be more rather than less human, and more available to deal with the out-of-the-ordinary problems (which, after all, are the most interesting).

The other big point of resistance is fear of "The Beast". Most secretaries start off by thinking that the computer will bite if mis-treated! - or more particularly, that they can wreck the whole system by one push of the wrong button. They need reassuring that

     a. they can't
     b. there's a back-up anyway
     (you have got a back-up, haven't you .....?)

Once these barriers have been overcome you can really get down to work. In general, make haste slowly. Introduce the system bit by bit, if you can. Start off with an easy, small part of the system, preferably with an instant output - word-processing is often a good idea. Try to avoid the situation in which a secretary is glued to the screen for eight hours a day, putting information in, but never getting anything out. Disillusionment quickly sets in if staff feel that there is nothing to show for their labours. If you want to enthuse staff, show them how it can make their job more interesting / productive / valuable.

Initial data entry can take ages - be warned! It can be a time of great disillusionment - you want to get the system working, yet it's taking a a long time to get data in and you're finding out the disadvantages of the system and you're slow, because you don't understand the system yet and you're making mistakes, for the same reason. If you expect to have this period of trauma you will be better equipped to weather it. There will come a time when things start to get better, the system starts to produce results, and suddenly the office is working as smoothly as it was before.

Then comes the day (gradually, and without ceremony) when you suddenly realise that things are working faster than before,and life is more efficient. There's time for some or the things that you never previously found time for. This is when you realise that computerisation was worthwhile after all.....

Never ever try to get efficiency by replacing a bad manual system with a computerised one. The third law of computing should be engraved on every businessman's heart "To err is human - but to really foul things up you need a computer". Computerise a bad system at your peril. Instead, get the manual system right (it doesn't matter if it's slow and tedious, the computer will sort that out for you): all that matters is that it is correct and efficient. Then you can computerise it.

Don't replace manual systems immediately with computerised ones - run the two side by side for a goodly time and see if they seem to keep in step. In this way, if there are any discrepancies you will be able to spot and correct them early on. If things go badly wrong, just continue with the manual system until the program has been fixed. Computerisation has bankrupted quite a few companies, usually because they got clever and threw away their manual system too early - then got in a mess and had nothing to fall back on.

Don't use the computer too much, especially for analysis. Just because you can easily produce graphs of telephone usage throughout the day, or lists of salesman by astrological sign, it doesn't mean that it's worth doing. Ask yourself, "What am I going to do with the data?" If the answer is "Not a lot..." then don't ask for it.

8. STAFF TRAINING

You need to spend enough time on this - by which we mean about five times more than you'd anticipated. You know your way round computers. You know what the implications of 'Can't extend' are, and what to do about it. Your secretary won't, not for ages, and when something goes wrong she will take her hands off the keyboard, not touch the machine at all, and ring you up! ("It's done it again...") Staff training involves the careful teaching of how to use the programs properly, and what they do (so your secretary can see how her work fits in with the rest of the work in the office.) Then she needs to be told what to do when things go wrong (and why). The more you can teach staff why something is done, (rather than just what to do), the more quickly will they be able to cope with crises.

9. AND ONWARDS.....

All computer systems develop. They tend to increase in size and complexity. If properly used they can get very addictive. If you've introduced computerisation properly you'll find your staff coming to you with ideas for how the system could be improved - better lay-out of screens, improved search facilities, ways of using the equipment to do things you never had time for in the past. Listen to them - they're the ones that use the thing!

As software develops you will need to spend time up-dating the training your staff have received. Sadly, complex systems are often under-used simply because no-one knows how to work the durn thing. (One of us has an advanced telephone system in his office, with automatic call re-routing, re-dial facilities, call reversion..... Hardly any of these facilities are used, simply because no-one has shown us just how to get the best out of the system. Half the problem is not understanding the times when the new procedures could be used, and the other half is not knowing what to do.)

Finally, don't forget to cater for break-downs. A big system needs a servicing and breakdown contract to ensure minimum down-time. If you are only using micros then you probably won't want to go this far - but consider what would happen if your printer failed or your computer developed a fault... how would you cope? This is where having a number of small micros has distinct advantages over a big system. Printed back-ups of your more important data save a lot of problems when there's a power cut!

Don't forget to backup your programs and data (see Chapter 11), because sooner or later a disc will get corrupted (or stolen, or lost in a fire). The value of a disc is not the disc itself, but the information on it. Make sure you have up-to-date copies.

27. PROGRAM PROTECTION, DATA THEFT & THE LAW

There are two aspects to protection - the protection you want to give your programs, and the protection that others have given to their programs to prevent you copying them! Although it should be obvious, illicit copying of someone else's program is theft - theft of the rewards they should have received from you for the effort and expertise used in writing the program.

This is a problem, however - it is very easy to damage or destroy programs which are stored in such a delicate medium as magnetic changes on the surface of tape or disc, and it is good practice to take up a back-up copy of any program or data against the possibility of this happening, but the protection that prevents illicit copying of a program also prevents legal back-ups being taken. It also stops you changing the program to customise it more exactly to your own requirements.

Some software is actually less efficient than it could be because of protection. It certainly is a lot more expensive because of the effort put in to make it pirate-proof. Equally, a lot of programs are more expensive than they need be because the programmer needs to get a decent return on his investment of time, effort and money. If he is to receive the same remuneration when half the users of his program have pirated versions, he will have to double the price to the legal user.

It is not always programs that need to be protected. Often data needs to be shielded from prying eyes. It is all too easy to fail to protect systems adequately against unauthorised usage. Confidential information comes in many forms. There is personal information, which can consist of addresses and telephone numbers, financial, medical, and legal details. Business information can be just as sensitive - customer lists, pricing structure, future plans and financial analyses, new product designs. It is for this reason that password systems are built into commercial software so that only correctly authorised personnel may access certain areas of a program. Also, passwords are often used to prevent "dangerous" commands being executed by unauthorised users (eg deleting files etc.)

Don't forget that confidential information is not confined to the screen. There is no point in protecting your system against unauthorised access if at the same time you leave piles of printout around. Don't forget the waste paper bin, either - if your information is that confidential then you ought to think about it being left on an open Council rubbish tip. Therefore, either burn it, or invest in a shredder.

METHODS OF PROTECTION

The area of protection is a jungle which changes from month to month. When buying ask what protection is operative and how it affects performance.

1. **Physical devices.** The obvious and most basic approach is to lock the room in which the computer sits! Variations on this theme include siting the computer inside a locking desk, and requiring a key to turn the computer on. More sophisticated devices include hardware (known as a dongle) that has to be fitted into a specific socket in the computer. Only those with the correct device may use the software/hardware (depending on the type of device). However, there is no point in locking the computer if you leave the discs around. Discs can be 'borrowed', copied, and returned to their rightful owner without anyone suspecting that a copy has been taken. You may have your machine locked - but an identical machine will have no difficulty in reading the discs.

2. **Software protection.** There are now so many methods of protection that it is acquiring the status of an art-form - unformatted tracks, 41 track discs, laser-burned holes in discs, discs with no write-protect hole, dual speed discs, block locking, limited number of access tries to a particular disc. One of our friends has arranged protection for his own programs by arranging for the discs to wipe themselves if any attempt is made to copy them or to alter the copyright notice!

These are all professional protection methods - and it is true that what one man can make, another can break. No protection can ever be absolute: though it is possible to make it so difficult to break programs that stops it being worth-while except as a mental exercise.

What can the average home micro user do to limit piracy of his programs, and security for his data?

INSTANT AND PERMANENT AMNESIA ON BREAK

Go on be nasty, *FX200, 3 Escape goes out of the window and the nice thing is that BREAK sweeps memory cleaner than a new pin! This is either a way of housekeeping and making certain that there are no odd bits hanging about, or a way of stopping people looking at your listings once a program is running.

If you want to call BREAK from within a program enter CALL !-4 within the program. Combining this with *FX200,3 wipes the memory clean on ending the program, thus making it un-listable. It also clears any odd changes you may have made via *FX calls - such as creating printer sinks etc which if left around untreated might interfere with the next program to be run.

Note, however, that this creates as a soft break, so the resident integer variables and contents of function keys remain unaltered.

Remember, If you just type NEW and feel a glow of satisfaction creeping over you, forget it. NEW only alters one byte of memory. Your 'stuff' is still in there. (As an aside, remember that if you 'wipe' a disc all of the material can still be recovered. Even if you re-format a disc the information is still on there and can be recovered, albeit with extreme difficulty. The only sure way is a socking great big magnet!! ... See Chapter 12)

NOW YOU SEE IT....

VDU 21 shuts off the screen display. Anything you do with the keyboard or program will not appear on the screen until you enter VDU 6 either from the keyboard or in the program, or else BREAK. This is very useful if you want to ask for a code word - the screen shuts down whilst the word is entered, and immediately afterwards opens up again with VDU6 - so no-one can sneak a look at the screen whilst you are entering your code.

However,VDU 21 generates a <Return> so if your printer is hooked up it will perform a line feed (which may put it out of alignment if you have it set up to use forms). If you have no printer on-line and you shut off the screen a lot you may fill the printer buffer with <Return>s - and if the printer buffer is full the program hangs when you next try to print to the screen. Therefore, prior to shutting down the screen the first time use *FX5 to create a printer sink - with this all output to the printer buffer disappears. You can select the printer again with other varieties of *FX5,n depending upon your printer type - see your machine User Guide.)

If you could manage to get VDU 21 at the beginning of your program you could prevent the whole lot LISTing on-screen - which gives a certain amount of protection against those who might want to copy bits of your program. Alternatively, if you place VDU21 at the beginning of a section, and VDU6 at the end of the section you could hide the section - useful for two things:-

1. Hiding portions of code you have already debugged so that during further programming you don't have to wade through it each time you LIST.

2. Hiding password sections of code. There's not much point in having a password system which stops the password being printed on the screen if it is possible to read the program listing! If you LIST the program and see

```
    30 UNTIL answer$="codeword"
```

it doesn't give your program all that much protection!

So - hide the password area. For example, if your program reads:-

```
10 REM Main program
20 PROCset_up: REM @@
21 REM hidden code section
22 VDU 21: REM turns the screen off when RUNning
23 *FX200, 3: REM now pressing <Break> will wipe memory
24 J = 0
25 REPEAT
26   J = J + 1: INPUT""answer$
27 UNTIL answer$ = "codeword" OR J = 3
28 IF NOT answer$ = "codeword": REPEAT:VDU7:UNTIL FALSE ELSE
   VDU6:REM If the codeword is correct,turns the screen back
   on - if not, makes a continuous beep, and if you hit
   <Break> the program wipes itself.
29 REM ``setting up arrays
30 ....rest of program
```

then when you have hidden lines 21 to 29 (see below) the program will read:

```
10 REM Main program
20 PROCset_up: REM setting up arrays
30 ....rest of program
```

Any attempt to LIST the program on screen or printer will give no indication that there are extra lines between 20 and 30, so not only does the actual codeword remains hidden but there is no indication of where it might be in the program because the line numbers increment by regular steps of 10.

To make the screen shut off on LISTing rather than RUNning it is not effective to write VDU21 in the listing - what you need is the character representing VDU21 to appear in the listing itself, so that when the character is read by the screen ROM it accepts the character as a direct command to be acted upon. Therefore, the character for VDU 21 has to be inserted directly into a listing in order to hide it. The method is as follows:-

Choose a pair of unlikely character: we use @ and #, as they hardly ever appear in our programs.

One of the characters (@) comes at the start of the section or sections you wish to hide, the other goes at the end of the section (#).

Lines 10 to 20 are just for demo. Lines 29000 onwards are the meat.

Each Procedure has a main loop which just searches the program in memory and, if it finds your chosen characters anywhere as a pair, changes them to the required VDU Codes. PROC_SHOW changes the VDU 21 back to @ for you: there is no need to change the VDU6 back.

The two procedures go at the top of your program and stay there. To hide your bits, type PROC_HIDE: to reveal all type PROC_SHOW. Note, you do this in command mode (did you know that you could call Procedures outside a program?).

Another use for this facility is to help edit programs in the making. Once you have a part complete, make it disappear. This way you don't have to watch thousands of lines flash past. However you must use *FX5 to create a printer sink (see above). LISTing the program generates a <Return> every time a 'hidden' part of the program runs through, and the printer buffer will fill with <Return>s in no time when you have LISTed the program a few times. If you don't use a printer sink the program will hang or the the LISTing will stop in mid-flight.

```
   10 REM Hello @@
   11 REM You can't see this!
   12 REM To make these lines disappear
   13 REM Print PROC HIDE in command mode
   14 REM To make them come back
   15 REM Type PROC SHOW in command mode
   16 REM##there!
   20 END
29000 REM@@
29010 DEFPROC_HIDE
29020   FOR ZZ% = PAGE TO TOP
29030     IF ?ZZ% = ASC("@") THEN IF ?(ZZ%+1) = ASC("@")
                                           THEN ?ZZ% = 21
29040     IF ?ZZ% = ASC("#") THEN IF ?(ZZ%+1) = ASC("#")
                                           THEN ?(ZZ%+1) = 6
29050   NEXT
29060 ENDPROC
29070 DEFPROC_SHOW
29080   FOR ZZ% = PAGE TO TOP
29090     IF ?ZZ%=21 THEN IF ?(ZZ%+1)=ASC("@") THEN ?ZZ%=ASC("@")
29100   NEXT
29110 ENDPROC
29120 ##REM"THE END"
```

Having entered the above, exactly, print PROC_HIDE <Return>. This is the result when you type LIST <RETURN> .

```
   10 REM Hello there!
   20 END
29120 REM"THE END"
```

PIRACY AND THE LAW

COMMERCIAL SOFTWARE - YOUR RIGHTS

Most reasonable companies accept that a back-up copy of a program is a necessity - it is all to easy for a disc to 'go down' and if it's the only version of an expensive program then you've got problems! However, few companies provide back-up copies: some stipulate that you must copy the disc and that you may not have more than three copies in existence at the same time. There may be clauses in the user agreement which say that the copy or copies may only be used on one specified machine - or you may have a site licence and have as many copies as you like, provided they remain on the premises.

If you are in any doubts about your rights, write to the company before buying and state your requirements - most will accommodate a reasonable variation of rules, usually for a nominal fee. The majority of responsible software houses will treat you fairly, which is all you want in the long run.

If you are going to work with a network this opens up a whole new can of worms. Whereas it is legal to have a disc in a single disc drive attached to one machine, it may not be if it is attached to two machines. If the disc drive is attached to a network it can be illegal. Look into it and be aware that there are not only pitfalls but hefty fines and prison sentences involved if you transgress the licensing or sale agreements.

PIRACY

Remember that if you breach the copyright agreement you are a thief. You are not stealing material but ideas and time and removing a deserved fee. After all, if it is worthwhile to have it it must be good and a good workman deserves his hire.

THE DATA PROTECTION ACT

The Data Protection Act was conceived to protect members of the public against damage to their reputation or credit-worthiness as a result of inaccurate information held on them in computers. Additionally, it was to regulate transfer of information so that data obtained for one purpose could not be transmitted to all and sundry. In order to do this a register of computer users has been set up, and if you hold personal data about other people you may need to register.

The overall effects of the law are roughly as follows:-

If you hold data on your home computer solely for personal, family, or household affairs or recreational purposes, you do not need to register.

If a business or a club holds information of any sort on other people, apart from just names and addresses, it may well need to register. Registration is in the name of the club or business - individual employees do not need to register.

It is up to the company or club to decide who in their organisation should have access to the data, bearing in mind the need to avoid unauthorised access, disclosure, or destruction of records.

If you are registered then members of the public on whom you hold information may have a legal right to see the information relating to themselves, and require you to change it, if it is inaccurate.

If you are registered, there are restrictions about where and to whom you may transmit data - essentially, you may only pass personal data to other properly registered organisations.

It is not our intention to attempt to interpret the law - we are not lawyers, and by the time you read this the regulations may have changed. For details of the current regulations, write to:-

> The Office of the Data Protection Registrar,
> Springfield House,
> Water Lane,
> Wilmslow,
> Cheshire SK7 5AX
> Tel. Wilmslow (06025)535777

The original concept was fine - no-one wants erroneous information to exist on anyone. Unfortunately, the way that the law was couched threw the net very wide. In the future it may well be that the regulations are amended to be less strict, so that the original spirit of the act is more closely attained.

28. SELLING YOUR PROGRAMS

There comes an exciting point where you feel that the program you have written is good enough to sell. Where do you go from here? Well, as always there are three routes:-

1. **Forget it, give up etc., etc**. We've given you this option first so you needn't read the rest of this. Selling your program requires a lot of time and hard work and may well not work out in the end. If your program isn't all that wonderful, then this is the route for you. Goodbye!

2. **Sell it or licence it to a publisher.** This can be difficult as it is not easy to know quite where to turn, or be certain whom you can trust. The vast majority of software houses are hard-working and honest, but does this apply to the one you have chosen? It could be too late by the time you have found out. However, this is the cheapest way to get a good return for your time, and if you strike lucky, the rewards can still be good.

3. **Do the whole shooting match yourself** - by far the most difficult way but also the most rewarding and exciting. The tips that follow are the result of doing it and enjoying it and making a lot of mistakes. Having ironed out most of them, things went quite smoothly!

Is your program any good? Of course it is - your friends have told you so, but does this cut any ice in the open market place? Hawk it around to one or two people who will tell you the truth.

OK., so it is a good program, but will anyone want it? Study what the magazines are saying and what they have been saying for the last couple of years. Read reviews of similar types of program, not only on the machine you have written for but for other machines (to see if there is a demand or unsuspected problems etc.).

Is your program sufficiently different to command sales? Points in its favour are as follows:-

1. There's nothing remotely like it in the market place
2. (Particularly for business software) It does the same
    job as another program, but
    a. significantly more quickly, or
    b. with a much greater ease of use, (and a much smaller
        manual!) or

c. a better screen display, or

d. many fewer key-strokes required for input or

e. is capable of upgrading and amendment of its files much
    more easily or

f. is more applicable to the direct office environment in
    which it is working. (The interaction between computer,
    secretaries, bosses and manual files is an area that is
    hardly ever considered, and in some ways is the most
    vital consideration in using a computer successfully in
    an office. It's not whether the program works as it is
    intended, it is whether the computerised work integrates
    well with the rest of the office work. This is why
    integrated suites of programs have mushroomed recently,
    because they don't need to dovetail in with manual files
    so much, but this is only one aspect of the problem.)

3. (Particularly for games) It develops aspects of a game
    that haven't been seen in any other game (for example, your
    little green men with laser blasters turn out to be
    friendly .... sometimes!

Is there a similar program being sold on PCs, IBMs etc - i.e. is your idea new
enough and interesting enough to be developed for the up-market field? (If so,
we'd advise that you go back to selling your idea to a software house: the PC field
can be an expensive area for the individual.)

ADVERTISING

Can you think up an advertising gimmick or name which is going to sell against the
opposition? You will most probably be starting with something like an eighth page
advertisement, which is small, and there is not a lot of room to make your product
stand out.

Beware the temptation to put too much in an advert - if it's cluttered it won't stand
out. Use 'white space' in your design. A completely blank advert, except for a
minutely printed 'Nemo Software' in the middle, may be much more arresting than a
cluttered description of your program.

Resist the temptation to describe everything about your software - if the basic idea
is interesting or different, hammer this point home. Therefore "Wordprocessing with
100K files on your Beeb", or "Arch Architect - design yourself a city, but watch out
for the planners who are out to get you.." or "Out-perform professional PC graphics
for only £34.50" will get those who are interested looking at your product further.
There is no point at this stage in telling them triumphantly how your system works
with sixteen extra commands.

Write in English, not computerspeak! It is amazing just how many clever ideas are around, but no-one knows about them because the adverts themselves are indecipherable

> "with our quint-fractured IO/UO
> peripheral buffer all redits are
> equalised and the quotient byte
> potential is greater than any other
> comparable program."

If you are writing software for people who are computer-naive (such as most small businesses who are looking for technological aid, then tell them in plain English what they will get if they buy from you.)

A market gardener looking for a micro to help run his business doesn't want to know anything about the internal workings of the machine - he just wants to know what the end product will be. So to say in your advert that "this is the biggest WYSIWYG W-P on the market with mail-merge" doesn't mean a thing, any more than Fisons No.2 and lawn-aerators mean to you! Instead, write something on the lines of "With this you can write individualized circulars to your customers automatically - what you see on the screen is just what your letter will look like. You can write longer letters on our equipment than with anyone else's". It's not as pithy, but it communicates much better to the man who may well buy it. (He skipped over the first advert because he didn't realise it could be relevant to him.)

Don't advertise in a particular magazine just because it is the best and most prestigious - look around and see which one will be most likely to sell for you. It is a good idea to find out if a particular magazine is going to charge you for the original typesetting. Some do - some don't. After your first advert you don't usually have to pay for small changes. Sometimes a magazine will take a copy of your advert from another magazine and not charge you for the typesetting.

Sell on tape or disc? If you have the equipment, discs are easier to produce..BUT.. If you are hoping to get shops to take your product don't forget that the packaging has to be fairly slick. One of the advantages of disc is that the size allows for a reasonably large Manual. The disadvantages revolve around the many disc options - what size (five and a quarter inch, three and a half inch, etc etc.), what format (40/80, single or double density, single or double sided). One way out is to sell on cassette with a disc loader included and an instruction on how to transfer to your type of disc. This covers all circumstances and gets good comments from the reviewers.

The worry with cassettes is - how do you copy them? The obvious answer is to get a professional copier to do the job. If you do, watch it! Get someone close at hand whose backside you can kick. One of us has had very bad experiences with two different, well known producers. One re-did the work when the errors were pointed out, the other was most unpleasant - though we do think that a 20% failure rate is a trifle high.

Eventually we made up a bank of 6 tape recorders (Ferguson 3T279, cheap and utterly reliable). On each one we drilled a little hole over the head adjusting screw so that they could be set them up accurately, though to be fair, they were all perfect when they arrived. These six recorders were joined in parallel to the BBC through a simple 10K resistance splitter. (We are not going to give details - if you don't know what we mean you shouldn't do it: get a competent electronics guy to tackle the job.) The recorders have automatic volume controls: this took care of any slight drop in signal level.

We never had a failure to load through the fault of the system, but did get problems through having un-labelled piles of tapes and muddling them up. Test one tape from each batch to check it loads completely (to allow for mains glitches, etc) Test every tape to see that it has something on it. If you find an error, scrap the batch, don't mess about. Don't try to record over the top - erase with a large permanent magnet or a specialist eraser. With the best will in the world different recorder heads are at different heights and the sliver of signal which may get left behind is going to mess up someone's tape. It doesn't happen often but once is enough to damage a reputation (it might be a review copy, or even more important, a customer's).

Labels. Photostated or hand written labels look all right in a club, but don't project a very good image. It will cost about £25 for 400-500 labels and is worth it. You can get thin labels and thick labels. Choose the thick ones, even if they cost more. The thin ones are a pain to get on the cassette as they wrinkle: thick ones are magic.

FINANCE

So you want to be rich? Balance greed with practicality. Write for the majority on a minority subject. A friend of ours laughs all the way to the bank on a program for the Spectrum which tells you when to plant your vegetables, information which is on the packet of seed you are going to plant! Look for an untapped market that the Big Boys are unlikely to think is big enough for them: get in and make a killing while the gap is still there.

......and good luck. You'll need it.....

INDEX

!BOOT		*FX 225	55,181
*BUILD	100	*FX 226	55
*OPT	100	*FX 227	55
limitations	102-103	*FX 238	181
RAM boards	277	*FX 254	181
RAM boards	103	*FX 255	
wordprocessing	275	Program speed	199
*ACCESS	249	*LOAD	
*APPEND	107	screens	170
*BACK	106	*MAP	107
*BACKUP	248	*MOTOR	92
40/80 discs	99	*MZAP	109
and faulty discs	245	*NORMALKEY	80
*BUILD	100,103,	*OPT	100
	107	*RECOVER	108
!BOOT	100	*REPAIR	109
*CDIR	106	*RESTORE	108
*CONFIGURE	111-112	*RMREINIT	75
*COPY		*SHOW	63
and faulty discs	245	*SPOOL	103,118
in ADFS	107	*SPOOLON	107
*CREATE	106	*STATUS	58,112
*DELETE	251	*SWAP	248
*DESTROY	248	*TAPE	205
*DZAP	244	*TITLE	
*ENABLE	248	in ADFS	107
*ENUM	72	*TV	24,112,123
*EXEC	103,118	*TYPE	103
*FORCE	63	*VERIFY	109,244-5
*FORMAT	248	*> rather than *.	127
*FREE	107	1 Megahertz Bus	53
*FX 6	112	ARCHIMEDES &	
*FX 6		COMPACT	53
printing defects	222	1770	54,80-81
*FX 15	179,222	2nd Processor	
*FX 138	207	(see Second Processor)	268
*FX 200	183	3-D images	12
*FX 200		3.5" drive	
wiping memory	287	ARCHIMEDES	65,67
*FX 202	182	32 bit	
*FX 210	122	ARCHIMEDES	54,59,79
*FX 211-214	193	32016 Co-processor	54,57

40/80
  problems   99
6502   54,79
  1 Megahertz Bus   53
  Byte?   230
6502 emulator
  ARCHIMEDES   66
6502 Second processor   52
8721   54
@%   165-166
  and machine code   188
A%
  and machine code   188
A300 series
  ARCHIMEDES   65
A400 series
  ARCHIMEDES   65
Abbreviations   123
  de-bugging   219
ACCELERATOR
  compatability   46
Accountancy   258
  BBC-B   55
  commercial use   258
  integrated accounts   258
  Word processing   9
ACORN   54
ACORN C
  compatability   46
Adapting software
  (see Customising)
Add-on boards   54
  BBC-B   54
  problems   39
Addresses   51
ADDROM
  compatability   46
ADE+
  compatability   46
ADFS   37-38,54,
                              247,248,
                              250,251
  *COPY   107
  *TITLE   107
  Adv' Disc Investigator   45
  ARCHIMEDES   59,65,67

compaction   107
double density   37
ECONET   62
ELECTRON   55
hard disc   37
libraries   108
networking   37
use of directories   37,94,
                              104-107
ADVANCED DISC INVESTIGATOR   42,43
ADVANCED DISC TOOLKIT
  compatability   46
Adventure writing in LOGO   47
Alarm   11,193
Amber
  VDU   20
AMX   259
AMX ROMs
  compatability   46
Analog-Digital Convertor   11
Analog-Digital Interface   53
AND   188-190
ANFS
  ARCHIMEDES   65
Animation   169-172
  ARCHIMEDES   170-171
  BBC-B   170-171
  flicker   70
  INKEY   171
  MASTER   170-171
  using EOR   189-190
  WAIT   70
APPEND   71
ARCHIMEDES   59,64-75,
                              251,258
  *REMOVE   251
  1 Megahertz Bus   53
  3.5" disc drive   59,65,67
  32 bit   64,79
  6502 emulation   59
  6502 emulator   66
  accountancy   258
  ADFS   37-38,59,
                              65,67
  animation   170-171
  ANFS   65

BASIC 5   69,161
Business & Education   269
commercial software   59
configuration   64
COLOUR   71
configuration   111-112
compatability   77
CP/M   268
CP/M   65
dBASE   268
desktop program   68
DFS   59,67
ECONET   66
educational software   59
ergonomics   19
fan   27
file system extension   67
GCOL   71
graphics   68-69
IBM podule & emulation   59
IBM emulator   74,268
languages   67
JAZZ   268
LISTO   145
LOTUS 1-2-3   268
memory   64
memory map   66
modes   68
mouse   69
modules   64,74
MS-DOS   65,268
poking to memory   81
podules   65
ports   65
Program speed   199
RISC   64
ROMS   66
sound   13
software compatability   66-67
sound   71
splitting
    multi-statement lines   145
sprites   64,68
SYMPHONY   268
syntax checking   211
transfer of software   67

types   64
video output   65
Winchester   65
windows   68-69
Archive   96
Arguments
    de-bugging   220
Aries shadow RAM board   254
Arithmetic
    multi precision   242
Arithmetic operations
    de-bugging   216
Array
    error mesage   225-226
Arrays   138,154-
                               157,238
    de-bugging   213
    DIM   155
    linked data   156
    one-dimensional   155
    passing in BASIC 5   73
    programming style   147
    putting information in   156
    READ   156
    saving space   202
    two-dimensional   156
ARTIST   259
Artwork
    mouse   51
ASCII   175,182
Assembly language
    saving space   204
Assessing programs   268
ATOM   54
Autodial   267

B128 (see BBC-B+)
Background colour
    with printing   163
Backing up programs   145-146
    (see also Backups)
    debugging   145
    duplication   146
    passing results   145
    saving memory   145

speed	146	
Backups	95-98	
TOOLKIT	96	
cassettes	96	
discs	95,97	
In business	95,285	
interval between	96	
library managers	96	
types	96	
Balanced line Networks	61	
Bank Manager business	264	
Banking	10	
Bad Program	208	
BASIC		
easy typing of listing	117	
flags	148	
functions	148	
getting the best from	148-161	
GET & GET$	148	
loops	148	
procedures	148	
structured programs	148	
BASIC 1	76-78	
BASIC 2	76-78	
BASIC 4	58,76-78	
BASIC 5	76-78	
*ENUM	72	
APPEND	71	
and ARCHIMEDES	69,161	
BY	70	
CASE	71-72	
CIRCLE	70	
EDIT	72	
ELLIPSE	70	
ELSE	72	
ENDCASE	71-72	
ENDWHILE	73	
error checking	73	
FILL	69	
flood-fill	69	
INPUT LINE	72	
INSTALL	73	
LINE INPUT	72	
LINE	70	
LISTO	72	
LIBRARY	73	
LOCAL ERROR	72	
MODE	70	
mouse	69	
OFF	69	
OTHERWISE	71-72	
passing arrays	73	
procedure libraries	73	
QUIT	72	
RECTANGLE	69	
SUM	72	
SWAP	73	
WAIT	70	
WHEN	71-72	
WHILE	73	
BASIC 40	57,76-78	
BAS 128	58	
BASIC EDITOR	43,58,74	
compatability	46	
BASIC interpreter	217	
BAUD & DATA	112	
BBC-A	54	
BBC-B	54-55,80	
2nd processors	54	
accountancy	55	
ADFS	37	
add-on boards	54	
animation	170-171	
convert programs		
to MASTER	58	
databases	55	
DFS	37	
function key		
memory area	191	
GXR	45	
PROWORD	255	
ROMs	41	
ROM compatability	46	
ROM cartridges	54	
separate keyboard	52	
software, education	55	
software, business	55	
user defined keys	226	
volume control	30	
wordprocessing	55	
BBC-B+	55-56	
ADFS	37	

DFS	37	crunching routine	202
function key		Buffer	
memory area	191	keyboard	179
GXR	45	Bugs	
PROWORD	255	due to static	23
ROM compatability	46	Bulletin boards	10,267
separate keyboard	52	Bundled software	
shadow RAM	55	COMPACT	58
sideways RAM	55	MASTER	58
BCPL	42	Business	
compatability	46	(see also Computerisation	
BEEBMON		of Business)	
compatability	46	ARCHIMEDES	269
BEEBUG C		backups	96-97
compatability	46	Bank manager	258,264
BEEP	122	computerisation	279-285
Benchmarks	271	databases	11,261
Bitstik	258	data, saving space	203
Blank files	275	disc backups	95
Blank lines	144	error trapping	185
Books		Networks	61
stacking	82	Word processors	252
Borders		writing programs	13
program to create	131	use	284
using windows	131	Business software	
windows	166-167	BBC-B	55
Brackets		BY	70
de-bugging	218		
Ease of use	190		
BREAK		C	42
C/BREAK	122	portable	48
D/BREAK	122	C/BREAK	
N/BREAK	122	*TAPE	122
CALL !-4	287	Cables	
PAGE	206	neatness & safety	31-32
wiping memory	287	screening	32
BREAK key		CAD	12,258
and variables	196	light pen	52
avoiding problems	82	mouse	51
guard	82	Calculator	51,88
lock	82	pull-down windows	88
re-defining	195-196	Calculating space	
BREAK key lock		saving space	204
MASTER	55	Calender	51
BROM PLUS	43,139	Capitals	127
compatability	46		

CARETAKER   43,55,
                                    80,139
    de-bugging   44
    problems   44
    splitting
        multi-statement line   145
Cartridge holders   41-42
CASE   71,72,79
Cassettes   91-92
    archive material   91-91
    ARCHIMEDES   91
    backing up   96
    COMPACT   91
    ease of use   92
Catalogues
    commercial   87
Ceefax   11
Centering headings
    MODE 7   162
    other MODES   164
CHAIN
    Resident Integer
    Variables   188
Chairs
    workstation design   18
Changing case   181-182
Changing Mode quickly   123
CHARDES
    font design   58
Check digits   84
Checking entry
    keyboard   133
    upper and lower case   133
Chip (see ROM)

Choosing hardware   268
CIRCLE   70
Circles   45,
                                    172-173
    speed   171
Cleaning   85-86
    disc drives   86
    keyboard   86
    printers   86
    screen   85
Cleaning equipment   87

CLEAR   73,74,207
    procedures   204
    and Resident Integer
        Variables   188
Clearing the screen   123
Clock rate
    Program speed   199
CLOSE#   249
Co-ordinates
    planning screen layouts   119
CODE
    direct entry
        from keyboard   57
CODE key
    MASTER   57
Colour
    editing   117,121
    grey scale   121
    more than two reds   168
    monochrome   121
    printer problems   120
    re-defining   169
    REMs   120
    rubbing out   168
    use of EOR   189-190
    VDU   20
Colour blindness   121
Columns of figures   164-166
COMAL   42,47
    compatability   46
Computing in business
    backups   285
    breakdowns (machine!)   285
    catalogues   87
    cost   282
    combining machine and
    non-machine operations   282-283
    data entry and time   281
    databases   281
    efficiency   285
    how to choose   280-282
    introduction
        to the office   283-285
    networks   281
    staff training   285
    up-dating   285

what to computerise 279-280

Comfort
    and VDU screen colour 20
    paperwork 19
    workstation 16-22
Command interpreters 180
Command line interpreter 251
Command mode checking
    variable 212-213
    array 212-213
Commercial programs
    altering the sound 193
    ARCHIMEDES 59
    assessment 268-273
    ease of use 272
    PAGE 207
    relocation 207
    'safety' 271-272
    second processor 52
COMMSTAR2
    compatability 46
Communications 10, 265-267
    databases 266
    mailboxes 266
COMPACT 58-59
    !BOOT 101
    1 Megahertz Bus 53
    accountancy 258
    ADFS 37
    bundled software 58
    configuration 111-112
    Compatability 77
    disc drive 58
    ergonomics 19
    keyboard 58
    ports 58
    ROM compatability 46
Compacting
    problems 44
    ADFS 107
Compatability 76-81
    3.5" disc drives 77
    40 & 80 track discs 35-36
    5.25" disc drives 77
    ARCHIMEDES 77

BASIC 1 & BASIC 2 76
    convert 81
    COMPACT 77
    CP/M 79-80
    density 80
    hardware 78-79 268-269
    hardware requirements 80
    language 76
    'legal' programming 81
    MASTER 77
    memory requirements 80
    MS-DOS 79-80
    of internal disc codes 79-80
    OPENIN 77-78
    OPENUP 77-78
    overcoming with
        RS242 78
        Mail banks 78
    poking to memory 81
    screen pokes 81
    second processor 76,81
    track format 77
    Winchester 77
    workspace clashes 80
Compiling
    Program speed 199
Computer aided design 12
Computerisation of
    businesses 279-285
Computer usage
    error trapping 185
    filing systems 6
    information Processing 6
    indexing 6
    matching 6
    reliability 7
    retrieval 6
    sorting 6
    statistics 6
    when not to use 6-7
    where to use 6
Conditions
    flags 140

Confidentiality	286
and the Law	286
Configuration	
!BOOT	101
CONFIGURE	
printing defects	222,223
Contrast	
VDU screen	16,20-21
VDU screen colour	20
Controlling equipment	11,53
Control variables	238,9
Controlling equipment	
disabled	14
hardware additions	53
User port	53
CONVERT	58
Convert	
compatability	81
Copyright	
licences	291
networks	60,291
piracy	291
software	291
CP/M	54,57
ARCHIMEDES	65,268
compatability	79-80
Crunch	220
Crunched programs	
de-bugging	216
Crunching routines	139
* commands	218
IF	217
saving space	202
tokens	216-218
CTRL/Function key	
resetting base values	181
CTRL/N	214
Cursor	
changing shape	162
vanishing	162
Cursor keys	
cursor	162
MASTER	55
Customising software	274-278
Wordwise	274
Wordwise Plus	274

D/BREAK	
*DISC	122
Daisy wheel printers	48
DATA	239-240
backups	95
cost of losing it	41
de-bugging	220
programming style	145
safety	95
saving space	203
siting	145
Data Protection Act	291-292
Databases	255,
	259-262
(see also	
Integrated suites)	
access to	9
BBC-B	55
business	11
charges	11 .
communications	266
effectiveness	12
in business	261
Networks	61
professional	11
searching	259-260
sorting	11,260
types	261-262
uses of	260
wordprocessing	9
Dates	182-183
American	183
arithmetic on	182
conversion to numbers	182-183
English	183
resident integers	183
Zellers congrunce	183
dBASE	261
dBASE III	74
DDFS	37
DFS	38
De-bugging	211-224
(see also	
program testing	
printing	
screen printing defects)	

1770 and BBC-B 80
ARCHIMEDES module 74
abbreviations 219
arguments 220
ARCHIMEDES
syntax checking 211, 212-218
arithmetic operations 216
backing up programs 145
brackets 218
CARETAKER 44
crunched programs 216
DATA 220
ELSE 215
EOR 220
examining
variable content 212-213
arrays 213
for IF 214
for GOTO 214
GET 222
keywords 216
keyboard setting 215
line numbers 220
locating errors 211
loops 214
loops (nested) 215
logic operations 216,220
minimising 211
MODE 218
No such variable 211
odd happenings 215,222, 242-2
out of data 212
programming style 143
procedures 150,154
printing defects 220
procedures
in command mode 211
printing errors 211
REMs 219
recursive procedures 215
see also
Program testing
Printing
Screen print defects

single statement lines 143
spaces 143-144, 219
structured programming 211
typing errors 218-220
using REM 212
using STOP 213
using TRACE 214
variable contents 215
windows 166,222
wordprocessing 276
Defaults 132
Density 35-38
disc quality 36
double & single 35-38
Design 12
Designing your workstation
(see Workstation design)
Desk-diary 51
Desktop
ARCHIMEDES 68
Desktop publishing 13
DFS 54,80,201 246,248, 249,2
1770 37
40/80 switching 38
8271 37
Adv' Disc Investigator 45
ARCHIMEDES 59
DDFS 38
double density 35-38
ENIGMA 44
PAGE 205
problems 38
shifting PAGE 205-207
single density (DFS) 35-38
use of directories 93-94
Watford Electronics 38
DIM 238
error 156
error message 225-226
saving space 157
space 156
zeroing an array 156
DIP switches 223

Directories	104-107, 251	Disc error messages	244-251
		Disc files	
ADFS	37, 104-107	PAGE	206
		Disc formats	
Disabled		TPI	41
assistance for	14	Discs	
controlling things	14	3.5" on COMPACT	57
games for	8,14	!BOOT files	
hardware	14	creating	100-103
special programs	14	problems	102
Disc access time		*OPT	100
program speed	199	Auto-start	100
Disc boxes	87	backups	95
dangers of	87	business	95
DISC DOCTOR	42,43,248	care	83-85
compatability	46	changing file names	127
menu	102	check digits	84
SWAP	37	colour coding	87
Disc drives		damaged, recovery from	
40 track	35	text files	109
40/80	22	BASIC programs	109-110
40/80 switchable		density	35,36
by switch	35	dust and smoke	84
by software	35	erasing	36
80 track	35	errors	84
advantages	33	labels	87
cleaning	86	printing	98
copying	34	writing	99
Compatab	77	pen	99
COMPACT	58	quality	40-41
ergonomics	35	rainbow	87
hard discs	40	safety	
head crash	85	of data	95
how many?	33	of programs	95
housing it	22-23	sizes	36
laser discs	40	storage	87
mechanical switching	22	working with	100-110
optical discs	40	write protect tab	250
setting head speeds	112	Domesday	7,40
sizes	36	Dot-matrix printers	48
solid state	38	Double height letters	163
software switching	22	Double density	
speed	33	ADFS	37
what type?	33	DOWHILE..ENDWHILE	158-159
Disc drive controller		Drums	13
(see DFS)		Dummy string	208

DUMP MASTER 2
   compatability 46
DUMP OUT 3 43
   compatability 46
Dust
   and cleaning 85
   and discs 84-85
E-NET 60,63
   and security 63
   and education 63
   PAGE 205
Earthing
   VDU screen 23
Ease of use 111-129
   *BACK 106
   Auto starting discs 100
   backing up cassettes 96
   butterfingers with *. 127
   changing MODE 123
   changing filenames 127
   clearing the screen 123
   databases in networks 61
   disc labels 98
   discs 93-95
   disc labels 98
   editing
      not in MODE 7 116-117
      in colour 116-117
   entering BASIC listings 117
   error trapping
   function keys 196
   Function keys 115-117
   in programming 196
   indexer programs 95
   keystrip colours 90
   length of files 248
   MASTER configuration 111
   minimum abbreviations 123
   moving cursor 122
   notepad 95,96,99
   planning screen layouts 118-119
   reverse shift 127
   shift key 122
ECONET 60,62
   ARCHIMEDES 66
   PAGE 205

EDIT 72
Editing
   MODEs other than 7 116-117
   colour 117
Education
   ARCHIMEDES 269
   E-NET 63
Educational software
   ARCHIMEDES 59
   BBC-B 55
Electricity
   clean 90-91
Electrostatic electricity 15
ELECTRON 55
   ADFS 37,55
   as a terminal 55
   single key entry 55
   with ROMs 55
ELLIPSE 70
Ellipses 45
ELSE 72
   De-bugging 215
ENDCASE 71-72
ENDWHILE 73
ENIGMA 42,43
   repair damaged discs 109
EOR 188-190
   and colour 189-190
   animation 189-190
   De-bugging 220
Epson 256
Ergonomics
   ARCHIMEDES 19
   COMPACT 19
   disc drives 35
   paperwork 19
   workstation design 16-19
Error
   DIM 156
Error checking 133
   BASIC 5 73
Error handling
   (see error trapping)
Error messages
   REMOVE 57

ERROR numbers & messages
    Please refer to
    chapter 22 pages   224-251
Error trapping   115,183-
                    187,196
    division by zero   231
    error numbers   184
Escape   183-184
    changing the key   183
    disabling   183
    intelligent use
    within programs   183
Exchange
    changing names
    in programs   139
EXEC (see *EXEC)
EXMON   43
EXMON (MASTER)
    compatability   46
EXMON2
    compatability   46
Eyestrain   20
    lighting   20

FALSE   139-141
Fanfold paper
    how to handle   88
Fans   27
Fatigue   20
    health hazard   15
    lessening
    for the operator   131-137
    VDU   15
File handling
    shifting PAGE   206
File searching   61
File-server
    Networks   60
Filenames
    changing   127
Filing systems
    computer useage   6
FILL   70
Fills   45
Filters
    electric main   91

Financial Planning
    spreadsheets   10
Flags
    BASIC   148
    meaningful programs   139-141
    TRUE & FALSE   139-140
Fleet Street Editor   13
Flexibility
    ROM images
    in Sideways RAM   50
Flicker
    reducing   16
    VDU   15
flood-fill   70
FLOPPYWISE MASTER
    compatability   46
Flush
    sound   192
Foam (conducting)   86
Font design
    CHARDES   58
Fonts   255
FOR .. NEXT   158-159,
                    215,242
Format of screen display   165
Formatting   245
Formatting errors   245
FORTH   42
    compatability   46
Functions
    (see also Procedures)
    allowed characters   226
    error messages   224-225,
                    226
Function keys   115-117,
                    196
    invisible messages   190-191
    memory area   191
    memory space
    BBC-B & MASTER   116
    resetting base value   181
    Wordwise   274
    Wordwise Plus   274
Function Keystrip
    (see Keystrip)   82
Furniture   87

Games
    and the disabled 7,14
    paddles 51
    teaching 8
    types 8
    writing your own 8
Gateway 11
GENIE
    information 51
GET 148,160,
    175,179,
    182
    de-bugging 222
    saving keystrokes 160
    to reduce keystrokes 132
GET$ 148,160
    to reduce keystrokes 132,160
Glasses (see spectacles) 20
GLOBAL variables
    procedures 151-154
Good programming 130-133
GOSUB 215,243
    and MODE change 227
    speed 187-188
GOTO 138
    avoidance of 141-143
    de-bugging 142,214
    errors 235,236,
    237,2
    in loops 220
    REMs 141
    speed 197
    turning REPEAT..UNTIL
    into WHILE 141
    use of 141
Grandfather, Father, Son
    (see Backups)
Graphics 258-259
    artwork creation 12
    ARCHIMEDES 68-69
    circles 45
    converting
    to MODE 7 screen 44
    ellipses 45
    fills 45
    LOGO 47

MODE 7 47
    mouse 51
    on printers 48
    palette 45
    packages available 258-259
    teletext 47
    uses 12
Graphics cursor
    windows 167
Graphics commands
    MASTER 58
Graphics package
    (see also
    Integrated suite)
Graphics pad 258
Green VDU 20
Grey scale 121
Grey scale indicator
    VDU testing and set up 25
Grid generator
    VDU testing 25
Grills 27
GXR
    (Graphics Extension ROM) 43,59
    BBC-B & BBC-B+ 45
    compatability 46

Handicapped
    paddles 51
Hard discs 40
    ADFS 37
    ARCHIMEDES 59
Hardware 33-35
    Compatability 78-79
    disabled 14
Hardware additions
    ports used 53
Hardware supplies 87
HCS
    ROMs 50
Head crash
    disc drive 85
Health hazards
    cables 32
    Computers 15
    fatigue 15

hum 28-28
migraine 15
positive 15
teno-synovitis 17
VDU 15
Heat
add-on boards 27
damage to chips 27
hardware bugs 27
Heat removal
fans & grills 27
HELP2
compatability 46
Hexadecimal 227
Hiding code
VDU 21 288-291
Home banking 10
Household budget program 263,264
Hum
health hazard 28-29
IBM-emulator
ARCHIMEDES 268
ICON MASTER
compatability 46
IF
de-bugging 214
IF..THEN 158-159
IMAGE 259
Indentation
LISTO 144
loops 144
program layout 144
Index files
saving space 203
Indexes 39
Indexing systems 7
Indexing
computer usage 6
narrative 7
Information
(see Oracle) 11
(see Ceefax) 11
(see Prestel) 11
(see Gateway) 11
acquiring it 10
access to databases 10-11

acquiring 264
Genie 51
Information processing
computer usage 6
Infra-red detector 11
INKEY
animation 171
INMAC 87
INPUT LINE 72
Input routines
(see Input vetting)
Input validation 133
Input vetting 174-181
alternative answers 178-180
changing case 175
numbers 177-178
programming style 147
INPUTLINE 113
INSTR 179,
180-181
Integer arithmetic
Program speed 198
Integer variables
CLEAR 204
Program speed 198
Saving space 202
Integrated programs 254
INTER - series 256
VIEW - series 254
Integrated suites
INTER series 264
VIEW series 264
INTER-BASE 112,261
compatability 46
INTER CHART
compatability 46
INTER-SHEET 262,263
compatability 46
INTER-WORD 31,254
compatability 46
Interlace 24
Internal disc codes
compatability 79-80
Invisible drawing 169
ISO-PASCAL
compatability 46

Joystick   258
    (see Paddles)

KEY database   261
Key-strip   82,89-90
    DIY   90
Keyboard   12,13
    buffer   179
    cleaning   86
    comfort   52
    COMPACT   58
    doing without
    (mouse,menus)   52
    separate   52
    setting case   127
    setting within program   182
    user defined codes   57
Keyboard entry
    and checking   133
Keystrokes
    Input vetting   178-180
    reducing   147
    with GET, GET$ 132
KEYWORD   216-218
Keywords
    de-bugging   216
    upper case   190
Keyword abbreviations   123
Labels
    for discs   98
    printing   257
        Word processors   257
Languages
    COMAL   47
    Micro-PROLOG   47
    PASCAL   47
    C   48
        portable   48
    Wordwise Plus   257
Laser discs   40
Laser printers   49
Law
    (see copyright)
    (see Data Protection Act)
Leads
    (see cables)

Legal programming
    Compatab   81
    Libraries   107-108
    ADFS   108
    machine code utilities   107-108
Library manager   96,146
Library programs   60
Library
    Utilities   146
Light
    (see also Electricity)   91
    comfort   20
    eyestrain   20
    paperwork & keyboard   20
    reflections   20
    the room   20
    Light pen   52-53,258
    CAD   52
    plotting board   52
    Lighting
    contrast   20
    workstation   20
LINE   70
Line feeds
    COMPACT configuration   112
    MASTER configuration   112
    printing defects   222
LINE INPUT   72
Linked data
    arrays   156
LISP
    compatability   46
List processing
    LOGO   47
Listings in BASIC
    using a wordprocessor   117
Listing
    VDU 21   288-291
LISTO   72,144
    ARCHIMEDES   145
    BBC-B   145
LOAD
    Resident
    Integer Variables   188

LOCAL	225,238		Magnets	
problems with			dangers with discs	84
nested procedures	153		Magnifying glasses	88
LOCAL ERROR	72		MAGSCAN	261
LOCAL variables			Mail merge	234,255,
procedures	151-154			257
Locked programs	145-146		PROWORD	257
Logic			View	257
de-bugging	220		Wordwise Plus	257
Logic operations			Mailboxes	
de-bugging	216		communications	266-267
LOGO	42		compatability	266
adventure writing	47		wordprocessors	266
compatability	46		Mailmerge	
graphics	47		Word processing	9
list processing	47		Mailshot	264
turtle	47		Mains filters	91
LOOK	73		Mains plugs	32
Loops	158,160,		Mains spikes	214
	242,243		Manuals	82
BASIC	148		MASTER	57-58
converting	242,4		!BOOT	101
de-bugging	214		accountancy	258
DOWHILE..ENDWHILE	158-159		ADFS	37-38
FOR..NEXT	158-159		animation	170-171
IF..THEN..GOTO	158-159		BREAK key lock	55
layout	144		bundled software	58
REPEAT..UNTIL	158-159		CODE key	57
speed	159-160		compatability	77
WHILE..ENDWHILE	158-159		configuration	30,58,
Loops (nested)				111-112
de-bugging	215		cursor keys	55
LOTUS 1-2-3	74		DFS	37
Lower case	127,175,		DFS & ADFS	57
	179		graphics commands	58
checking	133		keypad	
setting within program	182		resetting	181
variables	190,220		stopping	181
Machine code			numeric keypad	55
modules in ARCHIMEDES	74		PAGE	55
Machine code programs			poking to memory	81
ROMs	42		PROWORD	255
MACRO's	257		ROM compatability	46
MACROM			ROMs	57
compatability	46		second processors	57
			shadow RAM	55

user defined keys	226	compatability	46
VIEW	254	Minimum abbreviations	123
volume control	30	MISCO	87
MASTER 128		MODE	70,74
(see MASTER)		De-bugging	218
MASTER 512	57	No room	228
MASTER COMPACT		Saving space	203
(see COMPACT)		MODE 7	
MASTER REPLAY		centering headings	162-163
compatability	46	graphics	44
MASTER series	56-59	MODE change	
MASTERFILE 2	261	and GOSUB	227
Matching		Modem	267
computer usage	6	Modes	
MAX		ARCHIMEDES	68
compatability	46	Modules	
MEGA - 3	254	ARCHIMEDES	64,74
MEGA ROM		Monitor (see VDU)	
compatability	46	Monochrome VDU	20
MEGAROM	43	and colour	121
Memory map	66	MORLEY	
Memory space		solid state drive	39
BBC-B, BBC-B+		Mouse	51-52,70,
ELECTRON, MASTER	201		258
Memory rubbishing		artwork	51
to save space	207	ARCHIMEDES	69
Memory		CAD	51
wiping with *FX 200	287	commands	69
wiping with BREAK	287	graphics	51
Menus	132,179	menus	51
mouse	51	non-keyboard	51
program	102	MS-DOS	74
Merging programs	194-195	ARCHIMEDES	59,65,268
Micro Trader	258	compatability	79-80
Micro-PROLOG	47	Multi-column	255
compatability	46	Multi-precision arithmetic	242
list processing	47	Multiple statement lines	
pattern matching	47	program speed	198
MicroCODIL	42	saving space	202
Microtext	8	splitting	
MIDI	13	ARCHIMEDES	145
Migraine	15	Caretaker	145
Minerva Systems		Toolkit	145
Personal Accounts	258	Music	12
Delta	262	printing	12
MINI OFFICE 2	261,262	Music 5000	12

N/BREAK
   *NET   122
Narrative indexing   7
National Insurance   9
Nesting   242
Networks   60-63,268
   advantages   61-62
   business   61
   compacting   61
   Copyright   60
   databases   61
   E-NET   60
   Econet   60
   file-server   60
   file searching   61
   hard disc   37
   Star,Ring,Spur,Balanced   61
   teaching   60
   Winchesters   61
NEW   73,74
   Resident
     Integer Variables   188
Newspapers   13
NLQ printers   48
No room
   MODE   228
Non-reflecting screen
   VDU   22,25
Notebooks   99
Notepad   51
NOVOCAD   258
Numbers
   Input vetting   177-178
Numeric variables   139
Numeric
   changing to sign   182
Numeric keypad
   MASTER   55
Numerical constants
   programming style   147
OFF   70
OLD   82
ON ERROR
   division by zero   231
OPENIN   249
   compatability   77-78

OPENOUT
   and compatability   77-78
OPENUP   249
   and compatability   77-78
Operating system   190,201
Operator
   lessening fatigue   131-137
   reducing
     keystrokes   132
     errors   133
Optical discs   40
OPUS
   solid state drive   39
OR   188-190, 210
   de-bugging   220
Oracle   11
Organizing your work   82-92
OSCLI   251
OTHERWISE   71-72
P%
   and machine code   188
Paddles   51,52
   children   51
   games   51
   the handicapped   51
PAGE
   and BREAK   206,229
   and Bad program   229
   commercial programs   207
   DFS   205
   disc files   206
   E-NET   205
   ECONET   205
   shifting for files   206
PAGE mode   214
Palette   45
Paperwork
   comfort   19
   ergonomics   19
PASCAL   42,47
Passing
   arrays
   BASIC 5   73
   parameters
     and error messages   224-225

procedures	150, 224-225
speed	150
results	
files	145
resident integers	145
Passwords	286
Password	
alarm	193
safety	286
Pathway (see Directories)	
Pattern matching	
Micro-PROLOG	47
PENDOWN SPELLMASTER	
compatability	46
Picture processing	7
Picture control	
(see Screen control)	
Plotting boar	
light pen	52
PMS GENIE(see Genie)	51
Poking to memory	
compatability	81
Portable languages	
C	48
Ports	
COMPACT	58
Ports for hardware	53
Presentation	130-132
Presentation	
borders	130
PRESTEL	11,44
Printers	48-49
cleaning	86
colour	48
control code problems	120
daisy wheel	48
DIP switches	223
dot-matrix	48
flat-bed plotter	49
graphics	48
Laser	49
memory	49
NLQ	48
parallel	49
serial	49
sink (with *CON.)	112
special listing effects	120-121
thermal	48
Printer buffer	
sideways RAM	50
Printer drivers	256
Printing defects	
*FX 6	222
Printing	
background colour	163
centered lettering	163
double height in MODE 7	163
labels	257
defects	
CONFIGURE	222
line feeds	222
Printing errors	
De-bugging	211
Printing music	12
Procedures	134-147, 149-153
allowed characters	226
arguments	151
de-bugging	150,154
de-bugging,command mode	211
error messages	224-225, 226
errors	236,7, 8,241
GLOBAL variables	151-154
Libraries in BASIC 5	73
LOCAL variables	151-154
nesting problems	153
overlaying	204
passing parameters	150
program layout	150
program speed	199
recursion	243
saving space	150
saving time	150
speed	187-188
testing	154
versus GOSUB	187-188
windows	166
Processor	
(see also Second processor)	

Programs
  assessing 268
  household budget 263
  shells 8
  increasing speed 197-200
  layout
  (see programming style)
    blank lines 144
    indentation of loops 144
    procedures 150
    spaces 144
  merging 194-195
  protection 286-291
  selling 293-296
  speed
    *FX 255 199
    and GOTO 197
    and REMs 197
    ARCHIMEDES 199
    assembly language 199
    clock rate 199
    compiling 199
    disc accessing 199
    disc access time 199
    hard discs 199
    integer variables 198
    multiple
     statement lines 198
    integer arithmetic 198
    INT 198
    procedures 199
    SOLIDISC 199
    through software 197-200
    through hardware 199
    through software 199
    variable names 198
    VDU statements 199
Program testing 113-115
  in Command Mode 114
Program
  writing
  on a wordprocessor 117
Programming 138-147
  flags 138
  meaningful programs 139-141
  style 130-133

  arrays 147
  de-bugging 143
  input vetting 147
  numerical constants 147
  presentation 130
  REMs 145
  single
    statement lines 143
    spaces 143
    utilities 146
PROWORD
  word processor 255
QUEST MOUSE & PAINT 31,41,259
  compatability 46
QUICKCALC 263
QUIT 72
Radiation
  health hazards 15
Rainbow discs 87
RAM boards
  speed of loading 276-278
RAM filing system
  ROMIT 45
RAM, sideways
  (see Sideways RAM)
RAMROD
  compatability 46
Random (RND) 194
Re-numbering (REN.)
  and RESTORE 195
READ 240
  arrays 156
Real variables 199
RECTANGLE 70
Recursive procedures
  de-bugging 215
Red Boxes 11
Red Keys
  (see Function Keys)
Reducing errors
  operator 133
Reference tables
  useful ones 89
Reflections
  lighting 20
  non-reflective screen 22

Reliability
    computer usage 7
REM 138
REM
    abbreviated commands 219
    colour 120
    de-bugging 212,219
    programming style 145
    Saving space 202
    speed 197
    use of 145
REMOVE 57
REPEAT .. UNTIL 158-159,
                    215,242
REPLAY
    compatability 46
Resident integers
    and machine code 145,188
Resident Integer Variables
    CHAIN 188
    CLEAR 188
    LOAD 188
    machine code 145,188
    NEW 188
    RUN 188
    to pass results 145
RESTORE 240
    and re-numbering 195
Retrieval
    computer usage 6,7
Reverse SHIFT 127
    setting within program 182
    lock 182
Ring
    Networks 61
RISC 59
    ARCHIMEDES 64
ROMs 41-47,74
    ARCHIMEDES 66
    BASIC editors 42
    BBC-B 41
    cartridge holders 41
    changing 31
    compatability
      with Acorn range 46
    database 43

    disc mnipulators 42
    dis-assemblers 42
    explanation 42
    extraction tool 30
    graphics 42
    HCS 50
    insertion 29
    keystrips 90
    languages 42
    NLQ printer ROM 48
    removal 30
    SPELLMASTER 257
    spreadsheet 42
    static electricity 86
    storage 86
    toolkits 42
    type of programs 42
    VIEW 254
    word processor 43
    ZIF 31,41
ROM boards 51
    and RAM chips 51
ROM cartridges
    BBC-B 54
ROM commands
    (see under ROM name
    pages 42-46)
ROM images
    DFS on ARCHIMEDES 59
    sideways RAM 55
ROM MANAGER
    compatability 46
ROM sockets
    in sideways RAM boards 50
ROM SPELL
    compatability 46
ROM/RAM board
    Watford Electronics 50
ROMAS
    compatability 46
ROMIT 43,50
    compatability 46
    RAM filing system 45
Root
    see Directories
RS232 11

Rulers 88
RUN
  Resident
    Integer Variables 188
Safety
  error trapping 185
  of data
    databases in networks 61-62
    file-locking 61
Saving memory
  backing up programs 145
Saving screens 170
Saving space 139,
    201-210
  arrays 202
  assembly language 204
  CLEAR 204
  crunching routine 202
  data 203
  disc files 203
  index files 203
  integer variable 202
  memory rubbishing 207
  MODE 203
  multiple
    numbers in one
  variable 208-210
    statement lines 202
  overlaying procedures 204
  passing parameters 150
  PAGE shifting 205-207
  procedures 150
  REMs 202
  reducing calculating
  space 204
  screen memory 203
  second processor 201
  shadow RAM 201
  splitting programs 204-205
  string handling 207
  text compression 203
  through software 202-210
Saving time
  procedures 150
  printer buffer 49-50
  colour coded discs 87

SCARF socket
  ARCHIMEDES 65
Scientific programs
  Second processor 52
Screen
  animation 168-169
  brightness VDU 15,16
  cleaning 85
  control 123
  design 130-131
  display
    format 165
  drawing invisibly 169-170
  dump 255
    ARCHIMEDES module 74
    DUMP OUT 3 45
  display
    @% 165-166
    columns of figures 164-166
  layout planning 118-119
  memory
    Saving space 203
  pokes Compatab 81
  printing defects
    colour alignment 221
    program hanging 221
    scrolling 221
    TAB 221
    windows 221
  save 170
  shut-down 288
SCRIBE 255
SCROLL 112
Searching database 259-260
Second processor 52,54,81
  6502 52
  80186 and the MASTER 52
  BBC-B 54
  commercial programs 52
  CP/M 52
  CP/M 268
  for MASTER 57
  IBM PC emulation 57
  MS-DOS 52,268
  scientific programs 52
  Z80 52

Sectors   36
Security   E-NET   63
Selling your program   293-296
    advertising   294-295
    assessment   293-294
    copying   25-296
    profitability   296
    presentation   295-296
Servo motors   53
Shadow   animation   170-171
Shadow RAM   201,254
    BBC-B+   55
    errors with   80-81
    MASTER   55
    sideways RAM   50
SHIFT   127
SHIFT key
    'upside-down'   122
SHIFT lock
    setting within program   182
SHIFT/CTRL/Function key
    resetting base values   181
SHIFT/Function key
    resetting base values   181
Sideways RAM   49-51
    and ROM sockets   50
    and Spellmaster   258
    as a printer buffer   49
    battery backed   50
    BBC-B+   55
    for ROM usage   50
    in ROM boards   50
    makes   50-51
    MASTER   55
    ROM images   55
    shadow RAM   50
    silicon disc   55
    solid disc   50
Sign changing to numeric   182
Silicon disc
    (see Solid disc)
SLEUTH   compatability   46
Software compatability
    ARCHIMEDES   66-67
Software
    copyright   291

disc housekeeping   93-95
ease of use   93-100
program names   94
use of directories,
    ADFS   94
    DFS   93-94
Solid disc   38,39
    MORLEY   39
    OPUS   39
    SOLIDISC   39
    sideways RAM   50,55
SOLIDISC   50
    program speed   199
    solid state drive   39
Sorting
    computer usage   6
    databases   11,260
Sound   192-193
    Archimedes   13
    changing the beep   193
    flushing the buffers   192
    synchronization   192
    volume control   30
    parameters   210
Spaces
    de-bugging   219
    program layout   144
Spectacles   20
SPEECH
    compatability   46
Speed
    GOSUB   187-188
    loops   159-160
    passing parameters   150
    procedure   187-188
    windows   166
Spell checkers
    (see Spelling checkers)
Spelling checkers   257-258
    available types   257-258
SPELLMASTER   31,41,
                                       61,257
Spikes   91
    (see also Electricity)
Splitting programs
    Saving space   204

SPOOL (see *SPOOL)
Spreadsheets   262-263
    (see also
        integrated suites)
    financial planning   10
    other uses   10
    word processing   9
Sprites   ARCHIMEDES   64,68
Spur Networks   61
Standard programs   252-267
    word processors   252
    spreadsheets   262
Star Networks   61
STARGRAPH compatability   46
STARSTORE compatability   46
STARWORD compatability   46
Static electricity
    ROM damage   86
    and the operator   23
    bugs caused   23
    earthing VDU screen   23
    ROMs   86
    VDU screen   23
Statistics
    computer usage   6
STOP
    use in de-bugging   213,214
Stop Press   13
Storage
    disc boxes, dangers of   87
    discs   87
    ROMs   86
String handling
    saving space   207
Structured languages   47,48
Structured programming
    de-bugging   135,138,
                                    211
    at the keyboard   135
    programs   134-147
Sub-directories
    (see Directories & ADFS)
Sub-routines   134
SUM   72
SUPASTORE   262
SUPERCALC 3   74

Surges
    see Electricity   91
SWAP   73
Synthesizer   12,13
SYSTEM DELTA
    (see also
        Minerva Systems)
    compatability   46
TAB   222
Tape filing system
    error message   229
Tape recorder
    head adjustment   229-230
Teaching
    games   8
    Networks   60
Technical drawing   12
TED
    compatability   46
    viewdata   44
    (Teletext Editor)   43
Telecom Gold   78
Telephone numbers   51
Terminals   60,61,62
Test grid generator   25
Testing programs
    (see Program testing)   113,268
Tests   (see conditions)   140
Text compression
    Saving space   203
Thick lines from windows   166-167
TIME with Random (RND)   194
Tokens   76-78
    and user defined keys   226
    de-bugging   216-217
    list of   124-127
TOOLKIT & TOOLKIT PLUS   43,139,218
    backing up   96
    compatability   46
    crunching routine   202
    splitting
        multi-statement lines   145
TPI
    disc formats   41
TRACE
    de-bugging   214

Trackerball	258	de-bugging	213
Tracks		in lower case	190
(see Discs & Disc drives)		Integer	238
Transfer of software		Real	238
ARCHIMEDES	67	wiping	214
Tree (see Directories)		VAT (Value Added Tax)	9
TRUE	139-141	VDU (Monitor .. TV)	
TURBO (see MASTER)		adjusting	20-21
Turtle		amber	20
LOGO	47	brightness	20-21
TV (see VDU)		choosing	16
ULTRACALC 2	262,263	contrast	16,20-21
compatability	46	colour	20
Up-lighters	20	comfort	19-22
Upper case	127,175,	dual purpose TV/	24
	129	electrostatic fields	15
keywords	190	ELF	15
setting within program	182	fatigue	15
and checking	133	flicker	15
User-defined key	226	green	20
(see also Function Keys)		health hazard	15
User defined characters		interlace	24
from the keyboard	55	moving the picture	24
User friendly		monochrome	20
error trapping	185	non-reflecting screen	22,25
input vetting	174	purchase	24-25
reducing keystrokes	178	radiation	15
User Port	53	reducing flicker	16
Utilities	138,146	screen brightness	15,16
library	146	set up	25
library manager	146	siting	19
LOCAL	146	static	23
programming style	146	testing before purchase	24-25
spooled	145-6	VDU operator	
procedure errors	236-237	static	23
Utility		VDU set up	
GXR	45	grey scale	25
LOCAL	152	VDU testing	
Variable names		grid generator	25
program speed	198	VDU 1	223
Variable		VDU 14	214
characters	234-235	VDU 21	228,288
storing several numbers		listing	288-291
in one variable	208-210	passwords	288-291
Variables		printer	288
characters allowed	226	VDU 22	228

VDU 24   131
VDU 28   131
VDU 6   288
Vetting (see Input vetting)
Video effects   7
VIEW   58,66, 254,262
VIEW 2.1
    compatability   46
VIEW 3
    compatability   46
VIEW PROFESSIONAL   254
Viewdata
    TED   44
VIEWSHEET   58,263
    compatability   46
VIEWSPELL   257
VIEWSTORE   262
    compatability   46
Virtual memory   255
    SCRIBE   255
    Word processors   253
Volume   122
Volume control   30
    with configure   111-112
Wages   9
WAIT   70
Warning
    audible   133
Watford Shadow RAM board   254
WATFORD DFS
    compatability   46
WATFORD DDFS
    compatability   46
WHEN   71-72
WHILE..ENDWHILE   47,73,79, 158-159
Winchester
    (see also Hard Disc)   37
    and compacting   60
    ARCHIMEDES   65
Windows   166-167, 191
    ARCHIMEDES   68-69
    borders   131, 166-167

de-bugging   166,222
graphics cursor   167
procedures   166
thick lines   166-167
Wiping memory
    *FX 200   287
    NEW   288
Word processors   252-258, 274-276
    (see also Integrated suites)
    !BOOT   275
    accountancy   9
    and databases   9
    creating !BOOT files   103
    de-bugging   276
    discs   275
    in business   252
    integrated accounts   9
    label printing   257
    mail merge   9,257
    non-WYSIWYG   255-256
    printer drivers   256
    spelling checkers   257-258
    and spreadsheets   9
    virtual memory   253
    writing BASIC programs   117
    WYSIWYG   254-255
Wordprocessing
    BBC-B   55
WORDWISE
    !BOOT   101
    Customising   274
WORDWISE PLUS
    compatability   46
    customising   274
    disc file recovery   109
    Function keys   274
    programming language   257
    word-wrapping   276
Workstation
    chairs   18
    construction   20-23
    comfort   16-22
    design   16-26
    ergonomics   16-19

lighting   20
work surface
height & width   18
wrist rest   18
Writing programs   13
business use   13
WYSIWYG   253-255
available programs   253-256
non-WYSIWYG   255-256
X%   and machine code   188
Y%   and machine code   188
Z80   54,57
bundled software MASTER   57
Second processor   52
Zellers congruence   183
Zero page   231
Zero, division by   231
Zeroing with DIM   156
ZIF socket   31,41
problems
with certain ROMs   31
Zip code
menus   179

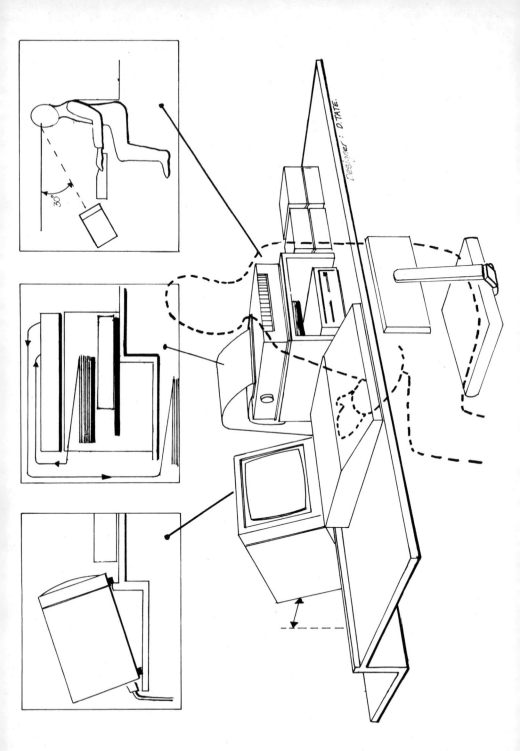

designer : D.TATE.